NO LONGER
PROPERTY OF PPLD

D0792373

The

GREAT
COOK

The GREAT COOK

ESSENTIAL TECHNIQUES AND INSPIRED FLAVORS TO MAKE EVERY DISH BETTER

JAMES BRISCIONE

WITH THE EDITORS OF CookingLight

Oxmoor House®

CONTENTS

Welcome!

On behalf of myself and the *Cooking Light* team, congratulations on taking a major step toward a tastier, healthier, happier meal time. In the following pages, you will find a cookbook experience unlike any other. The collection of tested, trusted recipes from the experts in the *Cooking Light* kitchen is only the beginning. The recipes are grouped into lessons, organized by category (breads, meats, desserts) and then by dish (rolls, pork medallions, layer cake). Each lesson kicks off with a master recipe—accompanied by detailed pictures of each and every step in the process—to guarantee that the dish is a success. Following each master recipe, you'll find variation recipes that will put your newly acquired epicurean expertise to use in different and delicious ways. Interspersed through each lesson you'll also find my best cooking advice: tricks and tips I've learned working in professional kitchens for more than 25 years. Together, these elements will make this feel less like a cookbook and more like having a trusted friend (who happens to be a professional chef) at your side, guiding you through each recipe.

My culinary journey began at the dishwashing station in a restaurant on Pensacola Beach, Florida. But with years of hard work and practice, I came to lead some of the nation's top restaurants. Along the way I learned a lot about food, cooking, and the joy that comes from feeding people. Over the years I have been happy to share my love for great food—whether it was writing my first cookbook with my wife, *Just Married and Cooking*, cooking on television, or working in my current position as Director of Culinary Development at the Institute of Culinary Education. But now, in the pages of this book, I am excited to share my passion and experience with you. Most of all, I'm happy to be there with you as you discover how simple and satisfying a healthful, home-cooked meal can be.

Enjoy!

James

How to Become a
GREAT COOK

To be honest, recipes can take you only so far. Great cooks rely on practice and experience, so cooking becomes almost instinct. The first and most critical step: Understand that most recipes act merely as guidelines to processes. Processes that need to be learned and mastered over time. As any trained chef will tell you, each dish has its own flavor arc, and the better cook learns to attend and guide a fixed series of recipe steps to an eventual, and usually delicious, end result. This might entail adjusting the temperature of the burner, stirring the sauce, or adding key flavors at just the right moment. Dried herbs, for instance, go into the pot early in the cycle of a stew, while fresh herbs (even the same herbs) go in near the end. To achieve light, exquisite dinner rolls, kneading bread dough by hand requires adding small amounts of flour until the dough reaches a texture that the experienced baker knows feels and looks just right. For the newbie cook, this knowing might seem mysterious. It's not; it's just a mark of experience. The resistance of a bread dough under the heel of the hand; how a dimple bounces back; the tough sort-of silkiness of developed gluten: Bread sends signals that the experienced baker receives.

Most of these signals are intercepted by the senses, which is why a great cook learns to use ears, eyes, nose, mouth, and fingers throughout the cooking process. Touching, tasting, smelling—these are key cooking strategies because the success of a dish often lies between the lines of a recipe, in the unwritten and almost indescribable things that help you know when a dish is cooking exactly the way it should. The goal of these 36 lessons, each with its own visual step-by-step process for mastering a dish, is to lead you along and through that cooking continuum so that you understand every single part of the process.

The first part of the process in these lessons begins with *mise en place*. This is a French term that means "everything in its place" and it is the most essential skill that a great cook learns. Doing your mise en place means getting all of your peeling, chopping, and organizing out of the way before you begin cooking. Most people marvel at how chefs make cooking look so effortless on TV, that's because they've got all their prepped ingredients and equipment ready to go. Plus, they've run through the steps of the recipe many times in their head—mise en place is mental, too. More than anything, good mise en place makes the act of cooking fun by getting rid of clutter and confusion.

Take these lessons at your own pace. Study each recipe with a critical eye, looking for anything unfamiliar. Shop for quality ingredients. Gather your mise en place. Make the recipes one or two or more times. Taste as you go. Eventually your practice and attention to detail will set you well on your way to gaining the experience it takes to catapult you from the realm of a good cook up to the level of a great one.

Kitchen
ESSENTIALS

Great kitchen tools and the best ingredients are invaluable to making cooking a more pleasurable experience; and that, in turn, can inspire you to cook more often. Make the investment to get good quality equipment; it really affects cooking results.

TOOLS

Whether stocking your kitchen from scratch or paring down to the basics, here are the tools and equipment we recommend you keep close at hand.

COLANDERS AND STRAINERS A well-stocked kitchen contains metal and plastic colanders in varying sizes. A large colander works well for draining pasta and salad greens and rinsing vegetables. A small strainer is great for separating fruit juice or pulp from seeds. Mesh strainers are the most versatile because nothing can get through the holes except liquid.

CUTTING BOARDS Both wood and plastic cutting boards work well. Whichever you choose, wash the board thoroughly to avoid food contamination. Wipe wooden boards with diluted bleach, and wash thoroughly; sanitize plastic ones in the dishwasher. Have a board for vegetables, another for fruit, and another for meat, fish, and poultry to prevent cross-contamination and keep tasks separate for an orderly kitchen.

FOOD SCALE To measure flour, the correct amount of cheese, or to make sure that pieces of meat, poultry, and fish are the specified size, use a scale. A digital scale is small, lightweight, and accurate. Food service–style balance scales are also good.

GRATERS A box-style grater gives you a choice of hole sizes. Use the smaller holes for grating hard cheese and chocolate and the largest holes for shredding foods like cheddar cheese and carrots. Microplane-style graters are essential in our kitchen for grating citrus rind and grating ginger, garlic, or hard cheese.

INSTANT-READ THERMOMETER Use an instant-read thermometer to check meringues, meat, and poultry to be sure they're cooked to the correct temperature. Don't leave the thermometer in the oven while the food is cooking; remove it from the food after you read the temperature.

KITCHEN KNIVES Great knives bring great joy and facilitate precision. They can be pricey, but they will last for many years if not abused. Start with an excellent chef's knife, paring knife, and serrated knife, then build your set as needed. The most important thing is that they feel good in your hand. For a quick primer, go to Knife Basics (page 16).

KITCHEN SHEARS Keep kitchen shears handy to mince small amounts of herbs, chop canned tomatoes, trim fat from meat and skin from poultry, and make slits in bread dough.

MANDOLINE We're not big on gadgets that clutter up the kitchen drawers, but the mandoline is one of those tools that does its job superbly. This efficient tool makes precise slices easy. You don't have to spend a lot on one, just buy a sturdy model and use the safety guard.

MEASURING CUPS Measuring cups, both dry and liquid versions, are crucial. Dry measuring cups, available in metal or plastic, are flat across the rim and are used for ingredients like flour, grains, and cereals. We use a set of nesting cups that includes 1-cup, ½-cup, ⅓-cup, and ¼-cup sizes. Liquid measuring cups, sized from 1 cup to 4 cups, are available in clear glass or plastic so that you can see the level of liquid.

MEASURING SPOONS Sometimes a "pinch of this" and a "dash of that" results in less-than-desired flavor. Measuring spoons ensure that your recipes come out just right. It's handy to have two sets—one for wet ingredients, one for dry.

PEELER A peeler removes the skin from both vegetables and fruits. Select one that has a comfortable grip and an eyer to remove potato eyes and other blemishes on vegetables and fruits. It's also handy for making Parmesan cheese shavings and chocolate curls.

PEPPER MILL Give your food a bit of pungent flavor with a sprinkle of cracked or freshly ground pepper from a pepper mill. A variety of pepper mills are now readily available in the spice section of supermarkets or in the kitchenware department of discount stores.

SPATULAS Two will do. A heat-resistant silicone spatula works for any pan, nonstick or not. And a fish spatula is useful for getting cookies off a baking sheet.

STORAGE CONTAINERS Keep your pantry orderly with clear, sturdy, straight-sided stackable containers. For the freezer, zip-top freezer bags that can be labeled are very easy to stack.

TONGS A good pair of silicone-tip tongs will be one of your hardest-working tools, working with nonstick pans and hot grills.

WHISKS Whisks in assorted sizes are ideal for beating eggs and egg whites, blending salad dressings, and dissolving solids in liquids. We consider them essential when making creamy sauces. Whisks are available both in stainless steel and nylon; the nylon ones won't scratch nonstick surfaces.

POTS *and* PANS

From Dutch ovens to soufflé dishes, here's our list of the essentials.
Of course, you can improvise with what you already own, but start adding items
to help produce the best results for each type of dish.

NONSTICK SKILLETS For healthy cooking, a nonstick skillet is essential, since it requires little added fat. We recommend 8-, 10-, and 12-inch pans. Keep in mind that even the most expensive nonstick pans will eventually show wear (toss them when the coating gets heavily scratched or starts to peel). To keep the pan performing well, use plastic, silicone, and wooden utensils, avoid cranking the heat above medium-high, and try to skip the dishwasher.

STAINLESS-STEEL OR CAST-IRON SKILLET When you want to achieve a dark-brown surface on meats and leave browned bits behind for deglazing, a heavy copper, cast-iron, or stainless-steel skillet is essential. We find a 10-inch cast-iron skillet indispensible, and it's a quality pan that can last a lifetime. Seasoning with oil is necessary for a cast-iron pan so food won't completely stick, but you can now buy pre-seasoned pans.

DUTCH OVEN A Dutch oven is neither Dutch nor an oven, but a deep pot with a tight-fitting lid that can go from cooktop to oven. Most cookware sets include a pot that fits this description. It usually holds 3 to 6 quarts. Some versions come with a long handle, like a skillet. If you choose one with a handle, make sure there's also a "helper handle" on the side, since a hot Dutch oven full of food can be quite heavy.

SAUCEPANS AND STOCKPOTS Saucepans should be stainless steel or even aluminum, but you want good, even heat conduction and diffusion across the bottom. Get a high-quality pot with a heavy bottom and high sides. A 2½-quart and a 4-quart stainless steel saucepan should be sufficient for most of your needs. For a stockpot to cook pasta or soups, get an 8- to 10-quart size.

BAKING SHEETS AND JELLY-ROLL PANS Thick heavy baking sheets (cookie sheets) and jelly-roll pans (large, flat sheets with 1-inch sides) are kitchen workhorses. Look for heavy, light-colored aluminum, not dark or nonstick surfaces.

BAKING PANS In our recipes, baking pan means a metal pan. Stock 8- and 9-inch square pans for brownies, as well as 8- and 9-inch round cake pans, a 9 x 5-inch loaf pan, and a 13 x 9-inch pan. We prefer heavy, nonshiny aluminum baking pans.

BAKING DISHES Baking dishes, made of glass or ceramic materials, are typically used for casseroles. An 8-inch-square, 11 x 17-inch, and 13 x 9-inch dish should cover all your needs. Note: Glass conducts heat better than metal, so if you use a baking dish in a recipe that calls for a pan, remember to decrease the oven temperature by 25 degrees.

ROASTING PAN Roasting pans are designed for cooking large cuts of meat, such as a pork loin or turkey. These heavy pans come in large rectangular or oval shapes with 2- to 4-inch vertical sides, which keep the pan juices from overflowing. They sometimes come with racks to keep the meat raised above the drippings; if your pan doesn't have one, you can elevate the meat with vegetables or get a wire rack that fits the pan. A good substitute is a broiling pan with a removable rack.

SOUFFLÉ DISH A soufflé dish is round and has tall, straight sides (5 to 7 inches high) so your egg mixture will climb the sides and rise high. And because it is designed to go from oven to table, a soufflé dish is usually attractive enough to use as a casserole or serving dish.

PANTRY STAPLES

Keeping some key staples on hand ensures there are endless ways to create a great dish.
So stock up and let your imagination go wild.

IN THE CUPBOARD:

All-purpose flour

Baking powder

Baking soda

Boil-in-bag or precooked brown rice or whole grains

Bottled roasted red bell peppers

Breads, pita bread

Canned artichoke hearts and bottoms

Canned minced clams

Canned no-salt-added whole or diced tomatoes

Canned organic beans: black, pinto, Great Northern

Canned water-packed tuna

Canola mayonnaise

Chile paste (sambal oelek)

Cooking spray

Cornstarch

Dried herbs and spices

Evaporated fat-free milk

Fat-free, less-sodium chicken broth

Flavored vinegars

Good-quality olive, vegetable, and sesame oils

Honey

Low-sodium soy sauce

Maple syrup

Noodles, couscous, and pasta

Nuts

Onions, shallots, garlic

Panko (Japanese breadcrumbs)

Pitted kalamata olives

Salt

Smoked paprika

Sugar

Unsweetened cocoa

Various wines and spirits

IN THE FRIDGE & FREEZER:

1% low-fat, 2% reduced-fat, and fat-free milks

Butter or margarine

Dried breadcrumbs

Fresh ginger

Fresh herbs

Fresh pasta

Frozen corn kernels

Frozen shelled edamame (soybeans)

Green onions

Homemade chicken or vegetable stocks

Large eggs

Lemons

Low-fat or fat-free cream cheese

Low-fat or fat-free sour cream

Orange juice concentrate

Plain low-fat or fat-free Greek yogurt

Spinach, baby or frozen

Various jams and jellies

Various mustards

HOW LONG WILL IT LAST?

Product	Shelf Life	Excess Storage Risk
High-acid canned goods *(fruit- or tomato-based)*	Up to 18 months	Metal from can dissolves into food
Low-acid canned foods *(meat, fish, vegetables)*	Up to 5 years	Quality deterioration
Oil	1 year	Rancidity
Starchy staples *(rice, pasta, beans, flour)*	Up to 18 months	Quality deterioration; pest infestation; mold growth
Sugar	Several years	If it gets wet, will clump and may grow mold

KNIFE BASICS

While cutting and chopping is routine kitchen work, the key to success starts with using the right knife. These three knives will prove invaluable assistants for any cutting task.

CHEF'S KNIFE The chef's knife (along with a cutting board) is the cook's workhorse. It's ideal for chopping herbs, onions, garlic, fruits, and vegetables and for cutting boneless meats (it even cuts through small bones, such as those of chicken and fish), slicing and dicing, and general cutting tasks.

SERRATED KNIFE The serrated knife, with its scalloped, toothlike edge, is ideal for cutting through foods with a hard exterior and softer interior. Like a saw, the teeth of the blade catch, and then rip, the exterior as the knife smoothly slides through the resistant skin and juicy flesh of a ripe tomato or a loaf of crusty bread.

PARING KNIFE Precise and delicate, the paring knife is the intricacy expert of the knife family. With its blade of 2½ to 4 inches, it looks like a miniature chef's knife, but its use is very different. Employ it for peeling fruits and vegetables; slicing a single garlic clove or shallot; or any type of controlled, detailed cutting.

HOW TO HOLD A KNIFE

BLADE GRIP: Grip the knife on the shaft of the blade (thumb and index finger grip the knife around the blade, with rest of the hand wrapped around handle). This provides maximum control.

With the opposite hand, hold the food to be chopped with your fingers safely curled under. As you cut and move your hand to expose sections of food, continue to keep your fingers curled.

HANDLE GRIP: Grip the knife around the entire handle. With the opposite hand, hold the food to be chopped with your fingers safely curled under.

HONING AND SHARPENING KNIVES

Regular sharpening is the most important aspect of maintaining your knives. Knives are a costly investment, so have them professionally sharpened if you don't want to chance ruining them. But for regular maintenance, use a sharpening steel to help hone and straighten the edge of a blade. Frequent use of this tool will maintain a good blade edge for up to two years.

To hone a blade: Hold the knife in one hand and the steel in the other, and slide the knife's blade on the steel at a 20-degree angle several times, either from the top of the steel to the bottom or vice versa. Turn the knife over and repeat the process. Take your time. Sliding the knife quickly doesn't result in better sharpening.

To maximize the performance of your knives, always wash them by hand and avoid soaking in water. Washing a knife in the dishwasher can dull the blade and prolonged immersion can loosen the handles.

HOW TO CHOP AN ONION

The onion is one of the most frequently used vegetables in the kitchen, whether it is simply chopped to add to a roasting pot or sliced and caramelized. Chopping can be tricky, but this method works well for uniform pieces.

1. Place the onion on its side with the root end toward your dominant hand. Cut the root end off with a sharp knife. Spin the onion around and cut off the top.

2. Place the onion top side down on the cutting board, halve the onion. Peel outer layers away.

3. Place one onion half, cut side down with the root end away from you. Following the curve of the onion, make downward slices all the way around the onion.

4. Spin the onion a quarter turn and make even, crosswise cuts toward the root.

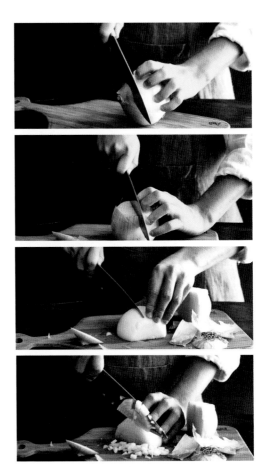

HOW TO MINCE GARLIC

Mincing results in finely chopped garlic (or vegetables and herbs) that distribute flavor to a dish without adding texture.

1. Place several peeled cloves of garlic on a cutting board.

2. Using a chef's knife, place the side of the knife over a clove and the palm of one hand on the other side of the knife. Gently lean on the clove and use your body weight to crush the clove.

3. Combine the crushed cloves in a small pile on the cutting board. Place the heel of the chef's knife over the cloves and the palm of your non-dominant hand on the front edge of the knife. Rock the knife back and forth until the garlic reaches a fine consistency.

Basic TECHNIQUES

To master cooking, especially light cooking, it's important to become adept at basic techniques that help build flavor without the need for large quantities of salt and fat. These three key techniques will set you up for success with the recipes in this book, and cooking in general.

MASTERING *the* BOIL *and* SIMMER

Boiling and simmering are essential techniques used to prepare everything from pasta to green vegetables to stewed meats. They both start with a heavy-bottomed pot or saucepan, but the effect each method has on food is profoundly different.

BASIC BOILING. This technique cooks food in a liquid (or involves cooking the liquid itself) at a relatively high temperature (212°), which is the boiling point for water at sea level. When liquids boil, bubbles break through and pop on the surface while the whole batch of liquid churns vigorously. Bubbles are caused by water vapor, a gas, rushing to the surface.

WHAT BOILING DOES. In the case of pasta, churning, boiling water keeps the food in motion, prevents sticking, and cooks it quickly so the pasta doesn't get soggy. Green vegetables are tossed into boiling water to cook as quickly as possible so they retain their flavor and bright color in the process called blanching; if they were to simmer gently in a covered pot, their color would dull, and they would lose much of their texture. Boiling causes speedy evaporation, a useful effect for reducing, where the volume of the liquid decreases and flavors are concentrated.

BEST BETS FOR BOILING. This intense cooking method is well suited for pasta, some grains, and green vegetables. Boiling is also useful for reducing sauces.

BASIC SIMMERING. A cooking method gentler than boiling, simmering refers to cooking food in liquid (or cooking just the liquid itself) at a temperature slightly below the boiling point (180 to 190°). A bubble breaks the surface of the liquid every second or two. More vigorous bubbling than that means you've got a boil going. The difference between the two can ruin a dish.

WHAT SIMMERING DOES. Simmering cooks food gently and slowly. Delicate foods such as fish are poached at or below a simmer to prevent them from breaking apart. Meats that are simmered remain moist and fork-tender, while boiled meats are often dry and tough because the heat of boiling liquid can cause their proteins to toughen. Stocks are simmered so the fat and proteins released by any cooking meat or bones float to the top, where they can be skimmed off instead of being churned back in, which can make the stock cloudy and greasy.

BEST BETS FOR SIMMERING. This technique is more versatile than boiling and lends itself to a variety of foods. Simmering is used to cook proteins (fish, poultry, and meats), often in the form of poaching (cooking in enough liquid to cover the food) and braising (cooking in a small amount of liquid). It's also essential when making broth or stock. Whereas boiling works well for tender green vegetables, tough, fibrous root vegetables (such as potatoes, turnips, and beets) are best simmered so they cook evenly throughout.

SIMMERING LIQUID. Food is usually simmered in flavored liquid, such as broth/stock or wine, but sometimes water is used. As a general rule, add meat to cold liquid and bring it up to a simmer. If you add uncooked meat to already-simmering broth, the meat immediately releases proteins that cloud the broth. When you start the meat in cold liquid, these proteins are released more gradually and become entangled with one another in a frothy mass that's easy to skim off the surface. Fish are an exception. If you start poaching small pieces of fish in cold liquid, by the time it comes to a simmer, the fish will be overcooked.

MASTERING *the* SAUTÉ

To sauté is to cook food quickly in a minimal amount of fat over moderately high heat.
The word comes from the French verb sauter, *which means "to jump," and describes not*
only how food reacts when placed in a hot pan but also the method of tossing in the pan.
The browning achieved by sautéing lends richness to meat and produce. And because it is
cooked quickly, the integrity of the flavor and texture remains intact.

BEST FOODS TO SAUTÉ. Time in the pan is brief, so it's important that the sautéed food be naturally tender. With meats, cuts such as beef tenderloin, fish fillets, and chicken breasts are good candidates. For produce, tender vegetables such as baby artichokes, sugar snap peas, mushrooms, and bell peppers lend themselves to this technique. That's not to say that denser, tougher vegetables can't be sautéed—they just may need to be blanched (briefly cooked in boiling water) first to get a head start on cooking.

SIZE MATTERS. Cutting food to a uniform thickness and size ensures that it will cook evenly. Vegetables should be no larger than bite-sized, meat no larger than portion-sized. Food that is too thick or large runs the risk of burning or forming a tough, overly browned outer crust in the time that it takes to completely cook them.

PREHEAT THE PAN. Be sure to thoroughly heat the pan over medium-high heat for a few minutes before adding ingredients. A hot pan is essential in order to cook the food properly. A barely heated pan can cause food to stick, and the food will end up releasing liquid and steaming rather than sautéing. A drop of water in the pan should sizzle.

CHOOSE A FAT. In general, use fats that have a high smoke point—peanut oil, regular olive oil, or canola oil. Or use a mixture of oil and butter to add more flavor. Once the pan is hot, add the fat and swirl enough to just coat the bottom of the pan. Heat the fat for 10 to 30 seconds—until oil shimmers or butter's foam subsides—and then add the food.

DON'T OVERCROWD THE PAN. All food releases steam as it cooks, so you need to leave room for the steam to escape, otherwise the food will steam instead of brown. It is better to work in batches or use a larger pan. Another common error is turning food too often. Meat (chicken, steaks, or pork medallions) won't develop a nice crust unless you allow it to cook, undisturbed, for the specified time.

MASTERING MARINATING

Marinating is a technique that's been around at least since the Renaissance, when acidic mixtures were commonly used to help preserve foods. Whether it's a short dip or a long soak, this method enhances a variety of foods. It boosts the flavor of lean cuts of meat and also works wonders with vegetables and fruits. It doesn't require special equipment and involves simple steps to produce unfussy-but-delicious food.

WHAT MARINATING DOES. Ideally a marinade flavors, not tenderizes, food. Though marinades are often purported to have tenderizing effects, the ingredients only permeate the surface of food and have little effect on the interior.

BEST BETS FOR MARINATING. Small or thin cuts of meat and poultry are generally good candidates. Larger cuts, such as roasts, may not benefit since they offer less surface area. Tender vegetables such as mushrooms, zucchini, yellow squash, and eggplant absorb flavor from marinades and taste especially good when grilled. A brief stint works well for fish and shellfish, and it's beneficial, too, for some tender fruits, such as berries, orange sections, and melons. (When it's fruit that is being marinated, the technique is called *macerating*.)

MARINADE INGREDIENTS. Many marinades include an acidic element, such as citrus juice or vinegar, which boosts flavor and may tenderize the surface proteins of meat. Oil is another common component, as it coats food, carries flavor, and helps food stay moist. Aromatics like garlic, herbs, and spices, along with other robust ingredients such as soy sauce, and Asian fish sauce enhance the savory qualities of meats and fish. A good basic marinade ratio is roughly equal parts acid, oil, and aromatics.

EQUIPMENT. Because many marinades are acidic, it's best to soak food in a nonreactive container like those made of glass, ceramic, plastic, or stainless steel. Reactive metals such as aluminum or copper will respond to acids by discoloring the food and giving it a metallic taste. For easy cleanup, a zip-top plastic bag works well.

MARINATING TIME. The length of time you marinate food depends on both the food and the marinade. Acidic marinades with citrus, wine, and vinegar can compromise the texture and subtle flavors of the meat if left on too long. In general, small or delicate foods, like fish, shellfish, and fruit usually only need 15 to 30 minutes to soak up the flavors. While meats can go longer, even the toughest cut doesn't need more than 12 hours, otherwise it might turn grainy.

SEASON LAST. Healthy cooks watching sodium levels use only a small amount of salt in a recipe. For our recipes that include added salt, we sprinkle it on after food is cooked instead of including salt in the marinade. Meat will only absorb a small amount of marinade and any salt and other subtle seasonings might be lost when the marinade is discarded. Seasoning after the food is cooked also allows the small amount of salt we use to have a bigger impact on the overall taste.

SOUPS

&

STEWS

CHICKEN STOCK

If you told any great chef to open a new restaurant tomorrow, the first thing he or she would do is put on a pot of stock. Chefs know a good stock is the base of many a great meal. Soups, sauces, braises, even rice pilaf and risotto are unimaginable without a good stock as a base. This simple liquid is the lifeblood of the kitchen.

Of course, chefs also have the luxury of serving dozens of chicken dishes a day, so bones or chicken parts for stock are never hard to come by. Fear not: You don't have to go on an all-chicken diet to get enough chicken parts to make a pot of stock. Keep a heavy-duty zip-top bag in the freezer and anytime you have chicken, reserve the wings, necks, and backs. When you've saved up enough, make a pot of stock. If you need to make some stock right away, look for value-sized packs of chicken necks, backs, or wings. Even just wings make great stock and are an economical way to go about it—as long as it's not Super Bowl week.

YOU'LL LEARN:

**HOW TO MAKE HOMEMADE STOCK • HOW TO KEEP STOCK CLEAR
HOW TO REMOVE FAT FROM STOCK**

MASTER RECIPE:

CHICKEN STOCK

VARIATIONS:

OLD-FASHIONED CHICKEN NOODLE SOUP • SPICY THAI COCONUT-CHICKEN SOUP

YOUR MISE EN PLACE

PROTEIN
CHICKEN BACKS, NECKS, OR WINGS

FRESH PRODUCE
FRESH PARSLEY SPRIGS

FRESH THYME SPRIGS

CARROTS, CHOPPED

CELERY STALKS, CHOPPED

LARGE ONIONS, CHOPPED

FLAVOR BOOSTERS/ STAPLES
BLACK PEPPERCORNS

BAY LEAVES

LIQUID
COLD WATER

EQUIPMENT NEEDED:
SHARP KNIFE

STOCKPOT

CHEESECLOTH

COLANDER

LARGE BOWL

CHICKEN STOCK

*Boiling your stock too rapidly will not only make a mess of your stove,
it will also leave you with a cloudy broth. Clear, clean-tasting stock
comes from a gentle simmer, so keep an eye on the heat.*

15 BLACK PEPPERCORNS

12 FRESH PARSLEY SPRIGS

10 FRESH THYME SPRIGS

**8 POUNDS CHICKEN BACKS, NECKS,
OR WINGS**

5 CARROTS, CHOPPED

5 CELERY STALKS, CHOPPED

4 BAY LEAVES

3 LARGE ONIONS, CHOPPED

5 QUARTS COLD WATER

*Hands-on time: 30 min.
Total time: 12 hr.*

*Freeze extra stock in 1- to
2-ounce portions (ice cube
trays work great) for up
to six months. Use it at
the last minute to make
pan sauces (see Mastering
Sauces, pages 122-123) or
steam veggies.*

1. Combine all ingredients in a 12-quart stockpot. Bring to
a boil over medium-high heat. Reduce heat to low. Simmer
4 hours, skimming and discarding foam as needed.

2. Strain through a cheesecloth-lined colander into a large
bowl; discard solids.

3. Cool stock to room temperature. Cover and refrigerate
6 hours or overnight.

4. Skim fat from surface; discard fat. Yield: 20 servings
(serving size: 1 cup)

CALORIES 28; FAT 1.1g (sat 0.3g, mono 0.3g, poly 0.3g); PROTEIN 3.6g; CARB 0.7g;
FIBER 0.1g; CHOL 15mg; IRON 0.2mg; SODIUM 23mg; CALC 12mg

OLD-FASHIONED CHICKEN NOODLE SOUP

Traditional egg noodles lend starchy body to flavorful home-made stock in this favorite soup loaded up with fresh-cooked chicken and vegetables. Make the stock the day before since it needs time to boil and chill.

---

8 CUPS CHICKEN STOCK (PAGE 30)

2 (4-OUNCE) SKINLESS, BONE-IN CHICKEN THIGHS

1 (12-OUNCE) SKINLESS, BONE-IN CHICKEN BREAST HALF

2 CUPS DIAGONALLY SLICED CARROT

2 CUPS DIAGONALLY SLICED CELERY

1 CUP CHOPPED ONION

6 OUNCES UNCOOKED MEDIUM EGG NOODLES

½ TEASPOON KOSHER SALT

½ TEASPOON BLACK PEPPER

CELERY LEAVES (OPTIONAL)

Hands-on time: 51 min.
Total time: 1 hr.

1. Combine the first 3 ingredients in a Dutch oven over medium-high heat; bring to a boil. Reduce heat; simmer 20 minutes. Remove chicken from pan; let stand for 10 minutes. Remove chicken from bones; shred meat into bite-sized pieces. Discard bones.

2. Add carrot, celery, and onion to pan; cover and simmer for 10 minutes. Add noodles, and simmer 6 minutes. Add chicken, salt, and black pepper; cook for 2 minutes or until noodles are done. Garnish with celery leaves, if desired. Yield: 4 servings (serving size: about 1½ cups)

CALORIES 423; FAT 7.7g (sat 2.2g, mono 1.6g, poly 1.4g); PROTEIN 44.4g; CARB 42.2g; FIBER 4.8g; CHOL 171mg; IRON 3.3mg; SODIUM 474mg; CALC 98mg

SPICY THAI COCONUT-CHICKEN SOUP

The Thai ingredients—lemongrass, fish sauce, and coconut milk—build big flavor into this soup, but the homemade stock lends an underlying richness.

2 TEASPOONS CANOLA OIL

1 CUP SLICED MUSHROOMS

½ CUP CHOPPED RED BELL PEPPER

4 TEASPOONS MINCED PEELED
   FRESH GINGER

4 GARLIC CLOVES, MINCED

1 (3-INCH) STALK LEMONGRASS,
   HALVED LENGTHWISE

2 TEASPOONS SAMBAL OELEK
   (GROUND FRESH CHILE PASTE)

3 CUPS CHICKEN STOCK (PAGE 30)

1¼ CUPS LIGHT COCONUT MILK

4 TEASPOONS FISH SAUCE

1 TABLESPOON SUGAR

2 CUPS SHREDDED COOKED CHICKEN
   BREAST (ABOUT 8 OUNCES)

½ CUP GREEN ONION STRIPS

3 TABLESPOONS CHOPPED FRESH
   CILANTRO

2 TABLESPOONS FRESH LIME JUICE

Hands-on time: 25 min.
Total time: 32 min.

1. Heat a Dutch oven over medium heat. Add oil to pan; swirl to coat. Add mushrooms and next 4 ingredients (through lemongrass); cook 3 minutes, stirring occasionally. Add chile paste; cook 1 minute. Add Chicken Stock, coconut milk, fish sauce, and sugar; bring to a simmer. Reduce heat to low; simmer for 10 minutes. Add chicken to pan; cook 1 minute or until thoroughly heated. Discard lemongrass. Top with onions, cilantro, and juice. Yield: 4 servings (serving size: about 1⅓ cups)

CALORIES 224; FAT 9g (sat 4.5g, mono 2.4g, poly 1.3g); PROTEIN 22.7g; CARB 15g; FIBER 1.1g; CHOL 58mg; IRON 1,1mg; SODIUM 463mg; CALC 35mg

FRENCH ONION SOUP

There's a lot of love in a bowl of French onion soup. There's the rich, homemade beef stock and the properly caramelized onions, both of which form the base of the soup. The onions take some time and a little attention: A satisfying bit of alchemy is involved in transforming the pungent, harsh raw onions into a tender, sweet, caramelized version of themselves. Like all good things, the perfect batch of onions (which leads to the perfect pot of soup) comes to those who wait. Properly caramelizing onions can take up to an hour.

But you don't need to clear your entire afternoon to make a pot of soup. After the first five minutes or so you only need to check in on the pot periodically until the onions reach golden perfection. Once they're cooked, you're off the hook until it's time to finish the soup off with bubbly melted cheese. While the classic onion soup may be the perfect example of the beauty of simple French cooking, we think you'll find our variations with sweet apples and earthy shiitake mushrooms equally delicious.

YOU'LL LEARN:

HOW TO MAKE BEEF STOCK • HOW TO CARAMELIZE ONIONS

HOW TO TAKE SOME SOUP SHORTCUTS

MASTER RECIPE:

FRENCH ONION SOUP

VARIATIONS:

FRENCH ONION AND APPLE SOUP • CARAMELIZED ONION AND SHIITAKE

SOUP WITH CHEESE TOASTS

YOUR MISE EN PLACE

PROTEIN
MEATY BEEF BONES

BEEF SHANKS

DAIRY
BUTTER

GRUYÈRE CHEESE, SHREDDED

FRESH PRODUCE
LARGE CARROTS, PEELED AND CHOPPED

CELERY STALKS, COARSELY CHOPPED

MEDIUM ONION, CUT INTO WEDGES

LARGE ONIONS, SLICED

FRESH THYME SPRIGS

FRESH FLAT-LEAF PARSLEY

FRESH CHIVES, CHOPPED

FLAVOR BOOSTERS/STAPLES
WHOLE BLACK PEPPERCORNS

BAY LEAF

OLIVE OIL

KOSHER SALT

BLACK PEPPER

FRENCH BREAD BAGUETTE

LIQUID
COLD WATER

EQUIPMENT NEEDED:

VEGETABLE PEELER

SHARP KNIFE

CHEESE GRATER

LARGE BAKING SHEET

DUTCH OVEN

FINE-MESH SIEVE

CHEESECLOTH

LARGE BOWL

PAPER TOWELS

JELLY-ROLL PAN

LADLE

BROILER-SAFE SOUP BOWLS

PREHEAT YOUR OVEN TO 450°.

FRENCH ONION SOUP

It's worth the effort to make your stock from scratch. If you substitute store-bought lower-sodium broth, not only will you need to reduce the amount of salt you add to the soup by half, but the final product won't taste nearly as good.

STOCK:

1½ POUNDS MEATY BEEF BONES

1 POUND BEEF SHANKS

2 LARGE CARROTS, PEELED AND COARSELY CHOPPED

2 CELERY STALKS, COARSELY CHOPPED

1 MEDIUM ONION, CUT INTO WEDGES

3 QUARTS COLD WATER

1 TABLESPOON WHOLE BLACK PEPPERCORNS

3 FRESH THYME SPRIGS

1 BUNCH FRESH FLAT-LEAF PARSLEY

1 BAY LEAF

SOUP:

2 TABLESPOONS OLIVE OIL

1 TABLESPOON BUTTER

3 LARGE ONIONS, VERTICALLY SLICED (ABOUT 13 CUPS)

1⅛ TEASPOONS KOSHER SALT

½ TEASPOON FRESHLY GROUND BLACK PEPPER

1 TEASPOON CHOPPED FRESH THYME

¼ CUP CHOPPED FRESH CHIVES

12 (½-OUNCE) SLICES FRENCH BREAD BAGUETTE

4 OUNCES GRUYÈRE CHEESE, SHREDDED (1 CUP)

Hands-on time: 1 hr. 20 min.
Total time: 5 hr. 39 min.

1. Preheat oven to 450°. To prepare stock, arrange first 5 ingredients in a single layer on a large baking sheet. Bake at 450° for 35 minutes or until browned.

2. Scrape beef mixture and pan drippings into a large Dutch oven. Stir in 3 quarts cold water and next 4 ingredients (through bay leaf); bring to a boil over medium heat. Reduce heat to low, and simmer 2½ hours, skimming surface as necessary.

3. Strain stock through a fine-mesh sieve lined with a double layer of cheesecloth over a large bowl; discard solids. Wipe pan clean with paper towels. Set stock aside.

4. To prepare soup, return Dutch oven to medium heat. Add oil to pan; swirl to coat. Melt butter in oil. Add sliced onion; cook for 5 minutes, stirring occasionally. Partially cover, reduce heat to medium-low, and cook 15 minutes, stirring occasionally.

5. Add salt and ground pepper; cook, uncovered, until deep golden brown, about 35 minutes, stirring frequently. Add reserved stock and chopped thyme; bring to a boil. Reduce heat, and simmer until reduced to 8 cups, about 50 minutes. Stir in chives.

6. Preheat broiler to high. Arrange bread slices in a single layer on a jelly-roll pan, and broil for 2 minutes or until toasted, turning after 1 minute.

7. Ladle 1⅓ cups soup into each of 6 broiler-safe soup bowls. Top each serving with 2 bread slices, and sprinkle evenly with cheese. Place bowls on jelly-roll pan; broil for 4 minutes or until tops are golden brown and cheese bubbles. Yield: 6 servings

CALORIES 346; FAT 14.1g (sat 5.9g, mono 6.2g, poly 1.2g); PROTEIN 16.1g; CARB 40.5g; FIBER 5.3g; CHOL 33mg; IRON 2.3mg; SODIUM 649mg; CALC 274mg

FRENCH ONION *and* APPLE SOUP

This quicker version relies on canned beef stock—enhanced and made richer in flavor with the addition of small amounts of Madeira, apple, and apple cider—to save some time.

---

3 TABLESPOONS UNSALTED BUTTER

4 POUNDS YELLOW ONIONS, SLICED (ABOUT 15 CUPS)

¾ TEASPOON BLACK PEPPER

1 HONEYCRISP OR PINK LADY APPLE, PEELED, QUARTERED, AND CUT INTO JULIENNE STRIPS

3 FRESH THYME SPRIGS

2 BAY LEAVES

½ CUP MADEIRA WINE OR DRY SHERRY

6 CUPS LOWER-SODIUM BEEF BROTH

½ CUP APPLE CIDER

1 TABLESPOON SHERRY VINEGAR

10 (½-OUNCE) SLICES SOURDOUGH BREAD, CUT INTO 1-INCH CUBES

8 OUNCES GRUYÈRE OR SWISS CHEESE, SHREDDED (2 CUPS)

FRESH THYME LEAVES (OPTIONAL)

Hands-on time: 25 min.
Total time: 2 hr. 10 min.

1. Melt butter in a Dutch oven over medium heat. Add onion to pan; cook 5 minutes, stirring frequently. Continue cooking 50 minutes or until deep golden brown, stirring occasionally. Add pepper, apple, thyme sprigs, and bay leaves; cook 3 minutes or until apples soften. Add wine; cook 2 minutes, scraping pan to loosen browned bits. Add broth and cider; bring to a boil. Reduce heat, and simmer 45 minutes. Discard bay leaves and thyme sprigs; stir in vinegar.

2. Preheat broiler.

3. Arrange bread cubes in a single layer on a jelly-roll pan; broil 2 minutes or until toasted, turning after 1 minute.

4. Preheat oven to 500°. Ladle 1 cup soup into each of 10 ovenproof soup bowls. Divide the bread cubes evenly among bowls, and top each serving with about 3 tablespoons cheese. Place bowls on jelly-roll pan. Bake at 500° for 8 minutes or until cheese melts. Garnish with thyme leaves, if desired. Yield: 10 servings

CALORIES 254; FAT 11g (sat 6.4g, mono 3.1g, poly 0.7g); PROTEIN 11.1g; CARB 29.2g; FIBER 4.1g; CHOL 33mg; IRON 1.1mg; SODIUM 426mg; CALC 278mg

CARAMELIZED ONION *and* SHIITAKE SOUP

with CHEESE TOASTS

SOUP:

1 TABLESPOON OLIVE OIL

2 POUNDS YELLOW ONION, VERTICALLY SLICED (ABOUT 8 CUPS)

10 OUNCES SHIITAKE MUSHROOM, STEMS DISCARDED, SLICED (ABOUT 5 CUPS)

4 GARLIC CLOVES, MINCED

2 FRESH THYME SPRIGS

½ CUP DRY WHITE WINE

1 (14-OUNCE) CAN FAT-FREE, LOWER-SODIUM CHICKEN BROTH

1 (14-OUNCE) CAN FAT-FREE, LOWER-SODIUM BEEF BROTH

½ TEASPOON SALT

½ TEASPOON FRESHLY GROUND BLACK PEPPER

TOASTS:

12 (½-INCH-THICK) SLICES FRENCH BREAD BAGUETTE (ABOUT 6 OUNCES), TOASTED

1 OUNCE GRUYÈRE CHEESE, SHREDDED (¼ CUP)

1 OUNCE CRUMBLED GORGONZOLA CHEESE (¼ CUP)

½ TEASPOON FINELY CHOPPED FRESH THYME

Hands-on time: 1 hr. 14 min.
Total time: 2 hr.

1. To prepare soup, heat oil in a large Dutch oven over medium-high heat. Add onion to pan; sauté 15 minutes or until almost tender, stirring frequently. Reduce heat to medium-low; cook until deep golden brown, about 40 minutes, stirring occasionally.

2. Increase heat to medium. Add mushrooms to pan; cook 10 minutes or until mushrooms are tender, stirring frequently. Stir in garlic and thyme sprigs; cook 2 minutes, stirring frequently. Increase heat to medium-high. Add wine to pan; cook 2 minutes or until most of the liquid evaporates. Add broths to pan; bring to a simmer. Reduce heat, and simmer 45 minutes. Stir in salt and pepper. Discard thyme sprigs.

3. To prepare toasts, preheat broiler. Arrange bread in a single layer on a baking sheet. Top each bread slice with 1 teaspoon Gruyère and 1 teaspoon Gorgonzola. Broil 2 minutes or until cheese melts. Sprinkle chopped thyme over cheese. Ladle about 1 cup soup into each of 6 bowls; top each serving with 2 toasts. Yield: 6 servings

CALORIES 208; FAT 5.4g (sat 2.3g, mono 2.2g, poly 0.4g); PROTEIN 8.9g; CARB 33.4g; FIBER 3.9g; CHOL 9mg; IRON 2.1mg; SODIUM 694mg; CALC 115mg

SAVORY STEWS

Have you ever heard someone refer to an old-fashioned stew as a meal that will "stick to your ribs"? What they mean is that unless you're heading out to do farm work for eight hours, eating a bowl of hearty stew packs on the pounds. Fortunately, it doesn't have to be that way. Stews can be hearty, warming, and comforting without being a giant pile of calories and fat.

Your secret weapon for flipping stews to the healthy side is replacing traditionally heavy ingredients with lighter versions. Butter gives way to olive oil, milk and cream get replaced with flavorful stock, and rich cuts of meat are swapped out for leaner versions. Vegetables play a major role too, adding satisfying bulk along with vitamins, nutrients, and fiber. And, slow simmering brings out their flavor. Basically, what we're saying is these deliciously healthy stews have more of what you want (nutrition and flavor) and less of what you don't (empty calories and fat).

YOU'LL LEARN:

HOW TO COOK STEW MEAT • HOW TO DEGLAZE A PAN
HOW TO MAKE DIFFERENT KINDS OF STEW

MASTER RECIPE:

ITALIAN BEEF STEW

VARIATIONS:

GUINNESS LAMB STEW • CHICKEN VERDE STEW WITH HOMINY

YOUR MISE EN PLACE

PROTEIN
BONELESS CHUCK ROAST, TRIMMED AND CUBED

FRESH PRODUCE
ONION, CHOPPED
CARROT, CHOPPED
CARROT, SLICED
GARLIC, MINCED
PLUM TOMATOES, CHOPPED
FRESH OREGANO, CHOPPED
FRESH THYME, CHOPPED
CREMINI MUSHROOMS, QUARTERED
FRESH BASIL, CHOPPED
FRESH PARSLEY, CHOPPED

FLAVOR BOOSTERS/STAPLES
OLIVE OIL
ALL-PURPOSE FLOUR
SALT
BLACK PEPPER
BAY LEAF

LIQUID
DRY RED WINE
FAT-FREE, LOWER-SODIUM BEEF BROTH
WATER

EQUIPMENT NEEDED:
SHARP KNIFE
DUTCH OVEN
WOODEN SPOON
LARGE BOWL
SHALLOW DISH

Italian
BEEF STEW

Tough cuts of meat that lend themselves to stews tend to be fatty, so you need to trim them well for healthy results. And don't try to hurry the process by boiling rather than simmering. Cooking low and slow helps flavors meld and lets the meat achieve a buttery texture.

7 TEASPOONS OLIVE OIL, DIVIDED

1½ CUPS CHOPPED ONION

½ CUP CHOPPED CARROT

1 TABLESPOON MINCED GARLIC

¼ CUP ALL-PURPOSE FLOUR

2 POUNDS BONELESS CHUCK ROAST, TRIMMED AND CUT INTO CUBES

¾ TEASPOON SALT, DIVIDED

½ TEASPOON BLACK PEPPER

1 CUP DRY RED WINE

3¾ CUPS CHOPPED SEEDED PEELED PLUM TOMATOES (ABOUT 2 POUNDS)

1½ CUPS FAT-FREE, LOWER-SODIUM BEEF BROTH

½ CUP WATER

2 TEASPOONS CHOPPED FRESH OREGANO

2 TEASPOONS CHOPPED FRESH THYME

1 BAY LEAF

1 (8-OUNCE) PACKAGE CREMINI MUSHROOMS, QUARTERED

¾ CUP (¼-INCH-THICK) SLICED CARROT

2 TABLESPOONS CHOPPED FRESH BASIL

1 TABLESPOON CHOPPED FRESH PARSLEY

Hands-on time: 40 min.
Total time: 2 hr. 40 min.

1. Heat a Dutch oven over medium-high heat. Add 1 teaspoon oil to pan. Add onion and chopped carrot; sauté 8 minutes, stirring occasionally. Add garlic; sauté for 45 seconds, stirring constantly. Transfer vegetables to a large bowl.

2. Add 1 tablespoon oil to pan.

3. Place flour in a shallow dish. Sprinkle beef with ½ teaspoon salt and pepper; dredge in flour. Add half of beef to pan; sauté 6 minutes, browning on all sides. Transfer meat to bowl with vegetables. Repeat procedure with remaining 1 tablespoon oil and beef.

4. Add wine to pan, and bring to a boil, scraping pan to loosen browned bits. Cook until reduced to ⅓ cup, about 5 minutes.

5. Return meat and vegetables to pan. Add tomato and next 6 ingredients (through mushrooms); bring to a boil. Cover, reduce heat, and simmer for 45 minutes, stirring occasionally.

6. Uncover, and stir in sliced carrot. Simmer, uncovered, for 1 hour or until meat is very tender, stirring occasionally. Discard bay leaf. Stir in remaining ¼ teaspoon salt, basil, and parsley. Yield: 8 servings (serving size: 1 cup)

CALORIES 334; FAT 13g (sat 3.9g, mono 0.8g, poly 6.6g); PROTEIN 40.6g; CARB 12.2g; FIBER 2.4g; CHOL 86mg; IRON 4.1mg; SODIUM 387mg; CALC 51mg

A light coating of flour not only helps the meat cubes brown beautifully, it will also aid in thickening your stew in less time.

8 TEASPOONS OLIVE OIL, DIVIDED

2 CUPS CHOPPED ONION

1 TABLESPOON CHOPPED FRESH THYME

1½ TEASPOONS CHOPPED FRESH
    ROSEMARY

3 TABLESPOONS ALL-PURPOSE FLOUR

2½ POUNDS BONELESS LEG OF LAMB,
    TRIMMED AND CUT INTO 1-INCH CUBES

1 TEASPOON SALT, DIVIDED

¾ TEASPOON FRESHLY GROUND BLACK
    PEPPER, DIVIDED

2 CUPS GUINNESS STOUT

1 TABLESPOON TOMATO PASTE

3 CUPS FAT-FREE, LOWER-SODIUM BEEF
    BROTH

1 BAY LEAF

2 CUPS CUBED PEELED YUKON GOLD
    POTATO

2 CUPS 1-INCH-THICK DIAGONALLY SLICED
    CARROT

8 OUNCES BABY TURNIPS, PEELED AND
    QUARTERED

1 TABLESPOON WHOLE-GRAIN DIJON
    MUSTARD

⅓ CUP CHOPPED FRESH PARSLEY

Hands-on time: 35 min.
Total time: 3 hr. 20 min.

GUINNESS LAMB STEW

1. Heat a large Dutch oven over medium-high heat. Add 2 teaspoons oil to pan; swirl to coat. Add onion, thyme, and rosemary; sauté for 5 minutes, stirring occasionally. Transfer onion mixture to a large bowl. Place flour in a shallow dish. Sprinkle lamb evenly with ½ teaspoon salt and ½ teaspoon pepper. Dredge lamb in flour, and shake off excess. Return pan to medium-high heat. Add 1 tablespoon oil to pan; swirl to coat. Add half of lamb mixture to pan; sauté for 6 minutes, turning to brown on all sides. Add browned lamb to onion mixture. Repeat procedure with remaining lamb and remaining 1 tablespoon oil.

2. Add stout to pan; bring to a boil, scraping pan to loosen browned bits. Cook until reduced to 1 cup (about 5 minutes). Return onion mixture and lamb to pan. Stir in the tomato paste; cook 30 seconds. Add broth and bay leaf; bring to a boil. Cover, reduce heat, and simmer for 1 hour and 15 minutes, stirring occasionally. Uncover and stir in potato, carrot, and turnips. Simmer, uncovered, for 1½ hours or until meat and vegetables are tender. Stir in mustard, remaining ½ teaspoon salt, and remaining ¼ teaspoon pepper. Discard bay leaf. Ladle about 1 cup stew into each of 7 bowls; sprinkle evenly with parsley. Yield: 7 servings

CALORIES 430; FAT 22.9g (sat 8.3g, mono 11g, poly 2g); PROTEIN 26.3g; CARB 24.2g; FIBER 3.4g; CHOL 83mg; IRON 3.3mg; SODIUM 702mg; CALC 50mg

CHICKEN VERDE STEW *with* HOMINY

2 ANAHEIM CHILES

COOKING SPRAY

1½ POUNDS TOMATILLOS, HUSKED AND RINSED

¼ CUP FINELY CHOPPED FRESH CILANTRO

1½ TEASPOONS GROUND CUMIN

1 TEASPOON DRIED OREGANO

2 CUPS FAT-FREE, LOWER-SODIUM CHICKEN BROTH, DIVIDED

2 TABLESPOONS OLIVE OIL, DIVIDED

1½ CUPS FINELY CHOPPED ONION

½ CUP CHOPPED CARROT

½ CUP CHOPPED CELERY

½ CUP CHOPPED RED BELL PEPPER

3 TABLESPOONS ALL-PURPOSE FLOUR

4 TEASPOONS FINELY CHOPPED GARLIC

1 POUND SKINLESS, BONELESS CHICKEN THIGHS, CUT INTO 1½-INCH PIECES

¾ TEASPOON KOSHER SALT, DIVIDED

½ TEASPOON BLACK PEPPER, DIVIDED

1 (29-OUNCE) CAN GOLDEN HOMINY, RINSED AND DRAINED

6 TABLESPOONS REDUCED-FAT SOUR CREAM

CILANTRO LEAVES (OPTIONAL)

Hands-on time: 35 min.
Total time: 1 hr. 20 min.

1. Preheat broiler to high. Halve, stem, and seed chiles. Place chiles, skin side up, on a foil-lined baking sheet coated with cooking spray; broil for 5 minutes or until charred. Place chiles in a paper bag; seal. Let stand for 15 minutes. Peel and discard skins. Arrange tomatillos on prepared baking sheet, and broil 14 minutes or until blackened, turning once. Combine the chiles, tomatillos, ¼ cup cilantro, cumin, and oregano in a blender. Add 1 cup broth; process until smooth.

2. Heat a large Dutch oven over medium-high heat. Add 2 teaspoons olive oil; swirl to coat. Add onion, carrot, celery, and bell pepper; sauté for 2 minutes, stirring occasionally. Stir in flour; sauté for 2 minutes, stirring frequently. Add garlic; sauté for 30 seconds, stirring constantly. Transfer onion mixture to a large bowl.

3. Sprinkle chicken with ½ teaspoon salt and ¼ teaspoon black pepper. Add 2 teaspoons oil to pan; swirl to coat. Add half of chicken; sauté 3 minutes. Add browned chicken to onion mixture. Repeat procedure with remaining chicken and remaining 2 teaspoons oil. Combine remaining 1 cup broth, tomatillo mixture, onion-chicken mixture, and hominy in pan over medium-high heat, and bring to a boil. Cover, reduce heat, and simmer for 45 minutes, stirring occasionally. Stir in remaining ¼ teaspoon salt and ¼ teaspoon black pepper. Ladle 1⅔ cups stew into each of 6 bowls, and top each with 1 tablespoon sour cream. Garnish with cilantro, if desired. Yield: 6 servings

CALORIES 322; FAT 14.1g (sat 3.6g, mono 6.3g, poly 2.7g); PROTEIN 18.7g; CARB 30.9g; FIBER 6.3g; CHOL 56mg; IRON 2.9mg; SODIUM 651mg; CALC 69mg

Today's Lesson

CHILI

Nothing says "party!" like a good pot of chili; even if it turns out to be just the company of two and not a party of six or ten. Steaming bowls of meaty, spicy chili are the ideal way to please everyone—and only dirty one pot in the process. But chili has many regional interpretations, and within each region almost as many recipes as there are cooks. No self-respecting Texan would consider adding beans, but in other regions, chili isn't chili without the beans.

But in the end, chili is a dish that's going to make everyone happy, including you, who won't be chained to the stove for hours cooking. The deep, slow-simmered flavor in these chili recipes happens in just an hour or two on your stovetop. Can't find dried chiles? Try substituting fresh versions of the same peppers—jalapeño for the chipotle and poblanos for the ancho chile. And for those times when you don't have a crowd to feed, keep in mind that chili is a soul-warming meal that tends to taste even better the next day.

YOU'LL LEARN:

HOW TO MAKE BASIC BEEF AND BEAN CHILI • HOW TO ADD HEAT WITH CHILES

HOW TO EXPLORE DIFFERENT FLAVOR COMBINATIONS

MASTER RECIPE:

BEEF AND PINTO BEAN CHILI

VARIATIONS:

CHILI CON CARNE • BISON CHILI WITH CHICKPEAS AND ACORN SQUASH

YOUR MISE EN PLACE

PROTEIN
BONELESS CHUCK ROAST, TRIMMED AND CUT

DAIRY
SOUR CREAM

FRESH PRODUCE
ONION, CHOPPED
JALAPEÑO PEPPERS, MINCED
GARLIC CLOVES, MINCED
RADISH, THINLY SLICED
AVOCADO, PEELED AND CHOPPED
FRESH CILANTRO LEAVES
LIME, CUT IN WEDGES

FLAVOR BOOSTERS/ STAPLES
COOKING SPRAY
SALT
CANOLA OIL
PAPRIKA
GROUND CUMIN
TOMATO PASTE
CANNED WHOLE PEELED TOMATOES, CHOPPED
CANNED PINTO BEANS, RINSED

LIQUID
BEER
FAT-FREE, LOWER-SODIUM BEEF BROTH

EQUIPMENT NEEDED:
SHARP KNIFE
COLANDER
SPATULA
DUTCH OVEN
LARGE BOWL
LADLE

Beef and Pinto Bean
CHILI

For a three-alarm chili, leave the seeds and membranes in the jalapeños.
Don't worry: The sour cream garnish has a cooling effect.

COOKING SPRAY

1 POUND BONELESS CHUCK ROAST, TRIMMED AND CUT INTO 1-INCH PIECES

⅜ TEASPOON SALT, DIVIDED

2 TABLESPOONS CANOLA OIL

4 CUPS CHOPPED ONION (ABOUT 2 MEDIUM)

¼ CUP MINCED JALAPEÑO PEPPERS (ABOUT 2 LARGE)

10 GARLIC CLOVES, MINCED

1 (12-OUNCE) BOTTLE BEER

1 TABLESPOON PAPRIKA

1 TABLESPOON GROUND CUMIN

2 TABLESPOONS TOMATO PASTE

3 CUPS FAT-FREE, LOWER-SODIUM BEEF BROTH

1 (28-OUNCE) CAN WHOLE PEELED TOMATOES, DRAINED AND CHOPPED

1 (15-OUNCE) CAN PINTO BEANS, RINSED AND DRAINED

½ CUP THINLY SLICED RADISH

1 AVOCADO, PEELED AND CHOPPED

6 TABLESPOONS SMALL FRESH CILANTRO LEAVES

6 TABLESPOONS SOUR CREAM

6 LIME WEDGES

Hands-on time: 1 hr.
Total time: 2 hr. 30 min.

1. Heat a Dutch oven over high heat. Coat pan with cooking spray. Sprinkle beef evenly with ⅛ teaspoon salt. Add beef to pan; sauté 5 minutes, turning to brown on all sides. Transfer beef to a large bowl.

2. Add oil to pan; swirl to coat. Add onion and jalapeño; cook 8 minutes or until lightly browned, stirring occasionally. Add garlic; cook 1 minute, stirring constantly.

3. Stir in beer, scraping pan to loosen browned bits; bring to a boil.

4. Cook until liquid almost evaporates (about 10 minutes), stirring occasionally. Stir in paprika, cumin, and tomato paste; cook 1 minute, stirring frequently.

5. Return beef to pan. Add broth, tomatoes, and beans; bring to a boil. Reduce heat, and simmer 1½ hours or until mixture is thick and beef is very tender, stirring occasionally. Stir in remaining ¼ teaspoon salt.

6. Ladle 1 cup chili into each of 6 bowls. Divide radish and avocado evenly among bowls. Top each serving with 1 tablespoon cilantro and 1 tablespoon sour cream. Serve with lime wedges. Yield: 6 servings

CALORIES 421; FAT 23g (sat 6.8g, mono 10.9g, poly 2.6g); PROTEIN 21.6g; CARB 30.4g; FIBER 8.5g; CHOL 53mg; IRON 4.1mg; SODIUM 565mg; CALC 123mg

This Texas-style chili packs a smoky punch from the mild poblanos and the hot chipotle chile. Rinsing the chipotle mellows the heat; skip that step for more fire.

---

8 POBLANO CHILES

3 TABLESPOONS ALL-PURPOSE FLOUR

3 POUNDS BONELESS CHUCK ROAST, TRIMMED AND CUT INTO ½-INCH CUBES

1½ TEASPOONS SALT

½ TEASPOON BLACK PEPPER

2 TABLESPOONS OLIVE OIL, DIVIDED

3 CUPS CHOPPED ONION

4 GARLIC CLOVES, MINCED

3 CUPS PEELED SEEDED CHOPPED PLUM TOMATO (ABOUT 10 MEDIUM)

1 TABLESPOON DRIED OREGANO

1 TABLESPOON GROUND CUMIN

1 CANNED CHIPOTLE CHILE IN ADOBO SAUCE

3 TABLESPOONS CHOPPED FRESH CILANTRO

6 TABLESPOONS SHREDDED REDUCED-FAT CHEDDAR CHEESE

Hands-on time: 50 min.
Total time: 2 hr. 10 min.

CHILI CON CARNE

1. Preheat broiler. Place poblanos on a foil-lined baking sheet; broil 8 minutes or until charred, turning after 6 minutes. Place poblanos in a zip-top plastic bag or paper bag; seal. Let stand 15 minutes. Peel and cut chiles into 1-inch pieces.

2. Place flour in a shallow dish. Sprinkle beef with salt and black pepper; dredge in flour. Heat 1 tablespoon olive oil in a Dutch oven over medium-high heat. Add half of beef to pan; sauté for 5 minutes, turning to brown on all sides. Transfer beef to a large bowl. Repeat procedure with remaining oil and beef.

3. Reduce heat to medium. Add onion to pan; cook 12 minutes, stirring occasionally. Add garlic; cook 3 minutes, stirring frequently. Return beef to pan. Stir in tomato, oregano, and cumin; bring to a simmer. Cover and cook 1 hour, stirring occasionally. Stir in poblanos; simmer for 45 minutes or until beef is tender, stirring occasionally. Rinse, seed, and chop chipotle. Stir in chipotle and cilantro. Ladle about 1 cup chili into each of 10 bowls. Sprinkle with cheese. Yield: 10 servings (serving size: about 1 cup chili and about 2 teaspoons cheese)

CALORIES 360; FAT 20.9g (sat 7.6g, mono 9.3g, poly 1.1g); PROTEIN 29.2g; CARB 13.8g; FIBER 2.6g; CHOL 84mg; IRON 3.6mg; SODIUM 442mg; CALC 83mg

BISON CHILI WITH CHICK-PEAS *and* ACORN SQUASH

2 DRIED ANCHO CHILES

2 CUPS UNSALTED BEEF STOCK (SUCH AS SWANSON)

1 (8-OUNCE) PACKAGE FRESH CREMINI MUSHROOMS

COOKING SPRAY

1½ POUNDS 90% LEAN GROUND BISON OR GROUND SIRLOIN

1 TEASPOON KOSHER SALT, DIVIDED

¾ TEASPOON BLACK PEPPER, DIVIDED

2 CUPS CHOPPED ONION

1 CUP CHOPPED GREEN BELL PEPPER

1 TABLESPOON MINCED GARLIC

1 TABLESPOON UNSALTED TOMATO PASTE

1 TABLESPOON CHILI POWDER

2 TEASPOONS DRIED OREGANO

1 TEASPOON GROUND CORIANDER

¾ TEASPOON CUMIN SEEDS, TOASTED

1 (12-OUNCE) BOTTLE DARK MEXICAN BEER

1 (28-OUNCE) CAN CRUSHED TOMATOES

2 CUPS (½-INCH) CUBED PEELED ACORN SQUASH

1 (14.5-OUNCE) CAN UNSALTED CHICKPEAS, RINSED AND DRAINED

½ CUP REDUCED-FAT SOUR CREAM

½ CUP CHOPPED FRESH FLAT-LEAF PARSLEY

Hands-on time: 40 min.
Total time: 1 hr. 50 min.

1. Combine chiles and stock in a microwave-safe bowl; microwave at HIGH 3 minutes. Let stand 10 minutes. Remove stems. Combine chiles and stock with mushrooms in a blender; process until smooth.

2. Heat a Dutch oven over high heat. Coat pan with cooking spray. Add bison, ½ teaspoon salt, and ½ teaspoon black pepper; cook 6 minutes or until browned, stirring to crumble. Transfer bison to a medium bowl. Reduce heat to medium-high. Add onion and bell pepper to pan; sauté 5 minutes. Stir in garlic; sauté 1 minute. Stir in tomato paste; cook 2 minutes, stirring frequently. Add chili powder, oregano, coriander, and cumin; sauté 30 seconds.

3. Return bison to pan. Stir in beer; cook 3 minutes or until liquid is reduced by half. Stir in mushroom mixture and tomatoes; bring to a simmer. Reduce heat, and simmer 25 minutes. Stir in squash and chickpeas; simmer 45 minutes. Stir in remaining ½ teaspoon salt and ¼ teaspoon black pepper. Top with sour cream and parsley. Yield: 8 servings (serving size: about 1½ cups chili, 1 tablespoon sour cream, and 1 tablespoon parsley)

CALORIES 295; FAT 9.3g (sat 3.8g, mono 3g, poly 0.8g); PROTEIN 24.3g; CARB 29.4g; FIBER 6.5g; CHOL 53mg; IRON 5.8mg; SODIUM 518mg; CALC 126mg

MEAT

&

POULTRY

FLANK STEAK

There was a time when cravings for beef and the task of maintaining a healthy diet led to one of two things. You either suffered through a tough beef cut that left more than a little to be desired in the flavor department, or you set off on a guilt-inducing binge on one of the heavily marbled "big three" cuts (filet, rib-eye, or strip). It was truly a bleak era for steak lovers. Thankfully, those dark days are behind us and we can confidently stride to the grill or stove, flank steak in hand.

Lower in fat and high in flavor, flank steak is also incredibly versatile. It readily takes on the flavors of Asia, Spain, or Latin America, as in the following recipes. But it's beefy enough to stand on its own as well. Cooking flank steak is best done with high heat like a grill or broiler. It's a thin cut, so intense heat gets you great browning on the outside without over-cooking. Why not kick back and toast the fact that you can have your healthier steak, and eat it too?

YOU'LL LEARN:

HOW TO MARINATE A FLANK STEAK • HOW TO COOK FLANK STEAK
THE CORRECT WAY TO SLICE FLANK STEAK

MASTER RECIPE:

MAPLE AND SOY–GLAZED FLANK STEAK

VARIATIONS:

FLANK STEAK WITH ROMESCO SAUCE • FLANK STEAK TACOS

YOUR MISE EN PLACE

PROTEIN
FLANK STEAK, TRIMMED

FLAVOR BOOSTERS/
STAPLES
LOWER-SODIUM SOY SAUCE
MAPLE SYRUP
SAKE
DARK SESAME OIL
SRIRACHA
BLACK PEPPER
COOKING SPRAY

EQUIPMENT NEEDED:
SHARP KNIFE
FORK
SHALLOW DISH
BROILER PAN
SMALL SKILLET
BASTING BRUSH
CUTTING BOARD

PREHEAT YOUR BROILER.

Maple and Soy-Glazed
FLANK STEAK

Letting your marinade pull double duty and act as a glaze or sauce is a simple way to amp up flavor. Just be sure the marinade boils well so it reduces to a glaze.

1 (1-POUND) FLANK STEAK, TRIMMED

3 TABLESPOONS LOWER-SODIUM SOY SAUCE

3 TABLESPOONS MAPLE SYRUP

2 TABLESPOONS SAKE (RICE WINE) OR DRY SHERRY

2 TEASPOONS DARK SESAME OIL

1 TEASPOON SRIRACHA (HOT CHILE SAUCE)

⅛ TEASPOON FRESHLY GROUND BLACK PEPPER

COOKING SPRAY

Hands-on time: 30 min.
Total time: 40 min.

Meat fibers run in lines known as grain; *this grain is very apparent in flank steak. Slicing across the grain, or perpendicular to the lines, makes steak tender.*

1. Preheat broiler. Pierce steak gently on both sides with a fork. Combine next 6 ingredients (through pepper) in a shallow dish; add steak and turn to coat. Marinate at room temperature 20 minutes, turning occasionally.

2. Remove steak from marinade, reserving marinade. Place steak on a broiler pan coated with cooking spray.

3. Pour marinade into a small skillet; bring to a boil, stirring well. Cook over medium-high heat 3 minutes or until thick and syrupy.

4. Brush steak with half of glaze; broil 5 minutes. Turn steak over, and brush with remaining glaze; broil 5 minutes or until desired degree of doneness.

5. Place steak on a cutting board; let stand 5 minutes. Cut steak diagonally across the grain into thin slices. Yield: 4 servings (serving size: 3 ounces)

CALORIES 232; FAT 9.1g (sat 3.2g, mono 3.6g, poly 1.2g); PROTEIN 23.4g; CARB 11.9g; FIBER 0.2g; CHOL 45mg; IRON 2mg; SODIUM 436mg; CALC 25mg

FLANK STEAK *with* ROMESCO SAUCE

A staple in the Catalan region of Spain, garlicky Romesco is a great flavor enhancer.

2 TABLESPOONS SLICED ALMONDS

2 (¾-OUNCE) SLICES WHOLE-GRAIN
   BREAD, TORN INTO 2-INCH PIECES

4 TEASPOONS EXTRA-VIRGIN OLIVE OIL

2 TEASPOONS CHOPPED FRESH GARLIC

¼ TEASPOON SPANISH SMOKED PAPRIKA

1 TABLESPOON SHERRY VINEGAR

1 (7-OUNCE) BOTTLE ROASTED RED BELL
   PEPPERS, DRAINED

½ TEASPOON SALT, DIVIDED

1 (1-POUND) FLANK STEAK, TRIMMED

¼ TEASPOON FRESHLY GROUND BLACK
   PEPPER

COOKING SPRAY

Hands-on time: 30 min.
Total time: 30 min.

1. Preheat broiler. Arrange almonds and bread in a single layer on a baking sheet. Broil 1 minute or until lightly browned. Transfer almonds and bread to a food processor; process until coarsely ground. Heat olive oil, garlic, and paprika in a small skillet over medium heat; cook for 1 minute or until garlic begins to brown. Add garlic mixture, sherry vinegar, bell peppers, and ⅛ teaspoon salt to bread mixture; process until smooth.

2. Sprinkle steak evenly with remaining ⅜ teaspoon salt and black pepper. Place on a broiler pan coated with cooking spray; broil 5 minutes on each side or until desired degree of doneness. Let stand 5 minutes. Cut steak diagonally across the grain into thin slices. Serve with sauce. Yield: 4 servings (serving size: 3 ounces steak and ¼ cup sauce)

CALORIES 262; FAT 13g (sat 3.2g, mono 6.5g, poly 1.4g); PROTEIN 27.1g; CARB 7.8g; FIBER 1.5g; CHOL 37mg; IRON 2.5mg; SODIUM 537mg; CALC 53mg

If you have leftover sauce, try it on grilled chicken or fish, toss with pasta, or use as a sandwich spread. Leftover sauce will keep in the refrigerator for up to a week.

FLANK STEAK TACOS

A spice mixture is rubbed into the steak before grilling to build in smoky, rich flavor; then it's tucked into warmed tortillas. If you don't feel like tacos, add the steak to a salad.

2 TABLESPOONS OLIVE OIL

2¼ TEASPOONS HOT PAPRIKA

2¼ TEASPOONS GROUND CUMIN

1½ TEASPOONS DARK BROWN SUGAR

½ TEASPOON SPANISH SMOKED PAPRIKA

½ TEASPOON GROUND RED PEPPER

¼ TEASPOON CELERY SEEDS

3 GARLIC CLOVES, MINCED

1 (1½-POUND) FLANK STEAK, TRIMMED

1 TEASPOON KOSHER SALT

½ TEASPOON BLACK PEPPER

COOKING SPRAY

12 (6-INCH) CORN TORTILLAS

Hands-on time: 30 min.
Total time: 2hr. 40 min.

1. Combine first 8 ingredients (through garlic) in a small bowl. Rub steak evenly with spice mixture. Cover and refrigerate at least 2 hours.

2. Preheat grill to high heat. Sprinkle steak evenly with salt and black pepper. Place steak on a grill rack coated with cooking spray, and grill for 6 minutes on each side or until desired degree of doneness. Remove steak from grill, and let stand for 10 minutes. Cut steak across the grain into thin slices.

3. Heat tortillas according to package directions. Divide steak evenly among tortillas. Yield: 6 servings (serving size: 2 tacos)

CALORIES 256; FAT 10.7g (sat 2.4g, mono 5g, poly 1.2g); PROTEIN 20.9g; CARB 20.7g; FIBER 2.8g; CHOL 28mg; IRON 2mg; SODIUM 380mg; CALC 54mg

Selecting
CUTS OF BEEF

Two cuts show up repeatedly in our recipes: tenderloin and flank steak. Tenderloin is the most tender, luxurious cut you can buy, and it's very lean. Flank steak is relatively tough, but delicious and tender when marinated, cooked rare or medium-rare, and sliced thinly against the grain. These are the leaner cuts we tend to favor, but don't limit yourself. Try different cuts. Experiment. You'll begin to understand the character and nuances of flavor and texture from cut to cut. Seek out recipes that best play to the strength of that cut.

● STEW   ● BRAISE   ● GRILL   ● SAUTÉ   ● ROAST   ● BROIL

CHUCK ROAST It's called a roast, but its toughness demands low, moist heat. ● ●

FLAT IRON STEAK The darling of savvy butchers, this specialty cut is very tender and well marbled. ● ● ●

BRISKET A fibrous cut that takes well to slow braising, roasting, or smoking on a low-heat grill. ● ● ●

OSSO BUCO Lower leg veal shanks become meltingly tender when braised. ●

RIB ROAST Great served whole for a special occasion; it's also where rib-eye steaks come from. ●

SHORT RIBS When slow-cooked, the tender meat falls off the bone. ●

TENDERLOIN Comparatively lean for a tender cut, so don't overcook—it dries out easily. ● ● ● ●

NY STRIP Classic grilling or pan-frying steak with full, meaty flavor. ● ● ●

TOP SIRLOIN Slightly less tender than strip steak, it still can handle high heat in a kebab. ● ● ●

TOP ROUND While often cut like a steak, it's tough and is best in dishes like pot roast. ● ●

FLANK STEAK A versatile recipe workhorse—just make sure to slice thinly or else it's too chewy. ● ● ●

SKIRT STEAK Better-marbled and more tender than flank; great for fajitas, tacos, and stir-fries. ● ●

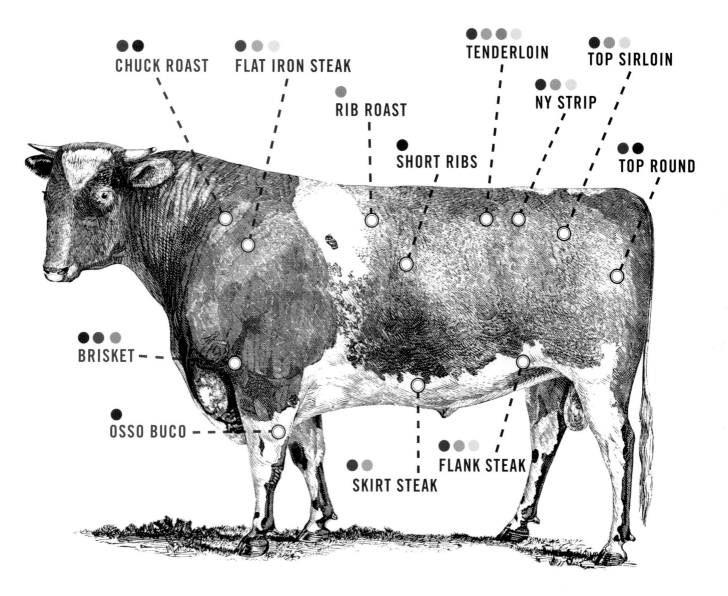

CHUCK ROAST

FLAT IRON STEAK

RIB ROAST

SHORT RIBS

TENDERLOIN

NY STRIP

TOP SIRLOIN

TOP ROUND

BRISKET

OSSO BUCO

SKIRT STEAK

FLANK STEAK

MEAT LOAF

Pause a moment for this unsung hero of family dinner tables around the country. Forget about the dense, gray scourge of school lunches past, and let's talk about really good meat loaf. That's right, meat loaf. It's a beautiful thing when done right, and with our help you'll have no trouble making it perfect. You can't go wrong starting with fresh breadcrumbs combined with tangy buttermilk to keep the meat moist. Then kick things up with spicy Dijon mustard and garlic, or maybe a different combination like pancetta and red wine.

Finish things off with gooey pockets of sharp cheddar cheese tucked into the loaf or, for variety, how about a creamy mushroom sauce on top? As far as variations go, it's all good.

Now that you're thinking about just how delicious meat loaf can be, think about how simple it would be to make for dinner tonight. Gather your fresh ingredients, spend a couple minutes chopping and then mixing, and it's ready for the oven. And you're on to more important things, like planning the meat loaf sandwich you'll make tomorrow.

YOU'LL LEARN:

HOW TO MIX A MEAT LOAF • HOW TO TEST A MEAT LOAF FOR DONENESS

HOW TO MAKE MINI MEAT LOAVES

MASTER RECIPE:

ALL-AMERICAN MEAT LOAF

VARIATIONS:

MEAT LOAF BOLOGNESE • CHEESY MEAT LOAF MINIS

YOUR MISE EN PLACE

PROTEIN
GROUND SIRLOIN
LARGE EGGS, LIGHTLY BEATEN

DAIRY
NONFAT BUTTERMILK
SHARP CHEDDAR CHEESE, DICED

FRESH PRODUCE
ONION, COARSELY CHOPPED
FRESH FLAT-LEAF PARSLEY, CHOPPED
FRESH GARLIC, MINCED

FLAVOR BOOSTERS/ STAPLES
KETCHUP
DIJON MUSTARD
BLACK PEPPER
KOSHER SALT
COOKING SPRAY
FRENCH BREAD, TORN

EQUIPMENT NEEDED:
SHARP KNIFE
FOOD PROCESSOR
BAKING SHEET
MEDIUM BOWL
WOODEN SPOON
LOAF PAN
BASTING BRUSH
MEAT THERMOMETER

PREHEAT YOUR OVEN TO 350°.

All-American
MEAT LOAF

*Chunks of diced cheddar and a surprise ingredient—tangy buttermilk—
help keep this healthier meat loaf moist and flavorful.*

1½ OUNCES FRENCH BREAD, TORN INTO PIECES

½ CUP KETCHUP, DIVIDED

1 CUP COARSELY CHOPPED ONION

5 TABLESPOONS CHOPPED FRESH FLAT-LEAF PARSLEY, DIVIDED

¼ CUP NONFAT BUTTERMILK

1 TABLESPOON MINCED FRESH GARLIC (ABOUT 3 CLOVES)

1 TABLESPOON DIJON MUSTARD

½ TEASPOON FRESHLY GROUND BLACK PEPPER

¼ TEASPOON KOSHER SALT

2 OUNCES SHARP CHEDDAR CHEESE, DICED

2 LARGE EGGS, LIGHTLY BEATEN

1 POUND GROUND SIRLOIN

COOKING SPRAY

*Hands-on time: 15 min.
Total time: 1 hr. 20 min.*

1. Preheat oven to 350°. Place bread in a food processor; pulse 10 times or until coarse crumbs measure 1 cup.

2. Arrange breadcrumbs in an even layer on a baking sheet. Bake at 350° for 6 minutes or until lightly toasted; cool.

3. Combine toasted breadcrumbs, ¼ cup ketchup, onion, 3 tablespoons parsley, and remaining ingredients except cooking spray in a bowl; gently mix until just combined.

4. Transfer mixture to a 9 x 5–inch loaf pan coated with cooking spray; do not pack. Bake at 350° for 30 minutes. Open oven and brush top of loaf with remaining ¼ cup ketchup.

5. Bake an additional 25 minutes or until thermometer inserted into the middle of the meat loaf registers 160°. Let stand for 10 minutes, and cut into 6 slices. Sprinkle with remaining parsley. Yield: 6 servings (serving size: 1 slice)

CALORIES 258; FAT 12.6g (sat 5.8g, mono 4g, poly 0.6g); PROTEIN 21.2g; CARB 14g; FIBER 0.8g; CHOL 119mg; IRON 2.6mg; SODIUM 557mg; CALC 104mg

---

Topping meat loaf with ketchup isn't just about nostalgia. The tomato-y glaze lends just the right touch of sweetness and keeps the meat from drying out in the oven.

MEAT LOAF BOLOGNESE

MEAT LOAF:

1 OUNCE FRENCH BREAD, TORN INTO PIECES

COOKING SPRAY

2 OUNCES PANCETTA, CHOPPED

½ CUP FINELY CHOPPED SHALLOTS

½ CUP FINELY CHOPPED CARROT

1 TABLESPOON TOMATO PASTE

¼ CUP FRUITY RED WINE

¼ CUP 2% REDUCED-FAT MILK

½ TEASPOON KOSHER SALT

½ TEASPOON FRESHLY GROUND BLACK PEPPER

1 LARGE EGG, LIGHTLY BEATEN

⅓ POUND GROUND SIRLOIN

⅓ POUND LEAN GROUND PORK

⅓ POUND GROUND VEAL

MUSHROOM SAUCE:

1 TABLESPOON BUTTER

4 OUNCES FINELY CHOPPED CREMINI MUSHROOMS

2 TABLESPOONS MINCED SHALLOTS

4 TEASPOONS ALL-PURPOSE FLOUR

1 CUP FAT-FREE, LOWER-SODIUM BEEF BROTH

2 TABLESPOONS HALF-AND-HALF

¼ TEASPOON GROUND BLACK PEPPER

DASH OF SALT

Hands-on time: 40 min.
Total time: 1 hr, 38 min.

1. Preheat oven to 350°. To prepare meat loaf, place bread in a food processor; pulse 10 times or until coarse crumbs measure ¾ cup. Arrange breadcrumbs on a baking sheet; bake at 350° for 8 minutes.

2. Heat a small skillet over medium-high heat. Coat pan with cooking spray. Add pancetta; sauté for 2 minutes. Add ½ cup shallots and carrot; sauté 8 minutes, stirring occasionally. Add tomato paste; cook 1 minute. Add wine; cook 2 minutes or until liquid almost evaporates, scraping pan to loosen browned bits. Remove pan from heat; cool 5 minutes. Combine the toasted breadcrumbs, pancetta mixture, milk, and next 6 ingredients (through veal) in a large bowl; gently mix until just combined.

3. Transfer mixture to a 9 x 5–inch loaf pan coated with cooking spray; do not pack. Bake at 350° for 40 minutes or until a thermometer inserted in the center of the meat loaf registers 160°. Let stand 10 minutes; cut into 6 slices.

4. To prepare sauce, melt butter in a medium saucepan over medium-high heat. Add cremini mushrooms and 2 table-spoons shallots; sauté for 6 minutes, stirring occasionally. Add flour, and cook for 1 minute. Add beef broth; cook for 2 minutes, stirring frequently. Stir in half-and-half, ¼ tea-spoon black pepper, and dash of salt. Cook for 30 seconds. Serve with meat loaf. Yield: 6 servings (serving size: 1 slice meat loaf and about 2 tablespoons sauce)

CALORIES 251; FAT 13.2g (sat 5.9, mono 4g, poly 0.8g); PROTEIN 20g;
CARB 10.5g; FIBER 0.8g; CHOL 100mg; IRON 1.6mg; SODIUM 597mg; CALC 47mg

The smaller shape helps bring these minis to the table in almost half the time of a classic loaf.

1 OUNCE BREAD, TORN INTO PIECES

COOKING SPRAY

1 CUP CHOPPED ONION

2 GARLIC CLOVES, CHOPPED

½ CUP KETCHUP, DIVIDED

¼ CUP CHOPPED FRESH PARSLEY

2 TABLESPOONS GRATED PARMESAN
    CHEESE

1 TABLESPOON PREPARED HORSERADISH

1 TABLESPOON DIJON MUSTARD

¾ TEASPOON DRIED OREGANO

¼ TEASPOON SALT

¼ TEASPOON FRESHLY GROUND BLACK
    PEPPER

3 OUNCES WHITE CHEDDAR CHEESE, DICED

1½ POUNDS GROUND SIRLOIN

1 LARGE EGG, LIGHTLY BEATEN

Hands-on time: 23 min.
Total time: 48 min.

CHEESY MEAT LOAF MINIS

1. Preheat oven to 425°. Place bread in a food processor; pulse 10 times or until coarse crumbs measure ¾ cup.

2. Heat a skillet over medium-high heat. Add bread-crumbs; cook 3 minutes or until toasted, stirring frequently.

3. While breadcrumbs cook, heat a large skillet over medium-high heat. Coat pan with cooking spray. Add onion and garlic; sauté 3 minutes. Combine breadcrumbs, onion mixture, ¼ cup ketchup, and remaining ingredients in a large bowl. Shape into 6 (4 x 2–inch) loaves on a broiler pan coated with cooking spray; spread 2 teaspoons ketchup over each. Bake at 425° for 25 minutes or until done. Yield: 6 servings (serving size: 1 mini meat loaf)

CALORIES 254; FAT 11.4g (sat 5.8g, mono 3.8g, poly 0.9g); PROTEIN 28.3g; CARB 11.1g; FIBER 0.9g; CHOL 112mg; IRON 2.6mg; SODIUM 607mg; CALC 150mg

Putting the mini loaves on a broiler pan lets excess fat drip away.

ROAST CHICKEN

Roasted chicken is the gold standard of the culinary world. Fussy French chefs may say they can tell everything about a cook by the way he or she makes an omelet. But we think if you want to prove yourself in the kitchen, roast a chicken. But the truth is, most cooks have a pale, soggy-skin chicken sob story or an undercooked chicken skeleton in their closet. In fact, we've all been deceived by the beautiful simplicity of the roasted chicken. Achieving that properly cooked, oh-so-tender meat is a task that should not be taken lightly. Luckily, you have a secret weapon—us.

We're going to hit you with all the tricks and tips you'll need to turn out a chicken that looks almost too good to eat. One of the most important strategies: Take the time to season chicken properly before putting it in the oven. Then, imagine that moment when you pull your perfectly roasted chicken out of the oven—with its golden skin and the amazing aromas filling the house. There's not much that can beat it. Perfect roast chicken ranks up there with some of the greater achievements in life. (Don't worry, we won't tell your kids, we get it.)

YOU'LL LEARN:

**HOW TO TRUSS A BIRD • HOW TO ROAST A WHOLE CHICKEN
HOW TO QUICKLY ROAST CHICKEN THIGHS AND BREASTS**

MASTER RECIPE:

CLASSIC ROAST CHICKEN

VARIATIONS:

ITALIAN-SEASONED ROAST CHICKEN BREASTS • ASIAN-GLAZED CHICKEN THIGHS

YOUR MISE EN PLACE

PROTEIN
ROASTING CHICKEN

DAIRY
UNSALTED BUTTER, SOFTENED

FRESH PRODUCE
FRESH THYME, MINCED
GARLIC CLOVES, MINCED
SHALLOTS, PEELED AND HALVED
FRESH THYME SPRIGS
LEMON, QUARTERED

FLAVOR BOOSTERS/ STAPLES
PAPRIKA
GROUND CORIANDER
EXTRA-VIRGIN OLIVE OIL
SALT
BLACK PEPPER

EQUIPMENT NEEDED:
SHARP KNIFE
SMALL BOWL
TWINE
CARVING BOARD
ROASTING RACK AND PAN
MEAT THERMOMETER

PREHEAT YOUR OVEN TO 350°.

Classic
ROAST CHICKEN

*Be prepared to turn on your vent. The high-heat method used
for finishing the chicken may generate some smoke.*

---

1 (4-POUND) WHOLE ROASTING CHICKEN

2 TEASPOONS UNSALTED BUTTER,
   SOFTENED

1½ TEASPOONS MINCED FRESH THYME

1 TEASPOON PAPRIKA

1 TEASPOON GROUND CORIANDER

2 TEASPOONS EXTRA-VIRGIN OLIVE OIL

¾ TEASPOON SALT

¼ TEASPOON FRESHLY GROUND BLACK
   PEPPER

2 GARLIC CLOVES, MINCED

3 SHALLOTS, PEELED AND HALVED

3 FRESH THYME SPRIGS

1 LEMON, QUARTERED

Hands-on time: 30 min.
Total time: 1hr. 40 min.

1. Preheat oven to 350°. Check for giblets and neck in the chicken's cavity; remove and discard or set aside for another use. Loosen skin from breasts and drumsticks by inserting fingers, gently pushing between skin and meat.

2. Combine butter and next 7 ingredients (through garlic) in a small bowl. Rub mixture under loosened skin, over flesh, and over top of skin.

3. Tie ends of legs together with twine.

4. Lift wing tips up and over back; tuck under chicken. Place chicken, breast side up, on a rack; place rack in roasting pan. Elevating the bird allows air to circulate and promotes even browning.

5. Place shallots, thyme sprigs, and lemon quarters in cavity of chicken. Roast at 350° for 45 minutes.

6. Increase oven temperature to 450° (do not remove chicken). Roast at 450° for 15 minutes or until a thermometer inserted in meaty part of leg registers 165°.

(continued)

Refrigerate raw chicken for up to two days and cooked chicken for up to three days. You can freeze uncooked chicken up to six months and cooked chicken up to three months.

*Resting is essential in the
roasting process. To keep
juices from being lost to
your cutting board, let the
chicken sit for at least 10
minutes before slicing, 25 to
30 minutes is ideal.*

7. Remove chicken from pan; let stand on carving board 10 minutes. Discard skin.

8. Place the roasted chicken breast side up. Pull each leg quarter away from carcass to expose the hip joint; cut through joint.

9. Cut to remove wings at their joint, cutting as close to the breast as possible.

10. Carve breast meat from top of breast to bottom, keeping knife almost parallel to center bone. Yield: 4 servings (serving size: 1 breast half or 1 leg quarter)

CALORIES 278; FAT 13.6g (sat 4.1g, mono 5.7g, poly 2.5g); PROTEIN 35.7g; CARB 0.9g; FIBER 0.3g; CHOL 111mg; IRON 1.9mg; SODIUM 563mg; CALC 23mg

Lean breast meat needs to be shielded as it cooks, so leave the skin on. With lean meat, you can eat the skin, if you want, and still keep calories and saturated fat within allowable limits.

1 TABLESPOON CHOPPED FRESH
   ROSEMARY

1 TEASPOON GRATED LEMON RIND

2 TABLESPOONS FRESH LEMON JUICE

4 TEASPOONS EXTRA-VIRGIN OLIVE OIL

½ TEASPOON FENNEL SEEDS, CRUSHED

½ TEASPOON SALT

¼ TEASPOON FRESHLY GROUND BLACK
   PEPPER

3 GARLIC CLOVES, MINCED

4 BONE-IN CHICKEN BREAST HALVES
   (ABOUT 3 POUNDS)

COOKING SPRAY

Hands-on time: 15 min.
Total time: 53 min.

ITALIAN-SEASONED ROAST CHICKEN BREASTS

1. Preheat oven to 425°. Combine first 8 ingredients (through garlic) in a small bowl, stirring well. Loosen skin from chicken by inserting fingers, gently pushing between skin and meat. Rub rosemary mixture under loosened skin over flesh; rub over top of skin. Place chicken, bone side down, on a broiler pan coated with cooking spray. Coat skin lightly with cooking spray.

2. Roast at 425° for 35 minutes or until a thermometer inserted into the thickest portion of the breast registers 155°. Remove chicken from pan; let stand for 10 minutes. Yield: 4 servings (serving size: 1 breast half)

CALORIES 240; FAT 12.2g (sat 2.8g, mono 6.3g, poly 2.1g); PROTEIN 29.5g; CARB 1.8g; FIBER 0.3g; CHOL 82mg; IRON 1.2mg; SODIUM 366mg; CALC 24mg

ASIAN-GLAZED CHICKEN THIGHS

Rich thigh meat is higher in fat than lean white meat, so the thighs stay moist even when they're roasted without skin.

⅓ CUP RICE VINEGAR

¼ CUP LOWER-SODIUM SOY SAUCE

3 TABLESPOONS HONEY

2 TABLESPOONS DARK SESAME OIL

1½ TABLESPOONS CHILE PASTE (SUCH AS SAMBAL OELEK)

10 GARLIC CLOVES, MINCED

12 BONE-IN CHICKEN THIGHS, SKINNED

COOKING SPRAY

½ TEASPOON SALT

Hands-on time: 22 min.
Total time: 1hr. 52 min.

1. Combine vinegar, soy sauce, honey, sesame oil, chile paste, and garlic in a small bowl, stirring until honey dissolves. Pour vinegar mixture into a zip-top plastic bag. Add chicken to bag; seal. Marinate in refrigerator 1 hour, turning occasionally. Remove chicken from bag, reserving marinade.

2. Preheat oven to 425°. Place reserved marinade in a small saucepan over medium-high heat; bring to a boil. Cook for 2 minutes or until syrupy, stirring occasionally.

3. Place chicken on a rack coated with cooking spray, and place rack in a roasting pan. Baste chicken with some of the reserved marinade; sprinkle evenly with salt. Roast at 425° for 10 minutes; baste with more of the marinade. Roast an additional 10 minutes; baste again with marinade. Discard remaining marinade. Roast an additional 10 minutes or until done. Let stand 5 minutes before serving. Yield: 6 servings (serving size: 2 thighs)

CALORIES 306; FAT 15.9g (sat 3.8g, mono 6.1g, poly 4.5g); PROTEIN 27.9g; CARB 12g; FIBER 0.2g; CHOL 99mg; IRON 1.7mg; SODIUM 646mg; CALC 24mg

Basting with this salty, sour, sweet, and spicy marinade will develop a rich, flavorful glaze and keep the chicken moist by slowing down the cooking process.

FLAVORFUL CHICKEN BREASTS

Skinless chicken breasts are a well-loved staple of the healthy kitchen, but, if we're honest, they could use a little help when it comes to bringing some excitement to the dinner table. Cue some amazingly flavorful and interesting sauces made in the same pan the chicken is cooked in. Pan-searing meats, then building a sauce out of the tasty bits that stick to the bottom of the pan, is a chef's technique that adds rich flavor to both the meat and the sauce. It lets you cook chicken breasts to perfect doneness without burning the exterior. And it creates *fond*, the brown bits on the bottom of the pan that is your secret ingredient for the tastiest sauces ever made in your kitchen.

Just remember these tips before you fire up the skillet. Check the temperature; think of it like dipping your toes in the pool before you hop in. Carefully place one corner of the chicken into the hot pan to make sure the oil sizzles before you lay the whole piece into the pan. Oh, and those flavorful brown bits (the key to your sauce) won't develop in a nonstick pan, so use stainless steel or enamel for the best-tasting sauces. Finally, trust your eyes. Watch the chicken as it cooks, being sure not to let it get too brown on either side, and be ready to reduce the heat as necessary.

YOU'LL LEARN:

HOW TO POUND CHICKEN INTO THIN PIECES • HOW TO DEGLAZE A PAN AND MAKE SAUCE • HOW TO FINISH COOKING IN EITHER THE SKILLET OR THE OVEN

MASTER RECIPE:

CHICKEN PICCATA

VARIATIONS:

CHICKEN WITH HONEY-BEER SAUCE • BALSAMIC AND SHALLOT CHICKEN BREASTS

PROTEIN
BONELESS CHICKEN BREAST
     HALVES

DAIRY
BUTTER

FRESH PRODUCE
SHALLOTS, CHOPPED
MEDIUM GARLIC CLOVES, SLICED
LEMON, JUICED
FRESH FLAT-LEAF PARSLEY,
     CHOPPED

FLAVOR BOOSTERS/
    STAPLES
ALL-PURPOSE FLOUR
KOSHER SALT
BLACK PEPPER
OLIVE OIL
DRY WHITE WINE
FAT-FREE, LOWER-SODIUM
     CHICKEN BROTH
CAPERS

EQUIPMENT
NEEDED:
SHARP KNIFE
CITRUS JUICER OR FORK
PLASTIC WRAP
MEAT MALLET (OR SMALL
     HEAVY SKILLET)
SMALL BOWL
SHALLOW DISH

CHICKEN PICCATA

In Italy, this classic dish is typically made with veal. But chicken breasts make a great substitute for the more expensive veal and go just as well with the lemon-caper sauce.

---

4 (6-OUNCE) SKINLESS, BONELESS CHICKEN BREAST HALVES

½ CUP ALL-PURPOSE FLOUR, DIVIDED

½ TEASPOON KOSHER SALT

¼ TEASPOON FRESHLY GROUND BLACK PEPPER

2½ TABLESPOONS BUTTER, DIVIDED

2 TABLESPOONS OLIVE OIL, DIVIDED

¼ CUP FINELY CHOPPED SHALLOTS

4 MEDIUM GARLIC CLOVES, THINLY SLICED

½ CUP DRY WHITE WINE

¾ CUP FAT-FREE, LOWER-SODIUM CHICKEN BROTH, DIVIDED

2 TABLESPOONS FRESH LEMON JUICE

1½ TABLESPOONS DRAINED CAPERS

3 TABLESPOONS COARSELY CHOPPED FRESH FLAT-LEAF PARSLEY

Hands-on time: 31 min.
Total time: 31 min.

1. Place each chicken breast half between 2 sheets of heavy-duty plastic wrap; pound to ½-inch thickness using a meat mallet or small heavy skillet.

2. Place 1 teaspoon flour in a small bowl, and place remaining flour in a shallow dish. Sprinkle both sides of chicken evenly with salt and pepper. Dredge chicken in flour in shallow dish; shake off excess.

3. Melt 1 tablespoon butter in a large skillet over medium-high heat. Add 1 tablespoon oil to pan; swirl to coat.

4. Add chicken to pan; sauté 4 minutes on each side or until done. Remove chicken from pan; keep warm.

5. Heat remaining 1 tablespoon oil in pan; swirl to coat. Add shallots to pan; sauté 3 minutes, stirring frequently. Add garlic; sauté 1 minute, stirring constantly.

6. Add wine; bring to a boil, scraping pan with wooden spoon to loosen browned bits. Cook until liquid almost evaporates, stirring occasionally.

(continued)

Proper heat is the key here, if the oil becomes dark or begins to smoke at the edges, reduce temperature so the chicken can cook through without burning on the outside.

When removing chicken from the pan, rest on a cooling rack rather than a plate to help the meat retain more juices.

7. Add ¼ cup broth to reserved 1 teaspoon flour; stir until smooth.

8. Add remaining ½ cup broth to pan; bring to a boil. Cook until reduced by half (about 5 minutes).

9. Stir in flour mixture; cook 1 minute or until slightly thick, stirring frequently.

10. Remove from heat; stir in remaining 1½ tablespoons butter, juice, and capers. Place 1 chicken breast half on each of 4 plates; top each serving with about 2 tablespoons sauce. Sprinkle each serving with about 2 teaspoons parsley. Yield: 4 servings

CALORIES 365; FAT 16.3g (sat 6.1g, mono 7.3g, poly 1.5g); PROTEIN 41.1g; CARB 9.3g; FIBER 0.7g; CHOL 118mg; IRON 2.1mg; SODIUM 574mg; CALC 41mg

An inexpensive, full-flavored domestic beer such as a wheat ale works nicely here. But you can use whatever beer you have in the house.

---

2 TEASPOONS CANOLA OIL

4 (6-OUNCE) SKINLESS, BONELESS CHICKEN BREAST HALVES

¼ TEASPOON FRESHLY GROUND BLACK PEPPER

⅛ TEASPOON SALT

3 TABLESPOONS THINLY SLICED SHALLOTS

½ CUP BEER

2 TABLESPOONS LOWER-SODIUM SOY SAUCE

1 TABLESPOON WHOLE-GRAIN DIJON MUSTARD

1 TABLESPOON HONEY

2 TABLESPOONS FRESH FLAT-LEAF PARSLEY LEAVES

Hands-on time: 4 min.
Total time: 20 min.

CHICKEN *with* HONEY-BEER SAUCE

1. Heat a large skillet over medium-high heat. Add oil to pan; swirl to coat. Sprinkle chicken evenly with pepper and salt. Add chicken to pan; sauté 6 minutes on each side or until done. Remove chicken from pan; keep warm. Add shallots to pan; cook 1 minute or until translucent. Combine beer and next 3 ingredients (through honey) in a small bowl; stir with a whisk. Add beer mixture to pan; bring to a boil, scraping pan to loosen browned bits. Cook 3 minutes or until liquid is reduced to ½ cup. Return chicken to pan; turn to coat with sauce. Sprinkle evenly with parsley. Yield: 4 servings (serving size: 1 breast half and 2 tablespoons sauce)

CALORIES 245; FAT 4.5g (sat 0.7g, mono 2g, poly 1.1g); PROTEIN 40g; CARB 7.8g; FIBER 0.2g; CHOL 99mg; IRON 1.6mg; SODIUM 544mg; CALC 27mg

BALSAMIC *and* SHALLOT CHICKEN BREASTS

Since they won't lay flat in a skillet, the bone-in chicken breasts need to be finished up in the oven for even cooking. But, it's still quick and easy.

---

6 (8-OUNCE) BONE-IN CHICKEN BREAST
  HALVES, SKINNED

1 TEASPOON FRESHLY GROUND BLACK
  PEPPER

½ TEASPOON SALT

1 TABLESPOON OLIVE OIL, DIVIDED

¼ CUP CHOPPED SHALLOTS

3 GARLIC CLOVES, CHOPPED

1 PLUM TOMATO, SEEDED AND CHOPPED

1½ TEASPOONS TOMATO PASTE

½ CUP FAT-FREE, LOWER-SODIUM
  CHICKEN BROTH

⅔ CUP BALSAMIC VINEGAR

¼ CUP CHOPPED GREEN ONIONS

Hands-on time: 23 min.
Total time: 43 min.

1. Preheat oven to 350°. Sprinkle the chicken evenly with pepper and salt. Heat a large skillet over medium-high heat. Add 2 teaspoons olive oil to pan. Add chicken, meat-side down; cook 7 minutes or until browned. Turn chicken over; cook 3 minutes. Place chicken on a jelly-roll pan. Bake at 350° for 23 minutes or until done.

2. Return the pan to medium-high heat. Add remaining 1 teaspoon oil, shallots, and garlic; sauté for 1 minute, stirring constantly. Add tomato and tomato paste; sauté for 1 minute, stirring constantly. Add broth; bring to a boil, scraping pan to loosen browned bits. Add vinegar; reduce heat to medium-low, and cook 20 minutes or until reduced to ⅔ cup, stirring occasionally. Sprinkle chicken with green onions and serve with the sauce. Yield: 6 servings (serving size: 1 chicken breast half and about 2 tablespoons sauce)

CALORIES 250; FAT 4.6g (sat 0.9g, mono 2.2g, poly 0.8g); PROTEIN 42.6g; CARB 6.9g; FIBER 0.4g; CHOL 105mg; IRON 1.8mg; SODIUM 372mg; CALC 39mg

COQ AU VIN

Those crafty French grandmothers, they certainly know how to whip together something amazing from whatever happens to be lying around. And if the resourceful ladies are from Burgundy, they certainly know their way with a chicken that is too tough to roast. They toss it in a pot and drown it in red wine, then pile on bacon and onions for good measure. Simmer together until the meat is falling-from-the-bone tender, and you've got one of the hallmark dishes of French cuisine.

In case you're wondering, coq au vin was originally made with older chickens that tended to be tough and a little gamey, so marinating the chicken two to three days was necessary to tenderize the meat and make it more mild. Today, we enjoy streamlined versions of the classic because modern chickens don't require excessive marinating or long six-hour cook times to turn out perfect. Another thing those wise women got right: Coq au vin is about the most luxurious one-pot meal a home cook can make. So to recap, here's a delicious, crowd-pleasing meal with more than a century of tradition behind it, and you're left with just one pot to wash. So get in the kitchen and make your—or someone's—grandmother proud!

YOU'LL LEARN:

HOW TO BROWN CHICKEN AND AROMATIC VEGETABLES • HOW TO DEGLAZE A DUTCH OVEN • HOW TO TAKE A FEW SHORTCUTS WITHOUT SACRIFICING FLAVOR

MASTER RECIPE:

COQ AU VIN

VARIATIONS:

BACON-BRANDY COQ AU VIN • CHICKEN WITH DARK BEER (COQ À LA BIÈRE)

YOUR MISE EN PLACE

PROTEIN
BONE-IN CHICKEN BREAST HALVES, SKINNED
BONE-IN CHICKEN THIGHS, SKINNED
CHICKEN DRUMSTICKS, SKINNED
BACON SLICES, CHOPPED

FRESH PRODUCE
YELLOW ONION, CHOPPED
CARROT, CHOPPED
PITTED DRIED PLUMS, QUARTERED
FRESH PARSLEY, CHOPPED

FLAVOR BOOSTERS/ STAPLES
RED WINE
SALT
DRIED THYME
DRIED ROSEMARY, CRUSHED
BLACK PEPPER
ALL-PURPOSE FLOUR
BAY LEAVES

EQUIPMENT NEEDED:
LARGE BOWL
SHALLOW DISH
DUTCH OVEN
SLOTTED SPOON
WOODEN SPOON

COQ AU VIN

Since the chicken marinates for eight hours (or overnight), the actual lesson time will be much shorter. Meat on the bone offers more flavor than boneless meat and holds up best in braises. You can purchase a whole chicken and cut it up (or have the butcher do so), or start with bone-in parts.

2 CUPS RED WINE

1 CUP CHOPPED YELLOW ONION

1 CUP CHOPPED CARROT

1 TEASPOON SALT

1 TEASPOON DRIED THYME

½ TEASPOON DRIED ROSEMARY, CRUSHED

½ TEASPOON FRESHLY GROUND BLACK PEPPER

2 (8-OUNCE) BONE-IN CHICKEN BREAST HALVES, SKINNED

2 (4-OUNCE) BONE-IN CHICKEN THIGHS, SKINNED

2 (4-OUNCE) CHICKEN DRUMSTICKS, SKINNED

½ CUP ALL-PURPOSE FLOUR

3 BACON SLICES, CHOPPED

½ CUP PITTED DRIED PLUMS, QUARTERED

2 BAY LEAVES

CHOPPED FRESH PARSLEY (OPTIONAL)

Hands-on time: 29 min.
Total time: 9 hr. 35 min.

1. Combine first 10 ingredients (through drumsticks) in a large bowl; cover and marinate in refrigerator at least 8 hours or overnight.

2. Remove the chicken from marinade, reserving marinade, and pat chicken dry.

3. Place flour in a shallow dish. Dredge the chicken in flour; set aside.

4. Cook bacon in a large Dutch oven over medium-high heat until crisp. Remove bacon from pan, reserving drippings in pan; set bacon aside.

5. Add half of chicken to pan; cook 4 minutes, browning on all sides. Remove chicken from pan. Repeat procedure with remaining chicken.

6. Remove onion and carrot from marinade with a slotted spoon, reserving marinade. Add onion and carrot to pan; sauté for 5 minutes or until softened.

7. Stir in marinade, scraping pan to loosen browned bits. Add chicken, bacon, dried plums, and bay leaves; bring to a simmer.

8. Cover, reduce heat, and simmer 1 hour and 20 minutes or until chicken is tender. Discard bay leaves. Garnish with parsley, if desired. Yield: 4 servings (serving size: 1 breast half, or 1 thigh and 1 drumstick, and about ¾ cup sauce)

CALORIES 353; FAT 11.2g (sat 3.5g, mono 4.4g, poly 1.7g); PROTEIN 34.2g; CARB 28.7g; FIBER 3.7g; CHOL 106mg; IRON 2.8mg; SODIUM 869mg; CALC 62mg

BACON-BRANDY COQ AU VIN

2 BACON SLICES, CHOPPED

4 (4-OUNCE) BONE-IN CHICKEN THIGHS, SKINNED

4 (4-OUNCE) CHICKEN DRUMSTICKS, SKINNED

½ TEASPOON SALT

½ TEASPOON FRESHLY GROUND BLACK PEPPER

¼ CUP FINELY CHOPPED FRESH FLAT-LEAF PARSLEY, DIVIDED

1½ CUPS SLICED CREMINI MUSHROOMS

1½ CUPS DRY RED WINE

1 CUP CHOPPED CARROT

½ CUP CHOPPED SHALLOTS

½ CUP FAT-FREE, LOWER-SODIUM CHICKEN BROTH

1 TABLESPOON BRANDY

1 TEASPOON MINCED FRESH THYME

2 TEASPOONS TOMATO PASTE

1 GARLIC CLOVE, MINCED

Hands-on time: 17 min.
Total time: 48 min.

1. Cook bacon in a large Dutch oven over medium-high heat for 2 minutes. Sprinkle chicken with salt and pepper. Add chicken to pan; cook 2 minutes. Stir in 3 tablespoons parsley, mushrooms, and remaining ingredients; bring to a boil. Cover, reduce heat, and simmer 25 minutes or until chicken is done.

2. Remove chicken with a slotted spoon; keep warm. Bring cooking liquid to a boil; cook until reduced to 3 cups (about 6 minutes). Return chicken to pan; cook 1 minute or until thoroughly heated. Sprinkle with remaining 1 tablespoon parsley. Yield: 4 servings (serving size: 1 thigh, 1 drumstick, and ¾ cup sauce)

CALORIES 345; FAT 12.7g (sat 3.7g, mono 4.7g, poly 2.7g); PROTEIN 43.7g; CARB 11g; FIBER 1.6g; CHOL 150mg; IRON 3.3mg; SODIUM 595mg; CALC 60mg

Even in quick versions of coq au vin like this one, browning the chicken is important. It helps seal in the chicken's juices and caramelizes the meat surface at the same time. A splash of brandy is all you need to add a bit of rich sweetness to the sauce.

CHICKEN *with* DARK BEER (COQ À LA BIÈRE)

3 TABLESPOONS ALL-PURPOSE FLOUR

½ TEASPOON SALT

¼ TEASPOON FRESHLY GROUND BLACK
  PEPPER

2 BONE-IN CHICKEN BREAST HALVES,
  SKINNED

2 BONE-IN CHICKEN THIGHS, SKINNED

2 CHICKEN DRUMSTICKS, SKINNED

2 TABLESPOONS BUTTER

1 TABLESPOON CANOLA OIL

3 TABLESPOONS DRY GIN

¾ CUP CHOPPED CELERY

¾ CUP CHOPPED PEELED CARROT

½ CUP CHOPPED SHALLOTS

3 JUNIPER BERRIES, CRUSHED

1 (8-OUNCE) PACKAGE MUSHROOMS,
  HALVED

3 SPRIGS FRESH THYME

3 SPRIGS FRESH FLAT-LEAF PARSLEY

1 BAY LEAF

1 CUP DARK BEER

¼ CUP WHOLE-MILK GREEK-STYLE YOGURT

2 TEASPOONS WHITE WINE VINEGAR

1 TABLESPOON CHOPPED FRESH FLAT-LEAF
  PARSLEY

Hands-on time: 30 min.
Total time: 1 hr. 15 min.

1. Combine first 3 ingredients; sprinkle evenly over both sides of chicken. Heat butter and oil in a large deep skillet over medium-high heat. Add chicken to pan; sauté 5 minutes on each side or until browned. Remove pan from heat. Pour gin into one side of pan, and return pan to heat. Ignite gin with a long match; let flames die down. Remove chicken from pan; keep warm.

2. Add celery, carrot, shallots, and juniper berries to pan; sauté 5 minutes or until vegetables are tender, stirring occasionally. Add mushrooms. Place thyme, parsley, and bay leaf on a double layer of cheesecloth. Gather edges of cheesecloth together; tie securely. Add cheesecloth bag to pan. Return chicken to pan, nestling into vegetable mixture. Stir in beer; bring to a simmer. Cover, reduce heat, and simmer 45 minutes or until a thermometer inserted in the meaty parts of chicken registers 160°. (Breasts may cook more quickly. Check them after 35 minutes, and remove them when they're done; keep warm.)

3. Discard cheesecloth bag. Remove chicken from pan; keep warm. Place pan over medium heat; stir in yogurt. Cook 1 minute or until thoroughly heated (do not boil, as the yogurt may curdle). Remove from heat; stir in vinegar. Serve chicken with sauce and vegetables. Sprinkle with chopped parsley, if desired. Yield: 4 servings (serving size: 1 chicken breast half, or 1 drumstick and 1 thigh, and about ¾ cup sauce and vegetable mixture)

CALORIES 370; FAT 16g (sat 6.6g, mono 5g, poly 3g); PROTEIN 30.8g;
CARB 15.1g; FIBER 1.4g; CHOL 103mg; IRON 2mg; SODIUM 465mg;
CALC 55mg

PORK PERFECTED

Pork tenderloin has long been a naturally lean, tender, and delicious staple of the family supper or the backyard cookout. But you can sometimes wait up to 30 minutes for a whole pork tenderloin to cook. Plus, its uneven shape means one or more pieces are likely to be either over- or under-cooked. Enter the medallion, a flat circular piece of pork without any bones.

Recipes with pork medallions are rare genius-level stuff. Every part of slicing your pork tenderloin before cooking it makes sense.

Slices create more surface area, meaning more room to season the meat with delicious things like coriander, cinnamon, and nutmeg; or mustard, breadcrumbs, and fresh herbs. It also means dinner will be ready faster since medallions cook in about one-third of the time of a whole tenderloin. And judging the doneness of medallions is way easier than trying to figure out when a whole tenderloin cut is properly cooked. So give these speedy, flavorful takes on pork a spin on any weeknight. You'll wonder what you've been waiting for.

YOU'LL LEARN:

HOW TO COOK PORK MEDALLIONS • HOW TO MAKE A QUICK PAN SAUCE

MASTER RECIPE:

SPICED PORK MEDALLIONS WITH SAUTÉED APPLES

VARIATIONS:

PORK MEDALLIONS WITH WHISKEY CUMBERLAND SAUCE AND HARICOTS VERTS

CRISPY PORK MEDALLIONS

YOUR MISE EN PLACE

PROTEIN
PORK TENDERLOIN, TRIMMED AND CUT
    INTO MEDALLIONS

DAIRY
BUTTER

FRESH PRODUCE
BRAEBURN OR GALA APPLES, SLICED

SHALLOTS, THINLY SLICED

FRESH THYME LEAVES

FLAVOR BOOSTERS/
STAPLES
SALT

GROUND CORIANDER

BLACK PEPPER

GROUND CINNAMON

GROUND NUTMEG

COOKING SPRAY

APPLE CIDER

EQUIPMENT NEEDED:
SHARP KNIFE

CAST-IRON SKILLET

SMALL BOWL

THERMOMETER

TONGS

SPATULA

SPICED PORK MEDALLIONS
with Sautéed Apples

Pork medallions just need a quick sear, so make sure your pan and oil are very hot before adding the meat. This will ensure that your meat browns nicely and will keep it from overcooking.

⅜ TEASPOON SALT

¼ TEASPOON GROUND CORIANDER

¼ TEASPOON FRESHLY GROUND BLACK PEPPER

⅛ TEASPOON GROUND CINNAMON

⅛ TEASPOON GROUND NUTMEG

1 POUND PORK TENDERLOIN, TRIMMED AND CUT CROSSWISE INTO 12 MEDALLIONS

2 TABLESPOONS BUTTER

2 CUPS THINLY SLICED UNPEELED BRAEBURN OR GALA APPLE

⅓ CUP THINLY SLICED SHALLOTS

⅛ TEASPOON SALT

¼ CUP APPLE CIDER

1 TEASPOON FRESH THYME LEAVES

Hands-on time: 20 min.
Total time: 20 min.

1. Heat a large cast-iron skillet over medium-high heat.

2. Combine first 5 ingredients (through nutmeg) in a small bowl; sprinkle spice mixture evenly over pork.

3. Add pork medallions to pan; cook 3 minutes on each side or until thermometer reaches 145°. Remove pork from pan with tongs; keep warm.

4. Melt butter in pan; swirl to coat. Add apple slices, shallots, and salt; sauté 4 minutes or until apple starts to brown.

5. Add apple cider to pan, and cook for 2 minutes or until apple is crisp-tender. Stir in thyme leaves. Serve apple mixture with pork. Yield: 4 servings (serving size: 3 pork medallions and about ½ cup apple mixture)

CALORIES 234; FAT 9.7g (sat 5, mono 3.2g, poly 0.7g); PROTEIN 24.4g; CARB 12.3g; FIBER 1.5g; CHOL 89mg; IRON 1.7mg; SODIUM 394mg; CALC 18mg

Don't be afraid of a little color. New guidelines advise cooking pork to 145°, which means the meat will still have a touch of pink.

PORK MEDALLIONS

with WHISKEY CUMBERLAND SAUCE AND HARICOTS VERTS

Fancy as it sounds, the sauce for these medallions is simple to assemble and cooks quickly.

2 TABLESPOONS FINELY CHOPPED SHALLOTS

2 TABLESPOONS SCOTCH WHISKEY OR BOURBON

2 TABLESPOONS RED CURRANT JELLY

1 TABLESPOON FRESH ORANGE JUICE

1 TABLESPOON FRESH LEMON JUICE

½ TEASPOON DRY MUSTARD

¼ TEASPOON GROUND GINGER

1 TABLESPOON OLIVE OIL

⅝ TEASPOON KOSHER SALT, DIVIDED

½ TEASPOON FRESHLY GROUND BLACK PEPPER, DIVIDED

1 (1-POUND) PORK TENDERLOIN, TRIMMED AND CUT CROSSWISE INTO 12 MEDALLIONS

2 (8-OUNCE) PACKAGES MICROWAVE-IN-A-BAG FRESH HARICOTS VERTS

1 TABLESPOON BUTTER

Hands-on time: 20 min.
Total time: 20 min.

1. Combine first 7 ingredients (through ginger) in a microwave-safe bowl. Microwave at HIGH 1 minute or until thoroughly heated; set mixture aside.

2. Heat a large skillet over medium-high heat. Add oil to pan; swirl to coat. Sprinkle ¼ teaspoon salt and ¼ teaspoon pepper evenly over both sides of pork. Add pork to pan; cook 3 minutes on each side or until a thermometer reaches 145°. Remove from pan; keep warm. Add whiskey mixture to pan; bring to a boil. Cook until reduced to ¼ cup (about 1 minute).

3. Cook haricots verts according to package directions. Combine haricots verts, butter, remaining ⅜ teaspoon salt, and remaining ¼ teaspoon pepper in a medium bowl; toss well to coat. Place 3 pork medallions and 4 ounces haricots verts on each of 4 plates; top pork with 1 tablespoon sauce. Yield: 4 servings

CALORIES 256; FAT 9g (sat 3.1g, mono 4.1g, poly 1g); PROTEIN 26.2g; CARB 16.5g; FIBER 4g; CHOL 81mg; IRON 2.4mg; SODIUM 388mg; CALC 53mg

Here the medallions are seared first on the stovetop and then finished off in the oven to promote even cooking and a crispy brown exterior. The whole process takes less than 30 minutes.

2 TABLESPOONS DIJON MUSTARD

1 (1-POUND) PORK TENDERLOIN, TRIMMED AND CUT INTO 8 MEDALLIONS

½ CUP PANKO (JAPANESE BREADCRUMBS)

1 TABLESPOON CHOPPED FRESH THYME

1 TABLESPOON MINCED FRESH PARSLEY

⅛ TEASPOON SALT

⅛ TEASPOON FRESHLY GROUND BLACK PEPPER

2 TABLESPOONS EXTRA-VIRGIN OLIVE OIL

Hands-on time: 15 min.
Total time: 26 min.

VARIATION

CRISPY PORK MEDALLIONS

1. Preheat oven to 450°. Rub mustard evenly over pork medallions. Combine panko, thyme, parsley, salt, and pepper in a large bowl. Dredge pork in panko mixture.

2. Heat a large ovenproof skillet over medium-high heat. Add oil to pan; swirl to coat. Add pork; sauté 2 minutes or until golden brown. Turn pork. Place skillet in oven; bake at 450° for 8 minutes or until a thermometer registers 145°. Let stand 3 minutes. Yield: 4 servings (serving size: 2 pork medallions)

CALORIES 210; FAT 9.4g (sat 1.7g, mono 5.8g, poly 1.1g); PROTEIN 24.5g; CARB 5.1g; FIBER 0.3g; CHOL 74mg; IRON 1.3mg; SODIUM 329mg; CALC 10mg

Already a virtuoso with medallions? Branch out to try this easy "oven-fried" version.

PAN-SEARED LAMB CHOPS

Poor, misunderstood lamb chops. In many ways, they've become a victim of their own greatness. For too long have they been relegated to the "special occasion" section of many cooks' repertoire. Or worse, abandoned completely over memories of tough, over-cooked, gamey meat. We are here to help teach you otherwise.

In the recipes that follow we school you in the simple joy of lamb chops. You'll realize that in the same time it takes to grill a chicken breast, you can sear up a memorable lamb chop. Chops are the ideal quick-cooking meat—they're cut thin so they cook fast, but the bone keeps them tender and succulent. You'll wonder why you went this long only serving them once in a while. So will your friends and family. Remember this day, as it will be known as the beginning of the Lamb Chop Era in your home.

YOU'LL LEARN:

HOW TO MAKE AN HERB RUB FOR LAMB • HOW TO COOK A LAMB CHOP

HOW TO MAKE A QUICK PAN SAUCE

MASTER RECIPE:

ROSEMARY LAMB CHOPS

VARIATIONS:

APRICOT LAMB CHOPS • CURRANT-GLAZED LAMB CHOPS WITH

PISTACHIO COUSCOUS

YOUR MISE EN PLACE

PROTEIN
LAMB RIB CHOPS, TRIMMED

FRESH PRODUCE
FRESH ROSEMARY, CHOPPED
GARLIC CLOVE, MINCED

FLAVOR BOOSTERS/
STAPLES
SALT
BLACK PEPPER
OLIVE OIL

EQUIPMENT
NEEDED:
SHARP KNIFE
SMALL BOWL
LARGE SKILLET
TONGS

Rosemary
LAMB CHOPS

Pressing gently on the lamb with your finger is the best way to test for doneness. Rare chops are springy to the touch; medium-rare are slightly more firm with a spongy texture; and firm to the touch meat is well done.

1½ TEASPOONS CHOPPED FRESH ROSEMARY

½ TEASPOON SALT

¼ TEASPOON FRESHLY GROUND BLACK PEPPER

1 GARLIC CLOVE, MINCED

8 (3-OUNCE) LAMB RIB CHOPS, TRIMMED

2 TEASPOONS OLIVE OIL

Hands-on time: 22 min.
Total time: 22 min.

Hot oil is essential for a really good sear. Pause a moment after adding the oil to the pan so it can heat completely before adding the lamb chops.

1. Combine rosemary, salt, pepper, and minced garlic in a small bowl.

2. Sprinkle herb mixture evenly over chops; gently rub into lamb.

3. Heat a large skillet over medium-high heat. Add oil to pan; swirl to coat.

4. Add lamb; cook 3 minutes on each side or until desired degree of doneness. Remove lamb from pan; let stand 5 minutes. Yield: 4 servings (serving size: 2 lamb chops)

CALORIES 157; FAT 9.7g (sat 3g, mono 4.6g, poly 0.9g); PROTEIN 16g; CARB 0.4g; FIBER 0.1g; CHOL 52mg; IRON 1.4mg; SODIUM 344mg; CALC 12mg

In this recipe, the chops are cooked slightly longer and sauced immediately before serving. The heat of the chops and the residual heat of the pan warm the sauce, which will keep the chops from overcooking.

½ CUP APRICOT PRESERVES

2 TEASPOONS DIJON MUSTARD

1 TEASPOON BOTTLED MINCED GARLIC

1 TEASPOON LOWER-SODIUM SOY SAUCE

½ TEASPOON WORCESTERSHIRE SAUCE

¼ TEASPOON SALT

⅛ TEASPOON GROUND CINNAMON

⅛ TEASPOON BLACK PEPPER

8 (4-OUNCE) LAMB LOIN CHOPS, TRIMMED

COOKING SPRAY

Hands-on time: 20 min.
Total time: 20 min.

APRICOT LAMB CHOPS

1. Combine first 5 ingredients in a small bowl; set aside. Combine salt, cinnamon, and pepper, and sprinkle over both sides of lamb.

2. Heat a large nonstick skillet over medium-high heat. Coat pan with cooking spray. Add lamb to pan; cook 5 minutes on each side or until desired degree of doneness. Remove skillet from heat; add apricot mixture, turning lamb to coat. Place 2 chops on each of 4 plates; spoon remaining apricot mixture evenly over chops. Yield: 4 servings (serving size: 2 lamb chops and about 2 tablespoons sauce)

CALORIES 287; FAT 8.6g (sat 3g, mono 3.8g, poly 0.6g); PROTEIN 26.1g; CARB 26.7g; FIBER 0.3g; CHOL 81mg; IRON 2.1mg; SODIUM 350mg; CALC 32mg

CURRANT-GLAZED LAMB CHOPS
with PISTACHIO COUSCOUS

1½ CUPS FAT-FREE, LOWER-SODIUM CHICKEN BROTH, DIVIDED

4 TEASPOONS OLIVE OIL, DIVIDED

½ TEASPOON SALT, DIVIDED

1 CUP UNCOOKED COUSCOUS

2 TEASPOONS MINCED FRESH ROSEMARY

½ TEASPOON GARLIC POWDER

¼ TEASPOON BLACK PEPPER

8 (3-OUNCE) LAMB RIB CHOPS, TRIMMED

COOKING SPRAY

⅓ CUP RED CURRANT JELLY

3 TABLESPOONS BALSAMIC VINEGAR

2 TEASPOONS WHOLE-GRAIN MUSTARD

¼ CUP UNSALTED SHELLED DRY-ROASTED PISTACHIOS, COARSELY CHOPPED

2 TABLESPOONS CHOPPED FRESH MINT

ROSEMARY LEAVES (OPTIONAL)

Hands-on time: 20 min.
Total time: 20 min.

1. Bring 1¼ cups broth, 2 teaspoons oil, and ⅛ teaspoon salt to a boil in a medium saucepan. Stir in couscous; cover. Remove pan from heat.

2. Combine remaining 2 teaspoons olive oil, remaining ⅜ teaspoon salt, rosemary, garlic powder, and pepper in a small bowl. Rub paste evenly into both sides of chops. Heat a large nonstick skillet over medium-high heat. Coat pan with cooking spray. Add lamb; cook for 3 minutes on each side or until desired degree of doneness. Remove from pan, and keep warm.

3. Add remaining ¼ cup broth, jelly, vinegar, and mustard to pan. Bring to a boil. Reduce heat; simmer for 90 seconds or until slightly syrupy. Fluff couscous with a fork; stir in pistachios, and sprinkle with mint. Spoon sauce over lamb. Garnish with rosemary leaves, if desired. Serve lamb with couscous. Yield: 4 servings (serving size: 2 chops and ⅔ cup couscous)

CALORIES 507; FAT 17.4g (sat 4.9g, mono 8.7g, poly 2g); PROTEIN 29.6g; CARB 56.4g; FIBER 3.5g; CHOL 70mg; IRON 2.9mg; SODIUM 595mg; CALC 42mg

The slow-cooked flavor of these lamb chops will have family or friends thinking you've been in the kitchen all day—not 20 minutes.

MASTERING SAUCES

A great cook can't afford to ignore the power of a good sauce. Sauces add richness to lean meats and fish, coat pastas, add zing to pizzas, and generally turn tasty meals into memorable ones. Yet sauce making has a reputation for being difficult, a culinary-school skill that separates the home cook from the pro, and not worth the time at home. Here is the good news: Most sauces are just not that hard. With these fundamental sauces in your repertoire, new horizons open up.

MUSHROOM GRAVY

Good with: chicken, pork loin, turkey, meat loaf
Hands-On Time: 20 min. Total Time: 35 min.

This uses fresh sage, but try chopped rosemary, tarragon, thyme, or parsley. If you prefer a thicker gravy, add 1 tablespoon flour to the slurry. If you substitute a fat-free, lower-sodium chicken broth, reduce the salt to $^1/_8$ teaspoon or add none at all.

1 TABLESPOON OLIVE OIL
½ CUP CHOPPED ONION
1½ TABLESPOONS CHOPPED FRESH SAGE
¼ TEASPOON SALT
1 (8-OUNCE) PACKAGE PRESLICED MUSHROOMS
¼ CUP MADEIRA WINE OR DRY SHERRY
3 CUPS CHICKEN STOCK (PAGE 30)
1½ TABLESPOONS ALL-PURPOSE FLOUR
2 TABLESPOONS WATER
2 TABLESPOONS BUTTER
⅛ TEASPOON FRESHLY GROUND BLACK PEPPER

1. Heat oil in a nonstick skillet over medium-high heat. Add onion to pan; sauté 1 minute. Add sage, salt, and mushrooms; sauté 11 minutes or until mushrooms are browned. Add wine; cook 30 seconds or until liquid almost evaporates. Stir in Chicken Stock. Boil; cook until reduced to 2 cups (about 14 minutes).

2. Combine flour and 2 tablespoons water in a bowl, stirring until smooth. Add flour mixture to pan, stirring constantly; return to a boil. Reduce heat; simmer 2 minutes or until slightly thickened, stirring occasionally. Remove from heat. Stir in butter,

1 tablespoon at a time, stirring until butter melts. Stir in pepper. Yield: 8 servings (serving size: about ¼ cup)

CALORIES 58; FAT 4.7g (sat 2.1g, mono 2.0g, poly 0.3g); PROTEIN 1.2g; CARB 3.2g; FIBER .51g; CHOL 7.8mg; IRON .25mg; SODIUM 103.9mg; CALC 9.4mg

BÉCHAMEL SAUCE

Good with: seafood lasagna, mac & cheese, moussaka
Hands-On Time: 15 min. Total Time: 30 min.

Béchamel, one of the "mother" sauces in classic French cuisine, is versatile: It can also serve as the base for soufflés, soups, and savory pie fillings. What's more, add a little Gruyère cheese, and voilà—you've got Mornay Sauce. We call for white pepper so it isn't visible in the sauce.

1¾ CUPS 2% REDUCED-FAT MILK
½ CUP THINLY SLICED ONION
DASH OF FRESHLY GRATED WHOLE NUTMEG
1 BAY LEAF
2 TABLESPOONS BUTTER
1½ TABLESPOONS ALL-PURPOSE FLOUR
¼ TEASPOON SALT
DASH OF GROUND WHITE PEPPER

1. Combine first 4 ingredients in a small saucepan over medium-high heat; bring to a simmer. Remove from heat; cover and let stand 15 minutes. Strain milk mixture through a sieve over a bowl; discard solids.

2. Wipe pan clean with paper towels. Melt butter in pan over medium heat. Add flour to pan; cook 1 minute, stirring constantly. Gradually add strained milk, stirring with a whisk until blended. Bring to a boil; cook 9 minutes or until thickened, stirring constantly. Remove from heat; stir in salt and pepper. Yield: 8 servings (serving size: about 2½ tablespoons)

CALORIES 57; FAT 3.9g (sat 2.4g, mono 1g, poly 0.2g); PROTEIN 2g; CARB 3.8g; FIBER 0.1g; CHOL 12mg; IRON 0.1mg; SODIUM 121mg; CALC 66mg

RED WINE REDUCTION

Good with: beef tenderloin, prime rib, duck
Hands-On Time: 45 min.   Total Time: 45 min.

You can use this recipe to make a pan sauce for steak: Remove the cooked steak from its pan, add the stock to the pan, and scrape to loosen browned bits, then proceed with the recipe. The deglazed bits add wonderful depth of flavor to the sauce.

2 CUPS CHICKEN STOCK (PAGE 30)
1 CUP ZINFANDEL OR OTHER FRUITY DRY RED WINE
⅓ CUP FINELY CHOPPED SHALLOTS
1 TABLESPOON TOMATO PASTE
1 THYME SPRIG
5 TEASPOONS BUTTER
⅛ TEASPOON SALT
⅛ TEASPOON FRESHLY GROUND
    BLACK PEPPER

1. Bring Chicken Stock to a boil in a small saucepan over medium-high heat. Cook until reduced to ½ cup (about 20 minutes). Place stock in a bowl; keep warm.

2. Combine wine and next 3 ingredients (through thyme) in pan over medium-high heat; bring to a boil. Cook until reduced to ⅓ cup, about 8 minutes. Stir in reserved stock; return mixture to a boil. Cook until reduced to ⅔ cup, about 7 minutes. Strain mixture through a sieve over a bowl; discard solids. Stir in butter, 1 teaspoon at a time, stirring until butter melts. Stir in salt and pepper. Yield: 4 servings (serving size: 2 tablespoons)

CALORIES 62; FAT 4.9g (sat 3.1g, mono 1.3g, poly 0.2g); PROTEIN .64g; CARB 3.3g; FIBER .64g; CHOL 12.9mg; IRON .37mg; SODIUM 153.7mg; CALC 13mg

TOMATO MARINARA

Good with: pizza, spaghetti with meatballs, baked ziti
Hands-On Time: 20 min.   Total Time: 7 hours 35 min.

Slow roasting concentrates the flavor in the tomatoes, making for a heartier sauce. If you don't have a food mill, puree the sauce in a blender and strain. Freeze the sauce in pint containers for up to six months.

1 TABLESPOON SUGAR
1 TABLESPOON EXTRA-VIRGIN OLIVE OIL
¾ TEASPOON DRIED BASIL
½ TEASPOON DRIED OREGANO
4 POUNDS PLUM TOMATOES, HALVED
    LENGTHWISE
COOKING SPRAY
⅓ CUP WATER
4 TEASPOONS EXTRA-VIRGIN OLIVE OIL
¾ CUP CHOPPED ONION
1 TEASPOON DRIED BASIL
½ TEASPOON DRIED OREGANO
3 GARLIC CLOVES, MINCED
⅓ CUP DRY RED WINE
⅔ CUP WATER
½ TEASPOON SALT
¼ TEASPOON FRESHLY GROUND BLACK PEPPER

1. Preheat oven to 250°.

2. Combine first 5 ingredients in a large bowl, tossing gently to coat. Arrange tomato halves, cut sides up, on a jelly-roll pan coated with cooking spray. Bake tomatoes at 250° for 7 hours. Remove pan from oven. Add ⅓ cup water to pan, scraping pan to loosen browned bits. Place a food mill over a large bowl; spoon tomato mixture into food mill. Press mixture through food mill; keep warm.

3. Heat 4 teaspoons oil in a saucepan over medium-high heat. Add onion and next 3 ingredients (through garlic); sauté 5 minutes or until tender. Add wine; cook 3 minutes or until liquid nearly evaporates. Stir in tomato mixture and ⅔ cup water; bring to a boil. Cover, reduce heat, and simmer 15 minutes, stirring occasionally. Remove from heat; stir in salt and pepper. Yield: 8 servings (serving size: about ½ cup)

CALORIES 99; FAT 4.9g (sat 0.7g, mono 3g, poly 0.9g); PROTEIN 2.3g; CARB 14.4g; FIBER 3g; CHOL 0mg; IRON 1.4mg; SODIUM 167mg; CALC 27mg

SEAFOOD

GRILLED FISH

Grilling fish seems deceptively simple. Sure, it looks as straightforward as adding food + fire. After all, cavemen could do it, right? Well, that might be the case when you're talking about a hunk of meat, but fish is different. To master fish on the grill, you need a strategy. Chefs call it *zone cooking* or using *direct and indirect heat*. This means building the fire so there is a hot and a cool side of the grill. Whether using a charcoal or gas grill, it goes like this: Make one side of your grill very hot by turning the knob to high, or mounding a majority of the coals on one side. This hot zone is where you'll do your initial searing, creating grill marks and reducing the chance of sticking. Set the other side of the grill to medium heat by turning the knob to medium or using just a few or no coals. The fish will finish cooking in this cooler zone, where indirect heat and convection-style airflow evenly cook the interior. There are a few important steps to take before tossing fish on the grill. First, give it a bath. Brining (soaking in a solution of salt and sugar) both seasons the fish and keeps it moist during cooking. Next, oil it: Pat the fish dry with paper towels, then lightly coat with oil. Dry food rarely sticks to cooking surfaces, and the oil will help the fish brown. It may seem like a lot to remember, but with a little bit of preparation, cooking fish is quick and simple, and the work is an easy trade-off for the sweet, smoky flavor.

YOU'LL LEARN:

HOW TO BRINE FISH • HOW TO GRILL FISH OVER DIRECT AND INDIRECT HEAT (HOT AND COOL ZONES)

MASTER RECIPE:

GRILLED TROUT

VARIATIONS:

CEDAR PLANK–GRILLED SALMON WITH MANGO KIWI SALSA

MAHIMAHI WITH BACON-TOMATO BUTTER

YOUR MISE EN PLACE

PROTEIN
RAINBOW TROUT, DRESSED

FRESH PRODUCE
DILL SPRIGS
MEDIUM LIMES, SLICED

FLAVOR BOOSTERS/
STAPLES
SEA SALT
SUGAR
COOKING SPRAY
TABLE SALT
BLACK PEPPER
WATER

EQUIPMENT
NEEDED:
SHARP KNIFE
SHALLOW DISH
CHARCOAL GRILL AND CHIMNEY
    STARTER, OR GAS GRILL
LARGE SPATULA

SET UP YOUR GRILL.

GRILLED TROUT

Dressed trout is a whole, scaled fish with the gills and internal organs removed. Most fishmongers will automatically clean and dress fish as it's purchased to make it ready for cooking.

2 CUPS WATER

1 TABLESPOON FINE SEA SALT

2 TEASPOONS SUGAR

4 (7-OUNCE) DRESSED RAINBOW TROUT

COOKING SPRAY

¼ TEASPOON TABLE SALT

¼ TEASPOON BLACK PEPPER

2 (1-OUNCE) BUNCHES DILL SPRIGS

2 MEDIUM LIMES, THINLY SLICED

Hands-on time: 20 min.
Total time: 40 min.

Easy does it when turning fish on the grill. To avoid tearing the skin, gently roll the fish over with a spatula instead of turning it with tongs.

1. Combine first 3 ingredients in a shallow dish, stirring until sea salt and sugar dissolve; add fish. Let stand 20 minutes. Drain; pat dry.

2. Prepare charcoal fire in a chimney starter; let coals burn for 15 to 20 minutes or until flames die down. Carefully pour hot coals out of starter; pile on one side of grill. Alternately, preheat a gas grill, turning one side to high heat and the other side to medium heat. Coat grill grate with cooking spray; put grate in place.

3. Sprinkle ¼ teaspoon salt and pepper over fish flesh. Divide dill and lime slices evenly among fish cavities.

4. Coat outside of fish with cooking spray. Place fish over direct heat (the hot zone); grill 4 minutes.

5. Turn fish over and move to indirect heat (the cool zone). Grill 12 minutes or until done. Yield: 4 servings (serving size: 1 fish)

CALORIES 230; FAT 8.9g (sat 2.5g, mono 2.7g, poly 2.8g); PROTEIN 35g; CARB 0.3g; FIBER 0g; CHOL 105mg; IRON 0.6mg; SODIUM 405mg; CALC 132mg

Before you add the fish, make sure the grate is very hot. This allows the radiant heat to begin cooking the fish before it even makes physical contact.

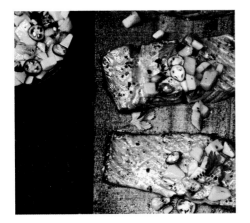

Wood planks offer a simple and elegant way to grill fish without worrying about zones and direct and indirect heating techniques. Flavor from the wood is typically subtle and lightly smoky. Look for food-safe cedar planks at large grocery or department stores.

1 LARGE CEDAR PLANK

1 CUP FINELY DICED PEELED RIPE MANGO

½ CUP DICED PEELED KIWIFRUIT

2 TABLESPOONS CHOPPED FRESH CILANTRO

1 TEASPOON EXTRA-VIRGIN OLIVE OIL

1 TEASPOON FRESH LIME JUICE

1 SERRANO CHILE, FINELY CHOPPED

½ TEASPOON KOSHER SALT, DIVIDED

½ TEASPOON FRESHLY GROUND BLACK PEPPER, DIVIDED

4 (6-OUNCE) SKINLESS SUSTAINABLE SALMON FILLETS (SUCH AS WILD ALASKAN)

Hands-on time: 25 min.
Total time: 40 min.

CEDAR PLANK– GRILLED SALMON *with* MANGO KIWI SALSA

1. Soak plank in water for 25 minutes.

2. Preheat grill to medium-high heat.

3. Combine mango and next 5 ingredients (through chile). Add ¼ teaspoon salt and ¼ teaspoon pepper; set salsa aside.

4. Sprinkle salmon with remaining ¼ teaspoon salt and remaining ¼ teaspoon pepper. Place plank on grill rack; grill 3 minutes or until lightly charred. Turn plank over; place fish on charred side. Cover; grill 8 minutes or until desired degree of doneness. Place each fillet on a plate; top each with ⅓ cup mango salsa. Yield: 4 servings

CALORIES 267; FAT 7.5g (sat 1.2g, mono 2.5g, poly 2.6g); PROTEIN 34.7g; CARB 14.8g; FIBER 2.2g; CHOL 88mg; IRON 1.6mg; SODIUM 356mg; CALC 42mg

MAHIMAHI *with* BACON-TOMATO BUTTER

The flavor of fish on the grill is always good, but a buttery-rich tomato sauce adds a depth and richness that turns simple grilled fish into an elegant dish for entertaining.

2 CUPS WATER

1 TABLESPOON FINE SEA SALT

2 TEASPOONS SUGAR

4 (6-OUNCE) MAHIMAHI FILLETS

COOKING SPRAY

⅛ TEASPOON TABLE SALT

1 SLICE CENTER-CUT BACON, FINELY CHOPPED

1 GARLIC CLOVE, THINLY SLICED

¼ TEASPOON HOT SMOKED PAPRIKA

2 PLUM TOMATOES, SEEDED AND DICED

2 TABLESPOONS BUTTER

Hands-on time: 25 min.
Total time: 45 min.

1. Combine first 3 ingredients in a shallow dish, stirring until sea salt and sugar dissolve; add fish. Let stand 20 minutes. Drain; pat dry.

2. Prepare charcoal fire in a chimney starter; let coals burn for 15 to 20 minutes or until flames die down. Carefully pour hot coals out of starter, and pile them onto one side of the grill. Alternately, prepare gas grill for zone cooking. Coat grill grate with cooking spray; put grate in place.

3. Sprinkle ⅛ teaspoon table salt evenly over fish. Lightly coat fish with cooking spray. Place fish, skin side down, over direct heat (the hot zone) on grill rack; grill 2 minutes or until well marked. Turn fish over and move to indirect heat (the cool zone); grill 12 minutes or until desired degree of doneness.

4. Heat a small skillet over medium heat; add bacon to pan. Cook 5 minutes or until bacon is almost crisp, stirring occasionally. Add garlic; cook for 2 minutes, stirring frequently. Add paprika, and cook for 20 seconds, stirring constantly. Add tomatoes, and cook for 3 minutes. Stir in butter. Remove from heat. Place a fillet on each of 4 plates; top each serving with about 2 tablespoons tomato mixture. Yield: 4 servings

CALORIES 211; FAT 8g (sat 4.4g, mono 1.7g, poly 0.5g); PROTEIN 31.5g; CARB 1.9g; FIBER 0.4g; CHOL 137mg; IRON 2mg; SODIUM 487mg; CALC 31mg

CRISPY-CRUNCHY FISH

A crispy, golden crust—whether the result of deep-frying in a pot of oil, shallow-frying in a skillet, or "frying" in the broiler—speaks the universal language of deliciousness. It makes fish perfect in every way: from crunchy and salty on the outside to tender and moist on the inside. Your secret m.o. for creating mouth-watering fried foods with minimal added fat is keeping things hot. Frying in oil at higher than normal temperatures—as in our master recipe Fried Catfish with Hush Puppies—makes your fish crisp quickly and prevents it from absorbing the cooking oil. In addition, coating fillets in breadcrumbs and crisping them under the blaze of a broiler keeps fish tender and moist while the exterior browns to crunchy perfection. Same thing for dunking fish in batter and pan-frying in a small amount of oil.

So whether you fry in a pot, in a pan, or under the broiler, remember that high heat is the shortest path to golden-brown goodness. And preheating is key. Always give yourself an extra minute or two to make sure your pot, pan, or oven is at the right temperature before adding your fish. A little too hot is better than not hot enough. Your patience will be deliciously rewarded.

YOU'LL LEARN:

HOW TO FRY FISH IN OIL • HOW TO PAN-FRY FISH • HOW TO "OVEN-FRY" FISH

MASTER RECIPE:

FRIED CATFISH WITH HUSH PUPPIES AND TARTAR SAUCE

VARIATIONS:

BEER-BATTERED FISH AND CHIPS • CRISPY FISH WITH LEMON-DILL SAUCE

YOUR MISE EN PLACE

PROTEIN
CATFISH FILLETS
LARGE EGGS

DAIRY
BUTTERMILK

FRESH PRODUCE
FRESH FLAT-LEAF PARSLEY, CHOPPED
LEMON, JUICED
ONION, GRATED

FLAVOR BOOSTERS/
STAPLES
CANOLA MAYONNAISE
DILL PICKLE RELISH
PREPARED HORSERADISH
SALT
PEANUT OIL
ALL-PURPOSE FLOUR
CORNMEAL
BLACK PEPPER
BAKING POWDER
RED PEPPER

EQUIPMENT NEEDED:
SMALL BOWL
CANDY/FRY THERMOMETER
DUTCH OVEN
3 SHALLOW DISHES
SLOTTED SPOON
PAPER TOWELS
MEDIUM BOWL

PREHEAT YOUR OIL TO 385°

FRIED CATFISH

with Hush Puppies and Tartar Sauce

Coat the fillets and prepare the batter for hush puppies while you wait for the oil to heat.

TARTAR SAUCE:

¼ CUP CANOLA MAYONNAISE

1 TABLESPOON DILL PICKLE RELISH

1 TABLESPOON CHOPPED FRESH
   FLAT-LEAF PARSLEY

1 TEASPOON PREPARED HORSERADISH

¾ TEASPOON FRESH LEMON JUICE

⅛ TEASPOON SALT

CATFISH:

8 CUPS PEANUT OIL

6 (6-OUNCE) CATFISH FILLETS

½ TEASPOON SALT

9 OUNCES ALL-PURPOSE FLOUR
   (ABOUT 2 CUPS), DIVIDED

1¼ CUPS CORNMEAL

1 TEASPOON GROUND BLACK PEPPER

2 CUPS BUTTERMILK

2 LARGE EGGS

HUSH PUPPIES:

3.4 OUNCES ALL-PURPOSE FLOUR
   (ABOUT ¾ CUP)

⅓ CUP CORNMEAL

⅓ CUP BUTTERMILK

3 TABLESPOONS GRATED ONION

1 TEASPOON BAKING POWDER

⅛ TEASPOON SALT

¼ TEASPOON GROUND RED PEPPER

1 LARGE EGG, LIGHTLY BEATEN

Hands-on time: 1 hr. 10 min.
Total time: 1 hr. 10 min.

1. To prepare tartar sauce, combine first 6 ingredients in a small bowl. Cover and chill.

2. To prepare catfish, clip a candy/fry thermometer to a Dutch oven; add oil to pan. Heat oil to 385°.

3. Sprinkle fillets evenly with ½ teaspoon salt. Place 4.5 ounces (1 cup) flour in a shallow dish. Combine remaining 4.5 ounces (1 cup) flour, cornmeal, and black pepper in a shallow dish. Combine 2 cups buttermilk and 2 eggs in a shallow dish.

4. Dredge 2 fillets in flour; dip in buttermilk mixture. Dredge in cornmeal mixture; shake off excess breading.

5. Place fillets in hot oil; cook 5 minutes or until done, turning occasionally. Make sure oil temperature does not drop below 375°. Remove fillets from pan using a slotted spoon; drain on paper towels. Return oil temperature to 385°. Repeat procedure twice with remaining fillets.

6. To prepare hush puppies, combine 3.4 ounces flour and remaining ingredients in a medium bowl until dough is thick and drops from a spoon slowly but easily.

7. Drop dough 1 tablespoonful at a time into pan; fry at 375° for 5 minutes or until browned, turning frequently. Remove hush puppies from pan using a slotted spoon; drain on paper towels. Yield: 6 servings (serving size: 1 fillet, 2 hush puppies, and 4 teaspoons tartar sauce)

CALORIES 507; FAT 23.8g (sat 4.1g, mono 8.4g, poly 9.4g); PROTEIN 29.4g; CARB 43g; FIBER 2.6g; CHOL 153mg; IRON 3.6mg; SODIUM 709mg; CALC 171mg

Firm-textured, sustainable fish varieties such as Alaskan cod or pollock work best for fish and chips. Serve with ketchup, tartar sauce, or—as Brits do—with a splash of malt vinegar.

---

1 POUND COD FILLETS, CUT INTO 3-INCH PIECES

1 CUP DARK BEER, DIVIDED

1 POUND BAKING POTATOES, CUT INTO (¼-INCH) STRIPS

COOKING SPRAY

¼ CUP CANOLA OIL, DIVIDED

¾ TEASPOON SALT, DIVIDED

3.38 OUNCES ALL-PURPOSE FLOUR (ABOUT ¾ CUP)

½ TEASPOON FRESHLY GROUND BLACK PEPPER

Hands-on time: 40 min.
Total time: 1 hr. 40 min.

BEER-BATTERED FISH *and* CHIPS

1. Preheat oven to 450°. Combine fish and ¼ cup beer in a medium bowl. Cover and chill for 1 hour.

2. Place potatoes on a jelly-roll pan coated with cooking spray. Drizzle with 1 tablespoon oil, and sprinkle with ¼ teaspoon salt; toss well. Bake at 450° for 20 minutes or until browned and crisp, stirring after 10 minutes.

3. Drain fish; discard liquid. Sprinkle fish with ¼ teaspoon salt. Weigh or lightly spoon flour into dry measuring cups; level with a knife. Combine remaining ¾ cup beer, flour, and black pepper in a medium bowl. Add fish to beer mixture, tossing gently to coat.

4. Heat remaining 3 tablespoons oil in a large non-stick skillet over medium-high heat. Remove fish from bowl, shaking off excess batter. Add fish to pan; cook 3 minutes or until browned. Turn fish over; cook 3 minutes or until done. Sprinkle fish with remaining ¼ teaspoon salt. Serve immediately with chips. Yield: 4 servings (serving size: about 4 ounces fish and about ½ cup chips)

CALORIES 398; FAT 15g (sat 1.1g, mono 8.4g, poly 4.6g); PROTEIN 24.6g; CARB 40.7g; FIBER 2.2g; CHOL 40mg; IRON 2.4mg; SODIUM 524mg; CALC 30mg

CRISPY FISH *with* LEMON-DILL SAUCE

Japanese breadcrumbs called panko are the secret ingredient that makes these oven-fried fish fillets nice and crispy. For sustainability reasons, choose Alaskan cod if you can find it. Or use halibut or tilapia instead of cod.

2 LARGE EGG WHITES, LIGHTLY BEATEN

1 CUP PANKO (JAPANESE BREADCRUMBS)

½ TEASPOON PAPRIKA

¾ TEASPOON ONION POWDER

¾ TEASPOON GARLIC POWDER

4 (6-OUNCE) SKINLESS COD FILLETS

1 TEASPOON BLACK PEPPER

½ TEASPOON SALT

COOKING SPRAY

¼ CUP CANOLA MAYONNAISE

2 TABLESPOONS FINELY CHOPPED DILL PICKLE

1 TEASPOON FRESH LEMON JUICE

1 TEASPOON CHOPPED FRESH DILL

LEMON WEDGES

Hands-on time: 13 min.
Total time: 21 min.

1. Preheat broiler. Place egg whites in a shallow dish. Combine panko, paprika, onion powder, and garlic powder in a shallow dish. Sprinkle fish evenly with pepper and salt. Dip each fillet in egg white, then dredge in panko mixture; place on a broiler pan coated with cooking spray. Broil 4 minutes on each side or until desired degree of doneness.

2. Combine mayonnaise, pickle, lemon juice, and dill. Serve sauce with fish and lemon wedges. Yield: 4 servings (serving size: 1 fillet and about 2 tablespoons sauce)

CALORIES 245; FAT 5.2g (sat 0.2g, mono 2.7g, poly 1.4g); PROTEIN 34.5g; CARB 11.5g; FIBER 0.8g; CHOL 63mg; IRON 0.7mg; SODIUM 654mg; CALC 18mg

Be sure to use a broiler pan, the air vents keep the fish from getting soggy.

How to Buy and Prep
FISH

BUYING FISH:

Often the fresh fish you buy has been frozen at some point to destroy parasites and preserve it. Fish sold as fresh can be anywhere from one day to two weeks out of the water. For top quality, look for "Frozen-at-Sea" (FAS)—fish that has been flash-frozen at extremely low temperatures in as little as three seconds onboard ship. When thawed, sea-frozen fish can be nearly indistinguishable from fresh fish in terms of quality. If you are shopping for fresh fish, ask what's freshest and best that day.

WHOLE FRESH FISH
LOOK FOR:

• Shiny skin, tightly adhering scales, bright clear eyes, firm taut flesh that springs back when pressed, and a moist, flat tail
• Cherry-red, not brownish, gills
• Saltwater fish should smell briny, like the ocean; freshwater fish should smell like a clean pond

FRESH FILLETS OR STEAKS
LOOK FOR:

• Translucent-looking fillets with a pinkish tint when buying white-fleshed fish
• Flesh that appears dense without any gaps between layers
• Plastic packages that contain little to no liquid

FROZEN FISH
LOOK FOR:

• Shiny, rock-hard frozen fish with no white freezer-burn spots, frost, or ice crystals
• Well-sealed packages from the bottom of the freezer case, not more than three months old

STORING FISH

Buy fish on your way out of the store, take it directly home, and cook (or freeze) it within 24 hours. Keep the fish as cold as possible until you're ready to cook it.

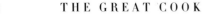

HOW TO FILLET A WHOLE FISH

Often buying whole fish instead of fillets or steaks means better quality and lower price. Ask the fishmonger to scale and gut the fish, then use this technique to fillet any kind of round fish.

1. REMOVE HEAD Place chef's knife behind the pectoral fin; make a diagonal cut through bone. Repeat on opposite side; discard head.

2. REMOVE TAIL Place chef's knife where the tail fin joins the body, and make a straight cut down through the flesh and bone; discard fin.

3. CUT FILLET Starting at head end, run a fillet knife along the backbone in a smooth motion. Cut around the rib cage to separate the fillet.

4. TRIM Cut away the thin belly portion of the fillet. It can be reserved for making stock or cooked separately.

5. REMOVE SKIN With fillet skin-side down, place chef's knife at the tail end between the skin and the flesh. Run the knife slowly along the fillet with the knife blade angled ever so slightly downward, firmly gripping the skin as you cut.

ROASTED WHOLE FISH

Roasting fish is an ideal way to show off a pristine fresh catch. No other meal is as dramatic, impressive, and utterly simple as roasting a whole fish. *Oohs* and *aahs* are guaranteed when the fish hits the table, and they'll continue long after the first bite. Just be sure that amongst all the accolades you don't let slip just how easy it was to pull off.

To start, you'll want to cozy up to the fisherman or fisherwoman in your life. They could provide the fish for you or help you clean it. If not, ask your fishmonger to lend a hand. Once you've got your fish, prep is as easy as making a few small cuts in each side (*scoring*), then seasoning and popping the whole thing into the oven. Scoring larger fish is a pro move as it not only helps the seasoning move into the fish, it's also the perfect place to test doneness. Simply insert the tip of your knife into one of the slits and look to see that the meat flakes easily and pulls cleanly from the bone.

YOU'LL LEARN:

**HOW TO ROAST FISH WHOLE • HOW TO SCORE AND SEASON WHOLE FISH
HOW TO MARINATE FISH**

MASTER RECIPE:

STUFFED WHOLE ROASTED YELLOWTAIL SNAPPER

VARIATIONS:

THAI-STYLE ROASTED TROUT • ROASTED WHOLE SNAPPER

YOUR MISE EN PLACE

PROTEIN
WHOLE YELLOWTAIL SNAPPERS, CLEANED

FRESH PRODUCE
LEMON, JUICED
ONION, CHOPPED
FENNEL BULB, CHOPPED
ROSEMARY SPRIGS
OREGANO SPRIGS

FLAVOR BOOSTERS/ STAPLES
EXTRA-VIRGIN OLIVE OIL
SALT
BLACK PEPPER
COOKING SPRAY

EQUIPMENT NEEDED:
CITRUS JUICER OR FORK
SHARP KNIFE
JELLY-ROLL PAN

PREHEAT YOUR OVEN TO 400°.

Stuffed Whole Roasted
YELLOWTAIL
SNAPPER

When buying whole fish, a good rule of thumb is that each pound of whole fish yields roughly $1\frac{1}{2}$ servings. Scoring the skin with long, shallow cuts keeps it from curling when it hits a hot oven.

2 (1½-POUND) WHOLE CLEANED YELLOWTAIL SNAPPERS (HEADS AND TAILS INTACT)

2 TABLESPOONS EXTRA-VIRGIN OLIVE OIL, DIVIDED

¼ CUP FRESH LEMON JUICE, DIVIDED

½ TEASPOON SALT

¼ TEASPOON GROUND BLACK PEPPER

COOKING SPRAY

6 TABLESPOONS CHOPPED ONION

2 TABLESPOONS CHOPPED FENNEL BULB

4 ROSEMARY SPRIGS

4 OREGANO SPRIGS

Hands-on time: 8 min.
Total time: 40 min.

Take time to season fish inside and out, especially along the slits you cut in the sides. These are the places salt will best penetrate and leave you with a tastier fish.

1. Preheat oven to 400°. Score skin of each fish with 3 diagonal cuts.

2. Rub inside flesh of each fish with 2½ teaspoons olive oil.

3. Drizzle each fish with 4½ teaspoons lemon juice. Sprinkle flesh evenly with salt and black pepper. Place both fish on a jelly-roll pan coated with cooking spray. Place 3 tablespoons onion, 1 tablespoon fennel, 2 rosemary sprigs, and 2 oregano sprigs inside each fish.

4. Rub skin of each fish with ½ teaspoon remaining oil; drizzle each with 1½ teaspoons remaining juice.

5. Roast at 400° for 30 minutes or until fish flakes easily when tested with a fork or until desired degree of doneness. Yield: 4 servings (serving size: about 5 ounces fish and ¼ cup vegetable mixture)

CALORIES 251; FAT 9.2g (sat 1.5g, mono 5.4g, poly 1.6g); PROTEIN 37.5g; CARB 2.7g; FIBER 0.4g; CHOL 67mg; IRON 0.4mg; SODIUM 378mg; CALC 63mg

Count on any fresh citrus to enhance the flavor of fish, but we think fresh lime juice best complements the sweet taste of trout.

2 TABLESPOONS FRESH LIME JUICE

1 TABLESPOON FISH SAUCE

2 TEASPOONS DARK SESAME OIL

½ TEASPOON CRUSHED RED PEPPER

4 (6-OUNCE) WHOLE CLEANED TROUT

COOKING SPRAY

¼ CUP COARSELY CHOPPED FRESH CILANTRO

LIME SLICES (OPTIONAL)

CILANTRO SPRIGS (OPTIONAL)

Hands-on time: 5 min.
Total time: 15 min.

THAI-STYLE ROASTED TROUT

1. Preheat oven to 450°. Combine first 4 ingredients in a small bowl; stir well.

2. Arrange trout on a jelly-roll pan coated with cooking spray. Brush half of juice mixture inside of fish. Roast at 450° for 5 minutes.

3. Brush remaining juice mixture over fish. Roast an additional 5 minutes or until fish flakes easily when tested with a fork or until desired degree of doneness. Sprinkle with chopped cilantro; garnish with lime slices and cilantro sprigs, if desired. Yield: 4 servings (serving size: 1 fish and 1 tablespoon cilantro)

CALORIES 280; FAT 12.2g (sat 3.1g, mono 3.9g, poly 4.1g); PROTEIN 39.3g; CARB 1g; FIBER 0.1g; CHOL 117mg; IRON 0.7mg; SODIUM 443mg; CALC 150mg

ROASTED WHOLE SNAPPER

1 (8-POUND) CLEANED WHOLE RED SNAPPER (HEAD AND TAIL INTACT)

1 CUP WATER

1 CUP FRESH LIME JUICE (ABOUT 8 LIMES)

½ CUP FRESH ORANGE JUICE (ABOUT 2 ORANGES)

1 TABLESPOON SALT

½ CUP (1-INCH) SLICED GREEN ONIONS

2 TABLESPOONS CHOPPED FRESH PARSLEY

1 TABLESPOON CHOPPED FRESH OR 1 TEASPOON DRIED THYME

2 TABLESPOONS FRESH LIME JUICE

1 TABLESPOON OLIVE OIL

½ TEASPOON SALT

½ TEASPOON GROUND ALLSPICE

¼ TEASPOON BLACK PEPPER

¼ TEASPOON GROUND RED PEPPER

6 GARLIC CLOVES, PEELED

COOKING SPRAY

2 LARGE RIPE TOMATOES, EACH CUT INTO 8 WEDGES

2 LARGE ONIONS, EACH CUT INTO 8 WEDGES

1 CUP DRY WHITE WINE

Hands-on time: 18 min.
Total time: 1 hr. 53 min.

1. Score skin of fish in a diamond pattern.

2. Combine 1 cup water, 1 cup lime juice, orange juice, and 1 tablespoon salt in an extra-large plastic bag. Add fish; seal and marinate in refrigerator 20 minutes, turning bag once. Remove snapper from bag; discard marinade.

3. Preheat oven to 425°.

4. Combine green onions and the next 9 ingredients (through garlic cloves) in a food processor or blender, and process until smooth. Spread spice rub evenly over both sides of fish. Place fish on a rack coated with cooking spray.

5. Place tomato wedges, onion wedges, and wine in a shallow roasting pan, and place rack with fish over vegetables in pan. Cover with foil; roast at 425° for 30 minutes. Uncover; roast an additional 45 minutes or until fish flakes easily when tested with a fork. Remove skin from top side of fish; discard skin. Remove tomato mixture from pan; serve with fish. Yield: 16 servings (serving size: 4 ounces fish and ¼ cup tomato mixture)

CALORIES 173; FAT 3g (sat 0.6g, mono 1g, poly 0.8g); PROTEIN 30.5g; CARB 4.9g; FIBER 0.8g; CHOL 53mg; IRON 0.6mg; SODIUM 142mg; CALC 58mg

TENDER SEARED SCALLOPS

A properly seared scallop is a thing of beauty, one of those perfect foods that demands to be celebrated. When you pull that first flawless scallop out of the pan, with its beautifully browned exterior, you'll definitely feel like celebrating. Which is a good thing, because pairing them with roasted vegetables, some wilted spinach, or a cabbage-apple sauté means you can whip up a special occasion meal any time.

There are a few simple points to keep in mind that will help you produce professional-looking scallops every time. Only well-dried scallops will take a proper sear; so dry your scallops before seasoning them, then pat the surface with paper towels again just before putting them into the pan. Speaking of that pan, make sure it's hot! Preheat your pan for a few minutes before cooking, then add the oil and give it a moment to heat as well. Keep the pan as hot as possible throughout the cooking process, but turn down the heat if the oil begins to smoke. Don't be tempted to move the scallops or the pan too much. Turning the scallops too often will only slow down their cooking and lead to a sear that is too light or scallops that are overcooked.

YOU'LL LEARN:

HOW TO SEAR SCALLOPS • HOW TO FLASH-ROAST VEGETABLES
HOW TO MAKE THE FRENCH BUTTER SAUCE CALLED BEURRE BLANC

MASTER RECIPE:

SEARED SCALLOPS WITH SUMMER VEGETABLES AND BEURRE BLANC

VARIATIONS:

SCALLOPS WITH SPINACH AND PAPRIKA SYRUP
SEARED SCALLOPS WITH BACON, CABBAGE, AND APPLE

YOUR MISE EN PLACE

PROTEIN
SEA SCALLOPS

DAIRY
BUTTER, CHILLED AND CUT

FRESH PRODUCE
SHALLOTS, CHOPPED
LEMON RIND, GRATED
MEDIUM ZUCCHINI
MEDIUM YELLOW SQUASH
ORANGE BELL PEPPER, CUT
SMALL RED ONION, CUT IN WEDGES
GRAPE TOMATOES
GARLIC CLOVES, SLICED
SMALL BASIL LEAVES

FLAVOR BOOSTERS/ STAPLES
DRY WHITE WINE
KOSHER SALT
OLIVE OIL
BLACK PEPPER

EQUIPMENT NEEDED:
SHARP KNIFE
GRATER
JELLY-ROLL PAN
SMALL SAUCEPAN
SIEVE
WHISK
LARGE BOWL
CAST-IRON SKILLET
PAPER TOWELS
TONGS

PLACE PAN IN OVEN AND PREHEAT YOUR
OVEN TO 500°.

SEARED SCALLOPS

with Summer Vegetables and Beurre Blanc

The luxurious sauce for these scallops is little more than butter emulsified with reduced white wine—keep the butter cold and whisk it in gradually for the creamiest sauce. Once it's done, keep the sauce warm, but don't let it simmer or it will quickly turn from silky sauce to greasy mess.

½ CUP DRY WHITE WINE

¼ CUP CHOPPED SHALLOTS

3 TABLESPOONS CHILLED BUTTER, CUT INTO SMALL PIECES

½ TEASPOON GRATED LEMON RIND

⅝ TEASPOON KOSHER SALT, DIVIDED

1 MEDIUM ZUCCHINI

1 MEDIUM YELLOW SQUASH

1 ORANGE BELL PEPPER, CUT INTO 1-INCH PIECES

1 SMALL RED ONION, CUT INTO WEDGES

2 TABLESPOONS OLIVE OIL, DIVIDED

1 CUP GRAPE TOMATOES

3 GARLIC CLOVES, THINLY SLICED

½ TEASPOON BLACK PEPPER, DIVIDED

1½ POUNDS LARGE SEA SCALLOPS

¼ CUP SMALL BASIL LEAVES

Hands-on time: 30 min.
Total time: 30 min.

1. Place a jelly-roll pan in oven. Preheat oven to 500° (leave pan in oven as it preheats). Combine wine and shallots in a small saucepan; bring to a boil. Cook 6 minutes or until mixture is reduced to 2 tablespoons.

2. Strain through a sieve into a bowl; discard solids. Return mixture to pan.

3. Gradually add butter, stirring with a whisk until smooth and emulsified. Stir in rind and ⅛ teaspoon salt; keep beurre blanc warm.

4. Cut zucchini and yellow squash in half lengthwise. Cut each half crosswise into 3 pieces; cut each piece lengthwise into 4 strips.

5. Combine zucchini, squash, bell pepper, onion, and 1 tablespoon oil in a large bowl; toss to coat. Arrange vegetable mixture carefully on preheated jelly-roll pan. Roast at 500° for 3 minutes.

(continued)

Dry-packed scallops are preferable to wet-packed because they sear better, are not chemically treated, and have lower sodium content.

A chef's trick: Try searing scallops a minute longer on the first side to ensure a good crust. But shorten your cooking time on the second side to avoid over-cooking.

6. Add tomatoes and garlic; toss gently. Roast at 500° for 4 minutes or until vegetables are lightly browned.

7. Remove from oven; sprinkle with ¼ teaspoon salt and ¼ teaspoon black pepper.

8. While vegetables cook, heat a large cast-iron skillet over high heat.

9. Pat scallops dry with paper towels; sprinkle evenly with remaining ¼ teaspoon salt and ¼ teaspoon black pepper.

10. Add remaining 1 tablespoon oil to pan; swirl to coat. Add scallops to pan; cook 1½ minutes on each side or until scallops are seared and desired degree of doneness. Serve scallops with vegetable mixture and beurre blanc sauce; garnish with basil leaves. Yield: 4 servings (serving size: about 4 ounces scallops, about 1 cup vegetables, and about 1 tablespoon sauce)

CALORIES 345; FAT 17g (sat 6.6g, mono 7.3g, poly 1.6g); PROTEIN 31.1g; CARB 14.9g; FIBER 2.5g; CHOL 79mg; IRON 1.5mg; SODIUM 660mg; CALC 85mg

The less you fuss with scallops, the better they'll taste. In this recipe, you'll make a sweet paprika-lemon sauce before quickly cooking the scallops and then combine the two just before serving.

¼ CUP SUGAR

¼ TEASPOON PAPRIKA

⅛ TEASPOON GROUND RED PEPPER

¼ CUP FRESH LEMON JUICE

2 TEASPOONS OLIVE OIL, DIVIDED

1½ POUNDS LARGE SEA SCALLOPS

¼ TEASPOON SALT, DIVIDED

¼ TEASPOON BLACK PEPPER

1 TEASPOON MINCED FRESH GARLIC

10 OUNCES FRESH BABY SPINACH

¼ CUP PINE NUTS, TOASTED

Hands-on time: 20 min.
Total time: 20 min.

SCALLOPS *with* SPINACH *and* PAPRIKA SYRUP

1. Bring first 4 ingredients to a boil in a saucepan; cook 4 minutes or until mixture thickens. Cool slightly.

2. While paprika mixture cooks, heat a large skillet over medium-high heat. Add 1 teaspoon olive oil to pan; swirl to coat. Pat scallops dry with paper towels; sprinkle with ⅛ teaspoon salt and black pepper. Add scallops to pan; cook 1½ minutes on each side or until done. Remove from pan; keep warm.

3. Add remaining 1 teaspoon oil and garlic to pan; cook 30 seconds, stirring constantly. Add half of spinach; cook for 1 minute, stirring constantly. Add remaining spinach; cook 2 minutes or until wilted. Stir in remaining ⅛ teaspoon salt.

4. Divide the spinach mixture evenly among each of 4 plates, and divide scallops evenly among servings. Drizzle paprika mixture evenly over scallops; sprinkle 1 tablespoon pine nuts over each serving. Yield: 4 servings

CALORIES 313; FAT 9.5g (sat 0.9g, mono 3.3g, poly 3.6g); PROTEIN 31.5g; CARB 27g; FIBER 3.8g; CHOL 56mg; IRON 3.3mg; SODIUM 535mg; CALC 94mg

SEARED SCALLOPS

with BACON, CABBAGE, *and* APPLE

Cook the vegetable mixture first, and then move on to the scallops, which as you're already learning, cook amazingly quick.

---

3 CENTER-CUT BACON SLICES, CUT CROSSWISE INTO ½-INCH PIECES

6 CUPS THINLY SLICED GREEN CABBAGE

1 TABLESPOON CHOPPED FRESH THYME

½ CUP WATER

1½ CUPS CHOPPED FUJI APPLE (1 MEDIUM)

3 TABLESPOONS CIDER VINEGAR

½ TEASPOON FRESHLY GROUND BLACK PEPPER, DIVIDED

1 TABLESPOON CANOLA OIL

16 LARGE SEA SCALLOPS (ABOUT 1 POUND)

¼ TEASPOON SALT

2 TEASPOONS CHOPPED FRESH DILL

Hands-on time: 20 min.
Total time: 20 min.

1. Cook bacon pieces in a Dutch oven over medium-high heat until crisp. Remove bacon pieces from pan, reserving 1½ tablespoons drippings in pan. Add sliced cabbage and chopped thyme to pan; sauté 2 minutes, stirring cabbage mixture occasionally. Add ½ cup water, scraping pan to loosen browned bits. Bring mixture to a boil. Reduce heat to medium; cover pan. Cook 5 more minutes. Stir in chopped apple and cider vinegar; cover. Cook 5 minutes. Stir in cooked bacon and ¼ teaspoon pepper.

2. Heat a large, heavy skillet over high heat. Add oil to pan; swirl to coat. Sprinkle scallops with ¼ teaspoon salt and remaining ¼ teaspoon black pepper. Add scallops to pan; cook 1½ minutes on each side or until scallops are done. Place about 1 cup cabbage mixture on each of 4 plates. Arrange 4 scallops on each serving. Sprinkle each serving with ½ teaspoon dill. Yield: 4 servings

CALORIES 201; FAT 6.1g (sat 1.2g, mono 2.3g, poly 1.3g); PROTEIN 22.4g; CARB 15.1g; FIBER 3.9g; CHOL 43mg; IRON 1.2mg; SODIUM 458mg; CALC 86mg

QUICK & DELICIOUS
STEAMED MUSSELS

Mussels are the chameleons of the culinary world. Unique and interesting on their own, they are also incredibly skilled at adapting to their surroundings, becoming more complex and exciting as they blend into their environment. Beer and bacon, curry and coconut milk, and tomatoes and pasta all make some pretty tasty "environments" in which they can shine. You've just got to guide them through a few basic steps before cooking.

The first step is cleaning. Rinse them well under cold water (use a brush to scrub if necessary), and then remove the "beard"—a tiny bundle of tough fibers that mussels use to attach themselves to things like ropes, posts, or boats, where they live in the wild. Always check to see that mussels are tightly closed, with no chipped or broken shells. If you come across open mussels, pinch the shells closed and hold for a moment; if they open again, discard the mussel. Once cleaned, store in a bowl in the refrigerator covered with a damp paper towel until ready to cook. Don't worry if some of the mussels open while in the refrigerator—they're perfectly safe to cook.

YOU'LL LEARN:

**HOW TO "DEBEARD" MUSSELS • HOW TO TEST MUSSELS FOR FRESHNESS
HOW TO COOK MUSSELS WITH DIFFERENT FLAVOR PROFILES**

MASTER RECIPE:

MUSSELS STEAMED WITH BACON, BEER, AND FENNEL

VARIATIONS:

CURRIED COCONUT MUSSELS • FETTUCCINE WITH MUSSELS

YOUR MISE EN PLACE

PROTEIN

MUSSELS

APPLEWOOD-SMOKED
BACON, CUT

FRESH PRODUCE

FENNEL BULB WITH STALKS

RED POTATOES, CUT

GREEN BEANS, TRIMMED
AND CUT

LEMON, JUICED

FLAVOR BOOSTERS/
STAPLES

KOSHER SALT

BLACK PEPPER

CAN OF BEER

EQUIPMENT NEEDED:

SHARP KNIFE

CITRUS JUICER

DUTCH OVEN

STIFF-BRISTLED BRUSH

MUSSELS STEAMED

with Bacon, Beer, and Fennel

*Most mussels are now farm-raised, so they're easier to clean
and may not even have a beard. If you can't find a 16-ounce beer (a "tall boy"),
you can use a 12-ounce beer plus ¹/₂ cup broth or water.*

1½ POUNDS MUSSELS (ABOUT 40)

1 (12-OUNCE) FENNEL BULB WITH STALKS

**1½ OUNCES APPLEWOOD-SMOKED
BACON, CUT CROSSWISE INTO THIN
STRIPS**

**10 OUNCES RED POTATOES, CUT INTO
½-INCH PIECES (ABOUT 2 CUPS)**

¼ TEASPOON KOSHER SALT

**¼ TEASPOON FRESHLY GROUND BLACK
PEPPER**

1 (16-OUNCE) CAN BEER

**4 OUNCES GREEN BEANS, TRIMMED AND
CUT INTO ⅓-INCH PIECES (ABOUT
¾ CUP)**

1 TABLESPOON FRESH LEMON JUICE

Hands-on time: 25 min.
Total time: 25 min.

---

*Mussels wait for no one.
So ring the dinner bell
right as the mussels go
into the pot. You'll want
to serve them immediately.*

1. Scrub mussels to remove anything clinging to the outside of shells. Remove the "beard," a tiny bundle of thin, rope-like brown fibers found where the two shells meet, by grasping it between your thumb and first finger; tug it out using a saw-like side-to-side motion.

2. Trim tough outer leaves from fennel; mince feathery fronds to measure 2 tablespoons. Remove and discard stalks. Cut fennel bulb in half lengthwise, and discard core. Vertically slice bulb.

3. Cook bacon in a large Dutch oven over medium heat for 3 minutes or until crisp, stirring frequently.

4. Add sliced fennel, potatoes, salt, and pepper. Cook 10 minutes or until fennel is lightly browned, stirring occasionally.

5. Increase heat to high. Add beer, scraping pan to loosen browned bits; bring to a boil.

6. Stir in mussels and green beans; cover and cook 4 minutes or until mussels open.

7. Discard any unopened shells. Stir in juice.

8. Divide mussel mixture evenly among 4 bowls, and spoon broth evenly over mussels. Sprinkle each serving with 1½ teaspoons chopped fennel fronds. Yield: 4 servings

CALORIES 237; FAT 7g (sat 2.2g, mono 2.9g, poly 0.9g); PROTEIN 18g; CARB 23.3g; FIBER 3.8g; CHOL 38mg; IRON 5mg; SODIUM 665mg; CALC 73mg

CURRIED COCONUT MUSSELS

For best results, have the lid to your pot next to the stove so you can cover the pot immediately after adding the mussels. Capturing the steam will help the mussels cook quickly and keep all their briny goodness in the pot.

---

1 TABLESPOON OLIVE OIL

2 CUPS CHOPPED ONION

1 TABLESPOON FINELY CHOPPED PEELED FRESH GINGER

2 GARLIC CLOVES, MINCED

1 JALAPEÑO PEPPER, CHOPPED

2 TEASPOONS RED CURRY PASTE

1 CUP LIGHT COCONUT MILK

½ CUP DRY WHITE WINE

1 TEASPOON DARK BROWN SUGAR

¼ TEASPOON KOSHER SALT

2 POUNDS SMALL MUSSELS, SCRUBBED AND DEBEARDED (ABOUT 60)

¾ CUP SMALL BASIL LEAVES, DIVIDED

3 TABLESPOONS FRESH LIME JUICE

4 LIME WEDGES

Hands-on time: 25 min.
Total time: 25 min.

1. Heat a large Dutch oven over medium-high heat. Add oil to pan; swirl to coat. Add onion, ginger, garlic, and jalapeño; sauté 3 minutes, stirring frequently. Stir in curry paste; cook 30 seconds, stirring constantly. Add coconut milk, wine, sugar, and salt; bring to a boil. Cook 2 minutes. Stir in mussels; cover and cook 5 minutes or until mussels open. Discard any unopened shells. Stir in ½ cup basil and juice.

2. Divide mussels mixture evenly among 4 bowls, and spoon the coconut mixture evenly over mussels. Sprinkle each serving with 1 tablespoon remaining basil; serve with lime wedges. Yield: 4 servings

CALORIES 241; FAT 9.9g (sat 4g, mono 3.2g, poly 1.3g); PROTEIN 20g; CARB 19.1g; FIBER 1.7g; CHOL 42mg; IRON 6.8mg; SODIUM 594mg; CALC 80mg

FETTUCCINE
with MUSSELS

*Timing is critical here, so have
everything ready for the sauce
before you even start cooking the
pasta. There's nothing finer than
a steaming pot of well-sauced
mussels tossed with al dente
pasta, and nothing worse than
lukewarm pasta and lukewarm
bivalves.*

8 OUNCES UNCOOKED FETTUCCINE

2 TABLESPOONS BUTTER

½ CUP FINELY CHOPPED ONION

6 GARLIC CLOVES, COARSELY CHOPPED

½ CUP DRY WHITE WINE

3 PLUM TOMATOES, CHOPPED

⅓ CUP BOTTLED CLAM JUICE

1½ POUNDS MUSSELS (ABOUT 40),
   SCRUBBED AND DEBEARDED

¼ CUP CHOPPED FRESH FLAT-LEAF
   PARSLEY

Hands-on time: 27 min.
Total time: 27 min.

1. Bring 6 quarts water to a boil in a large pot. Add pasta; cook until almost al dente. Drain through a sieve over a large bowl, reserving ⅓ cup pasta cooking water.

2. Melt butter in a large skillet over medium heat. Add onion to pan; cook 4 minutes, stirring occasionally. Add garlic to pan; cook 1 minute, stirring constantly. Add wine to pan; cook 3 minutes or until the liquid evaporates, stirring occasionally. Add tomatoes; cook 2 minutes, stirring occasionally. Stir in reserved pasta cooking water and clam juice; bring to a boil. Add mussels; cover and cook 4 minutes or until mussels open. Discard any unopened shells. Add cooked pasta to the tomato mixture; cook 1 minute or until thoroughly heated, tossing well to combine. Sprinkle with parsley. Serve immediately. Yield: 4 servings (serving size: about 2 cups)

CALORIES 415; FAT 10.1g (sat 4.5g, mono 2.3g, poly 1.2g); PROTEIN 27g; CARB 54g; FIBER 2.9g; CHOL 58mg; IRON 8.6mg; SODIUM 530mg; CALC 76mg

SAUTÉED SHRIMP

I admit I've long had a love/hate relationship with shrimp. As a teenager working in a seafood restaurant on the Florida Gulf Coast, I was sentenced to hours standing by the sink, peeling and deveining hundreds of pounds of shrimp in a weekend. But now shrimp is often my family's go-to for a quick-cooking, lean protein that is perfect for weeknight meals or dressed up to be the star at a dinner party.

Shrimp demand a little TLC during their short cooking time to turn out perfectly.

Keeping an eye on the time and temperature that your shrimp cook will ensure they don't wind up rubbery or tough. Always be sure to cook in a hot pan, but don't let the pan get too hot (hint: if you see the edges of the pan smoking, it's too hot), as shrimp will quickly toughen on the outside if cooked at too high a temperature. Watch the shrimp carefully as they cook. As soon as they curl (like a C) and turn white, remove them from heat; it doesn't take much time to go from perfectly cooked and tender to overdone and chewy.

YOU'LL LEARN:

HOW TO PEEL AND DEVEIN SHRIMP • HOW TO SAUTÉ SHRIMP
HOW TO COOK GRITS

MASTER RECIPE:

LEMON PEPPER SHRIMP SCAMPI

VARIATIONS:

SAUTÉED ASPARAGUS AND SHRIMP WITH GREMOLATA
SHRIMP AND GRITS

YOUR MISE EN PLACE

PROTEIN
JUMBO SHRIMP

DAIRY
UNSALTED BUTTER

FRESH PRODUCE
FRESH PARSLEY, CHOPPED
FRESH GARLIC, MINCED
LEMON, JUICED

FLAVOR BOOSTERS/ STAPLES
ORZO
SALT
BLACK PEPPER

EQUIPMENT NEEDED:
PARING KNIFE OR DEVEINING TOOL
LARGE POT
SIEVE
CITRUS JUICER
MEDIUM BOWL
LARGE NONSTICK SKILLET

Lemon Pepper
SHRIMP SCAMPI

Jumbo shrimp are sautéed in butter and lemon juice for an easy,
classic dish that can be prepared in just minutes.

1½ POUNDS JUMBO SHRIMP

1 CUP UNCOOKED ORZO

2 TABLESPOONS CHOPPED FRESH
    PARSLEY

½ TEASPOON SALT, DIVIDED

7 TEASPOONS UNSALTED BUTTER,
    DIVIDED

2 TEASPOONS MINCED FRESH GARLIC

2 TABLESPOONS FRESH LEMON JUICE

¼ TEASPOON FRESHLY GROUND BLACK
    PEPPER

Hands-on time: 20 min.
Total time: 20 min.

To save time, use a pair of kitchen shears to cut through the back side of the shrimp and quickly pull out the vein. Or buy prepeeled and deveined shrimp to further minimize prep time.

1. Take each shrimp and pull off the head (if still attached) and the legs. Peel off the outer shell and discard.

2. Using a sharp paring knife, cut about ¼ inch deep along the back of the each shrimp. Remove and discard the dark vein using the tip of the knife or deveining tool.

3. Bring 4 to 6 quarts water to a boil in a large pot. Add orzo; cook 10 minutes or until al dente; drain. Place orzo in a medium bowl. Stir in parsley and ¼ teaspoon salt; cover and keep warm.

4. While orzo cooks, melt 1 tablespoon butter in a large non-stick skillet over medium-high heat.

5. Sprinkle shrimp with remaining ¼ teaspoon salt. Add half of shrimp to pan; sauté 2 minutes or until almost done. Transfer shrimp to a plate. Melt 1 teaspoon butter in pan. Add remaining shrimp to pan; sauté 2 minutes or until almost done. Transfer to plate.

6. Melt remaining 1 tablespoon butter in pan. Add garlic to pan; cook 30 seconds, stirring constantly. Stir in shrimp, lemon juice, and pepper; cook 1 minute or until shrimp are done. Serve with orzo. Yield: 4 servings (serving size: ½ cup orzo and about 7 shrimp)

CALORIES 403; FAT 10.4g (sat 4.8g, mono 2.2g, poly 1.4g); PROTEIN 40.1g;
CARB 34.7g; FIBER 1.7g; CHOL 276mg; IRON 4.3mg; SODIUM 549mg; CALCIUM 97mg

VARIATION

SAUTÉED ASPARAGUS *and* SHRIMP *with* GREMOLATA

The shrimp and asparagus are sautéed separately to make for even cooking. The fresh lemon-herb topping is added after cooking to help build flavor.

GREMOLATA:

¼ CUP FINELY CHOPPED FRESH FLAT-LEAF PARSLEY

2 TEASPOONS GRATED LEMON RIND

⅛ TEASPOON SALT

⅛ TEASPOON FRESHLY GROUND BLACK PEPPER

3 GARLIC CLOVES, MINCED

SHRIMP:

4 TEASPOONS OLIVE OIL, DIVIDED

3 CUPS (1½-INCH) SLICES ASPARAGUS (ABOUT ½ POUND)

1½ POUNDS PEELED AND DEVEINED MEDIUM SHRIMP

⅛ TEASPOON SALT

⅛ TEASPOON FRESHLY GROUND BLACK PEPPER

Hands-on time: 25 min.
Total time: 25 min.

1. To prepare gremolata, combine all 5 ingredients; set aside.

2. To prepare shrimp, heat a large nonstick skillet over medium-high heat. Add 2 teaspoons oil to pan, swirling to coat; heat 20 seconds. Add asparagus to pan; sauté 3 minutes, stirring frequently. Remove asparagus from pan; keep warm.

3. Add remaining 2 teaspoons oil to pan, swirling to coat; heat 20 seconds. Add shrimp to pan; sauté 3 minutes or until done, stirring occasionally. Add asparagus, salt, and pepper to pan; sauté 1 minute or until thoroughly heated. Sprinkle evenly with gremolata. Yield: 4 servings (serving size: 1½ cups)

CALORIES 240; FAT 7.6g (sat, 1.2g, mono, 3.7g, poly, 1.7g); PROTEIN 36.1g; CARB 5.2g; FIBER 1.6g; CHOL 259mg; IRON 5.6mg; SODIUM 403mg; CALC 115mg

This is a quick version of the Southern classic. Add hot pepper sauce or chipotle chiles for an extra kick.

3 CUPS WATER

1 TABLESPOON BUTTER

¾ CUP UNCOOKED QUICK-COOKING GRITS

2 OUNCES GRATED PARMESAN CHEESE (ABOUT ½ CUP)

⅝ TEASPOON KOSHER SALT, DIVIDED

¾ TEASPOON FRESHLY GROUND BLACK PEPPER, DIVIDED

2 CENTER-CUT BACON SLICES, CHOPPED

1 CUP CHOPPED WHITE ONION

1 TABLESPOON MINCED GARLIC

1 (8-OUNCE) PACKAGE PRESLICED MUSHROOMS

1 POUND MEDIUM SHRIMP, PEELED AND DEVEINED

½ TEASPOON CRUSHED RED PEPPER

¼ CUP HALF-AND-HALF

1 TABLESPOON ALL-PURPOSE FLOUR

¾ CUP FAT-FREE, LOWER-SODIUM CHICKEN BROTH

⅓ CUP CHOPPED GREEN ONIONS

Hands-on time: 29 min.
Total time: 29 min.

SHRIMP *and* GRITS

1. Bring 3 cups water and butter to a boil in a small saucepan. Whisk in grits; cover and cook 5 minutes, stirring frequently. Remove from heat. Stir in cheese, ¼ teaspoon salt, and ½ teaspoon black pepper; cover. Keep warm.

2. Cook bacon in a large nonstick skillet over medium-high heat until crisp. Add white onion, garlic, and mushrooms to pan; cook 8 minutes or until mushrooms begin to brown and give off liquid, stirring frequently. Add shrimp and red pepper; cook 3 minutes.

3. Combine half-and-half and flour in a small bowl, stirring with a whisk until smooth. Add flour mixture, broth, remaining ⅜ teaspoon salt, and remaining ¼ teaspoon black pepper to pan; bring to a boil. Cook 2 minutes or until slightly thickened. Top with green onions. Serve shrimp mixture with grits. Yield: 6 servings (serving size: ½ cup grits and about ½ cup shrimp mixture)

CALORIES 236; FAT 7.9g (sat, 4.1g, mono 1.4g, poly, 0.5g); PROTEIN 18.4g; CARB 22.8g; FIBER 2.1g; CHOL 115mg; IRON 1.3mg; SODIUM 583mg, CALC 173mg

This creamy, saucy shrimp is also good over pasta or brown rice.

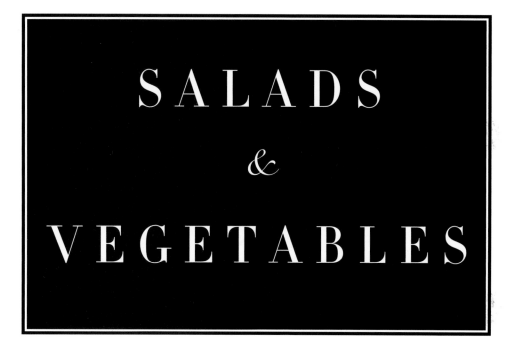

SALADS

&

VEGETABLES

LEAFY MAIN SALADS

If there's one thing that all nations have in common, it's main-dish salads. They're universal, popping up in every culture around the globe. And it's no wonder why: Salads are quick and easy to prepare and packed with all the elements that make food exciting. The array of colors, textures, and flavors makes every bite different and interesting. With the following recipes, we'll take an around-the-globe look at salads that will get you excited about eating your leafy greens.

Who else but the French would think to top their salad with crunchy croutons, crispy bits of bacon, and a delicate, creamy, poached egg? Take a spin through Thailand for a cabbage-and-sprout salad brilliantly tossed with sliced steak and bright herbs such as cilantro, mint, and basil. Then, go Greek, where classics like tangy feta, olives, and sweet tomatoes add up to one delicious meal that can be topped off with just about any meat. Global flavors. Hearty ingredients. You'll never think of salads as boring again.

YOU'LL LEARN:

HOW TO MAKE DIFFERENT KINDS OF SALADS AND DRESSINGS
HOW TO MAKE CROUTONS • HOW TO POACH EGGS

MASTER RECIPE:

FRENCH FRISÉE SALAD WITH BACON AND POACHED EGGS

VARIATIONS:

THAI STEAK SALAD • GREEK SALAD BOWL

YOUR MISE EN PLACE

PROTEIN
APPLEWOOD-SMOKED BACON, CUT
LARGE EGGS

FRESH PRODUCE
FRESH TARRAGON, CHOPPED
FRISEE, TORN

FLAVOR BOOSTERS/ STAPLES
RYE BREAD, CUBED
WHITE WINE VINEGAR
OLIVE OIL
KOSHER SALT
GROUND BLACK PEPPER
WHITE VINEGAR
CRACKED BLACK PEPPER

EQUIPMENT NEEDED:
SHARP KNIFE
BAKING SHEET
LARGE SKILLET
SLOTTED SPOON
LARGE BOWL
WHISK
SMALL CUP (FOR POACHING
    THE EGGS)
PAPER TOWELS

PREHEAT YOUR OVEN TO 400°.

French
FRISÉE SALAD
with Bacon and Poached Eggs

Also known as curly endive, frisée is a slightly bitter green with crisp, lacy leaves.
If you can't find it sold separately, substitute a bagged salad blend that includes frisée
or radicchio. Put water on to boil for poaching the eggs while the croutons toast.

---

4 (1-OUNCE) SLICES RYE BREAD,
    CUT INTO ½-INCH CUBES

6 SLICES APPLEWOOD-SMOKED BACON,
    CUT CROSSWISE INTO ½-INCH-THICK
    PIECES

⅓ CUP WHITE WINE VINEGAR

1 TABLESPOON CHOPPED FRESH
    TARRAGON

3 TABLESPOONS OLIVE OIL

⅛ TEASPOON KOSHER SALT

¼ TEASPOON FRESHLY GROUND BLACK
    PEPPER

1 HEAD FRISÉE (ABOUT 8 OUNCES), TORN

1 TABLESPOON WHITE VINEGAR

4 LARGE EGGS

CRACKED BLACK PEPPER (OPTIONAL)

Hands-on time: 23 min.
Total time: 48 min.

A chef's trick for poach-
ing eggs: Crack your eggs
first into a small cup, then
carefully slip them into the
simmering poaching water.

1. Preheat oven to 400°. Arrange bread cubes in a single layer on a baking sheet; bake at 400° for 20 minutes or until toasted, turning once. Let croutons cool.

2. Cook bacon in a large skillet over medium heat until crisp, stirring occasionally. Remove bacon from pan with a slotted spoon, reserving 1 tablespoon drippings; set bacon aside.

3. Combine 1 tablespoon drippings, white wine vinegar, and next 4 ingredients (through ground pepper) in a large bowl, stirring with a whisk.

4. Add croutons, bacon, and frisée to dressing in bowl, tossing to coat. Place 2 cups salad mixture on each of 4 plates.

5. Add water to a large skillet, filling two-thirds full; bring to a boil. Reduce heat; bring to a simmer. Add white vinegar. Break eggs into pan; cook 3 minutes or until desired degree of doneness.

6. Carefully remove eggs from pan using a slotted spoon; drain on paper towels. Top each salad with a poached egg. Sprinkle with cracked pepper, if desired. Yield: 4 servings

CALORIES 344; FAT 23.5g (sat 5.6g, mono 12.5g, poly 2.6g); PROTEIN 14.5g;
CARB 18g; FIBER 2.3g; CHOL 227mg; IRON 2.4mg; SODIUM 765mg; CALC 101mg

Give your steak a few minutes to rest before slicing so all the juices from the meat don't wind up on your cutting board.

COOKING SPRAY

1 (1½-POUND) FLANK STEAK, TRIMMED

½ TEASPOON FRESHLY GROUND BLACK PEPPER

¼ TEASPOON KOSHER SALT

¼ CUP FRESH LIME JUICE

1 TABLESPOON BROWN SUGAR

2 TABLESPOONS LOWER-SODIUM SOY SAUCE

1 TABLESPOON FISH SAUCE

2 TEASPOONS MINCED FRESH GARLIC

1 TEASPOON SRIRACHA (HOT CHILE SAUCE)

1½ CUPS THINLY SLICED RED CABBAGE

1¼ CUPS FRESH BEAN SPROUTS

¾ CUP JULIENNE-CUT CARROTS

⅓ CUP FRESH MINT LEAVES

⅓ CUP FRESH CILANTRO LEAVES

⅓ CUP FRESH BASIL LEAVES

Hands-on time: 15 min.
Total time: 20 min.

THAI STEAK SALAD

1. Heat a large grill pan over medium-high heat. Coat pan with cooking spray. Sprinkle steak evenly with pepper and salt. Add steak to pan; cook 6 minutes on each side or until desired degree of doneness. Remove steak from pan; let stand 5 minutes. Cut steak diagonally across grain into thin slices.

2. Combine juice and next 5 ingredients (through Sriracha) in a large bowl; stir with a whisk.

3. Combine cabbage and remaining ingredients in a medium bowl. Add 6 tablespoons juice mixture to cabbage mixture; toss well. Toss steak in remaining 2 tablespoons juice mixture. Add steak to cabbage mixture; toss to combine. Yield: 6 servings (serving size: 3 ounces steak and ⅔ cup salad)

CALORIES 198; FAT 6.5g (sat 2.4g, mono 2.2g, poly 0.3g); PROTEIN 26.3g; CARB 8.4g; FIBER 1.5g; CHOL 37mg; IRON 2.4mg; SODIUM 498mg; CALC 57mg

Check the nutrition labels of the hearts of palm and artichoke hearts if you are watching your sodium intake; sodium levels vary greatly among brands.

8 CUPS TORN ROMAINE LETTUCE

2 CUPS CHOPPED COOKED CHICKEN BREAST (ABOUT ¾ POUND)

1 (14-OUNCE) CAN HEARTS OF PALM, DRAINED AND SLICED

1 (14-OUNCE) CAN QUARTERED ARTICHOKE HEARTS, DRAINED

1 CUP GRAPE TOMATOES, HALVED

½ CUP PITTED KALAMATA OLIVES, HALVED

½ CUP THINLY SLICED RED ONION

⅓ CUP LIGHT BOTTLED GREEK VINAIGRETTE WITH OREGANO AND FETA CHEESE

Hands-on time: 12 min.
Total time: 12 min.

VARIATION

GREEK SALAD BOWL

1. Combine all ingredients in a large bowl; toss well to coat. Serve immediately. Yield: 6 servings (serving size: 2 cups)

CALORIES 182; FAT 8g (sat 1.4g, mono 3.7g, poly 2.1g); PROTEIN 18.1g; CARB 11.1g; FIBER 3.2g; CHOL 40mg; IRON 3.4mg; SODIUM 695mg; CALC 67mg

KALE

For years leafy green kale sat ignored, a throwaway garnish on the side of our plates, or tucked behind an orange slice or the lemon wedges in our baskets of fried seafood. It was a vegetable on the fringe. But it's finally moved to the center of our plates and winning the hearts of healthy eaters. Trendy no longer, it's now considered a leafy green with lots of possibility. Only one question remains: What took us so long to fall in love?

Kale is one of the most nutritious and versatile vegetables you'll ever find. Hardly any other veggie can easily go from starring role in a crisp salad to tender braised green to salty, crunchy snack. Not to mention that a serving of kale has more (and better absorbed) calcium than a glass of milk, and way more vitamin C than an orange. Healthy fats—like olive oil and pumpkin seeds or a small amount of cheese—enhance kale's nutritional value. The carotenoids (powerful antioxidants) in kale are better utilized in the body when taken in with a little fat. Oh yeah, and kale tastes really good. So hop on the kale bandwagon and enjoy its many shades of green.

YOU'LL LEARN:

HOW TO PREPARE KALE FOR SALAD • HOW TO BRAISE KALE
HOW TO MAKE KALE CHIPS

MASTER RECIPE:

LEMONY KALE SALAD

VARIATIONS:

KALE CHIPS • BRAISED KALE

YOUR MISE EN PLACE

DAIRY
FRESH PECORINO ROMANO CHEESE, SHAVED

FRESH PRODUCE
KALE

LEMON, JUICED

SWISS CHARD LEAVES, TORN

GREEN ONIONS, SLICED

FLAVOR BOOSTERS/
STAPLES
OLIVE OIL

SUGAR

BLACK PEPPER

KOSHER SALT

PUMPKINSEED KERNELS

EQUIPMENT NEEDED:
JUICER OR FORK

SHARP KNIFE

COLANDER

LARGE SERVING BOWL

WHISK

SMALL SKILLET

SALAD TOSSERS

Lemony
KALE SALAD

Some varieties of kale have fairly tender, edible stems. But if stems are large and tough, remove them with a knife or kitchen shears. Or try this chef's tip: Loosely grasp the base of the stem between your fingers and pull the leaf through the fingers with your opposite hand.

1 SMALL BUNCH KALE (ABOUT 8 OUNCES)

1 TABLESPOON FRESH LEMON JUICE

1 TABLESPOON OLIVE OIL

½ TEASPOON SUGAR

½ TEASPOON FRESHLY GROUND BLACK PEPPER

¼ TEASPOON KOSHER SALT

2 CUPS TORN SWISS CHARD LEAVES

4 TEASPOONS UNSALTED PUMPKINSEED KERNELS

¼ CUP SLICED GREEN ONIONS (ABOUT 2)

1 OUNCE SHAVED FRESH PECORINO ROMANO CHEESE

Hands-on time: 10 min.
Total time: 20 min.

Store washed kale leaves (torn or whole) in a salad spinner or wrap with a damp paper towel and tuck inside a plastic bag in the fridge.

1. Rinse kale leaves to remove any dirt; drain well.

2. Fold each leaf in half lengthwise; cut out hard stem. Tear kale into small pieces.

3. Combine lemon juice and next 4 ingredients (through salt) in a large serving bowl, stirring with a whisk until sugar dissolves.

4. Add kale and chard; toss. Let stand 10 minutes.

5. Heat a small skillet over medium heat. Add pumpkinseed kernels; cook 5 minutes or until browned, stirring frequently.

6. Add toasted seeds, onions, and cheese to greens; toss. Yield: 6 servings (serving size: 1 cup)

CALORIES 65; FAT 4g (sat 0.8g, mono 2g, poly 0.8g); PROTEIN 2.6g; CARB 6.3g; FIBER 1.4g; CHOL 2mg; IRON 1.4mg; SODIUM 234mg; CALC 87mg

These chips are crispy, crunchy, salty, and truly easy to make. For a different flavor, try sprinkling the kale with grated Parmesan, red pepper flakes, or sweet paprika before baking.

1 LARGE BUNCH CURLY KALE (ABOUT 1 POUND), TORN INTO 2-INCH PIECES

1 TABLESPOON OLIVE OIL

¼ TEASPOON KOSHER SALT

Hands-on time: 8 min.
Total time: 23 min.

KALE CHIPS

1. Preheat oven to 350°. Rinse kale; drain well, and pat dry with paper towels. Place in a large bowl. Drizzle with olive oil, and sprinkle with salt. Toss well. Place kale in a single layer on 3 (16 x 13–inch) baking sheets.

2. Bake at 350° for 15 minutes. (Watch closely to prevent leaves from burning.) Cool completely. Store in an airtight container. Yield: 4 servings (serving size: 1 cup)

CALORIES 67; FAT 4g (sat 0.5g, mono 2.5g, poly 0.6g); PROTEIN 2.5g; CARB 7.5g; FIBER 1.5g; CHOL 0mg; IRON 1.3mg; SODIUM 152mg; CALC 101mg

If you've ever bought kale, you know the size of a bunch can vary widely. Weight measurements are a good place to start, but don't agonize if the size of your bunch is off by a couple of ounces. The recipes will still work.

1 TABLESPOON OLIVE OIL

1½ CUPS THINLY SLICED ONION

⅓ CUP THINLY SLICED GARLIC

2 LARGE BUNCHES KALE (ABOUT 2 POUNDS), CHOPPED

1 CUP FAT-FREE LOWER-SODIUM CHICKEN BROTH

1 CUP WATER

¾ TEASPOON CRUSHED RED PEPPER

2 TEASPOONS RED WINE VINEGAR

¼ TEASPOON SALT

¼ TEASPOON BLACK PEPPER

Hands-on time: 15 min.
Total time: 35 min.

BRAISED KALE

1. Heat olive oil in a Dutch oven over medium heat. Add onion and garlic; cook 10 minutes or until golden, stirring frequently. Add kale, broth, 1 cup water, and red pepper; cover and bring to a boil. Reduce heat, and simmer 20 minutes if you like it chewy; add another 5 to 10 minutes if you like it soft. Stir in vinegar, salt, and black pepper. Yield: 8 servings (serving size: ¾ cup)

CALORIES 88; FAT 2.6g (sat 0.4g, mono 1.3g, poly 0.6g); PROTEIN 4.5g; CARB 14.8g; FIBER 2.9g; CHOL 0mg; IRON 2.1mg; SODIUM 173mg; CALC 167mg

GRILLED VEGETABLES

If you're firing up the grill for your favorite cut of meat, why would you dream of cooking your vegetables anywhere else? Grilling is not only one of the quickest, no-fuss ways to cook vegetables, it's also one of the most flavorful. Grilling brings out the natural sweetness of vegetables, gives them a light smoky flavor, and, simply put, promotes all-around deliciousness.

And just like meats, grilled vegetables definitely benefit from being seasoned before they cook. At the very least, salt and a light coating of fat are a must before any veggie hits the grill. Salt draws out water and enhances flavor while the fat promotes browning and helps those fabulous grill marks develop. You'll see the recipes here offer suggested cooking times, but as any grill master soon learns, every grill is a little bit different. So don't be afraid to sample the veggies as they cook to help you determine doneness. Consider it a bit of healthy snacking!

YOU'LL LEARN:

DIFFERENT WAYS TO SEASON VEGETABLES FOR GRILLING

HOW TO GRILL VEGETABLES

MASTER RECIPE:

GRILLED ASPARAGUS WITH CAPER VINAIGRETTE

VARIATIONS:

GRILLED STUFFED JALAPEÑOS • MISO-GRILLED VEGETABLES

YOUR MISE EN PLACE

FRESH PRODUCE
ASPARAGUS SPEARS, TRIMMED
GARLIC CLOVE, MINCED
FRESH BASIL LEAVES

FLAVOR BOOSTERS/
STAPLES
EXTRA-VIRGIN OLIVE OIL

KOSHER SALT

COOKING SPRAY

RED WINE VINEGAR

DIJON MUSTARD

BLACK PEPPER

CAPERS, CHOPPED

EQUIPMENT
NEEDED:
SHARP KNIFE

GRILL

SHALLOW DISH

SMALL BOWL

TONGS

WHISK

PREHEAT YOUR GRILL TO
MEDIUM-HIGH.

GRILLED ASPARAGUS

with Caper Vinaigrette

*Thinner asparagus cooks beautifully directly on the grill, but bigger stalks
(aka jumbo asparagus) need to be precooked to keep them from losing their bright color.
If all you can find is jumbo asparagus, dunk those thicker stalks in a pot
of boiling salted water for 2 minutes, then refresh in cold water before grilling.*

1½ POUNDS ASPARAGUS SPEARS, TRIMMED

3 TABLESPOONS EXTRA-VIRGIN OLIVE OIL, DIVIDED

½ TEASPOON KOSHER SALT, DIVIDED

COOKING SPRAY

1 TABLESPOON RED WINE VINEGAR

½ TEASPOON DIJON MUSTARD

¼ TEASPOON FRESHLY GROUND BLACK PEPPER

1 GARLIC CLOVE, MINCED

2 TEASPOONS CAPERS, COARSELY CHOPPED

¼ CUP SMALL FRESH BASIL LEAVES

Hands-on time: 30 min.
Total time: 30 min.

Spread veggies out on trays or cooling racks after grilling. A pile of freshly cooked veggies quickly turns to mush if all that heat is trapped together.

1. Preheat grill to medium-high heat. Place asparagus in a shallow dish. Add 1 tablespoon oil and ¼ teaspoon salt, tossing well to coat.

2. Place asparagus on grill rack coated with cooking spray; grill 4 minutes or until crisp-tender, turning after 2 minutes.

3. Combine remaining ¼ teaspoon salt, vinegar, and next 3 ingredients (through garlic) in a small bowl; stir with a whisk. Slowly pour remaining 2 tablespoons oil into vinegar mixture, stirring constantly with a whisk. Stir in capers.

4. Arrange asparagus on a serving platter; drizzle with vinaigrette, and sprinkle with basil. Yield: 6 servings (serving size: about 4 asparagus spears and about 2 teaspoons vinaigrette)

CALORIES 91; FAT 7.2g (sat 1.1g, mono 5g, poly 1.1g); PROTEIN 2.6g; CARB 4.8g; FIBER 2.5g; CHOL 0mg; IRON 2.5mg; SODIUM 198mg; CALC 32mg

If making these poppers for a party, you can stuff the peppers, cover, and chill. Then pop them on the grill just before your guests arrive. They're a healthy, fresh alternative to the popular breaded and fried version.

2 SLICES CENTER-CUT BACON

½ CUP (4 OUNCES) CREAM CHEESE, SOFTENED

½ CUP (4 OUNCES) FAT-FREE CREAM CHEESE, SOFTENED

¼ CUP (1 OUNCE) SHREDDED EXTRA-SHARP CHEDDAR CHEESE

¼ CUP MINCED GREEN ONIONS

1 TEASPOON FRESH LIME JUICE

¼ TEASPOON KOSHER SALT

1 SMALL GARLIC CLOVE, MINCED

14 JALAPEÑO PEPPERS, HALVED LENGTHWISE AND SEEDED

COOKING SPRAY

2 TABLESPOONS CHOPPED FRESH CILANTRO

2 TABLESPOONS CHOPPED SEEDED TOMATO

Hands-on time: 30 min.
Total time: 40 min.

GRILLED STUFFED JALAPEÑOS

1. Preheat grill to medium-high heat.

2. Cook the bacon in a skillet over medium heat until crisp. Remove bacon from pan, and drain on paper towels. Crumble bacon. Combine crumbled bacon, cheeses, and next 4 ingredients (through garlic) in a bowl, stirring to combine. Divide cheese mixture evenly and fill the pepper halves.

3. Place peppers, cheese side up, on grill rack coated with cooking spray. Cover and grill peppers 8 minutes or until bottoms of peppers are charred and cheese mixture is lightly browned. Place the peppers on a serving platter. Sprinkle with cilantro and tomato. Yield: 14 servings (serving size: 2 pepper halves)

CALORIES 56; FAT 4.1g (sat 2.2g, mono 1.1g, poly 0.2g); PROTEIN 2.9g; CARB 2.1g; FIBER 0.5g; CHOL 13mg; IRON 0.2mg; SODIUM 157mg; CALC 55mg

The vegetable amounts that are suggested below are just guidelines; it's fine to double or triple amounts for a crowd. Just make sure to keep the proportions in the marinade: 1 to 2 tablespoons miso and 1 tablespoon water to about 3 tablespoons olive oil.

2 TABLESPOONS RED OR WHITE/YELLOW MISO (SOYBEAN PASTE)

1 TABLESPOON LUKEWARM WATER

3 TABLESPOONS OLIVE OIL

1 POUND ZUCCHINI, CUT LENGTHWISE INTO ⅓-INCH-THICK SLICES

8 OUNCES JAPANESE EGGPLANT, CUT LENGTHWISE INTO ⅓-INCH-THICK SLICES

1 RED BELL PEPPER, CUT INTO 6 PIECES

1 ORANGE BELL PEPPER, CUT INTO 6 PIECES

1 SMALL RED ONION, CUT INTO WEDGES

COOKING SPRAY

2 TABLESPOONS FRESH MINT LEAVES

1 LIME, CUT INTO WEDGES

Hands-on time: 25 min.
Total time: 25 min.

MISO-GRILLED VEGETABLES

1. Preheat grill to high heat.

2. Combine miso and 1 tablespoon water. Gradually add oil, stirring with a whisk. Place zucchini, eggplant, and bell peppers on a jelly-roll pan. Add 5 tablespoons miso mixture; toss to coat. Brush onion with remaining miso mixture.

3. Place vegetables on a grill rack coated with cooking spray. Grill zucchini, eggplant, and bell pepper 4 minutes on each side or until tender. Grill onion 6 minutes on each side or until tender. Sprinkle with mint. Serve with lime wedges. Yield: 6 servings (serving size: about 3 zucchini pieces, 2 eggplant pieces, 2 bell pepper pieces, and 1 onion wedge)

CALORIES 112; FAT 7.1g (sat 1g, mono 4.9g, poly 0.8g); PROTEIN 1.8g; CARB 11.4g; FIBER 4.5g; CHOL 0mg; IRON 0.6mg; SODIUM 221mg; CALC 22mg

HEIRLOOM TOMATOES

There's really nothing more exciting than the first day heirloom tomatoes arrive at your local market. Perfectly imperfect, with all sorts of funky shapes and colors that range from red to orange to yellow to green—even shades of purple—heirloom tomatoes are a great connection to our foodie past. What makes a tomato heirloom? The term is used to describe any tomato plant that's openly pollinated (by wind and bees) and has been cultivated for more than 50 years. But these vibrant, colorful, flavorful tomatoes began to disappear in the 1940s, in favor of modified varieties that were disease resistant and had a longer shelf life. Trouble is, those changes also meant a reduction in flavor.

Thankfully heirloom varieties are making a comeback, in all their misshapen, multi-colored glory. Isn't that delicious news? And there's something you can do to make sure they stick around. The surefire way to make farmers keep growing—and markets keep selling—wildly colorful and good-for-you heirloom tomatoes is to buy them. Buy them whenever you can and make these outrageously delicious recipes.

YOU'LL LEARN:

HOW TO IDENTIFY DIFFERENT HEIRLOOM VARIETIES

DIFFERENT WAYS TO USE HEIRLOOM TOMATOES

WHY TOMATOES DON'T STORE WELL IN THE REFRIGERATOR

MASTER RECIPE:

TOMATO STACK SALAD WITH CORN AND AVOCADO

VARIATIONS:

SUMMER PEACH AND TOMATO SALAD • HEIRLOOM TOMATO SALSA

YOUR MISE EN PLACE

PROTEIN
BACON SLICES

DAIRY
BUTTERMILK

FRESH PRODUCE
FRESH CHIVES, CHOPPED
FRESH BASIL, CHOPPED
GARLIC CLOVE, MINCED
CORN, SHUCKED
HEIRLOOM TOMATOES, SLICED
GLOBE TOMATOES, SLICED
AVOCADO, PEELED AND SLICED

FLAVOR BOOSTERS/ STAPLES
CANOLA MAYONNAISE
CIDER VINEGAR
BLACK PEPPER
COOKING SPRAY
KOSHER SALT
EXTRA-VIRGIN OLIVE OIL

EQUIPMENT NEEDED:

SHARP KNIFE
GRILL
SPATULA
LARGE NONSTICK SKILLET
TONGS
PAPER TOWELS
WHISK
SMALL BOWL

PREHEAT GRILL TO HIGH.

TOMATO STACK
Salad with Corn and Avocado

Look for larger heirloom tomato varieties (Brandywine, Mr. Stripey, Cherokee Purple) to make the slices needed for this stack salad. Firm flesh that yields slightly to gentle pressure is the best test of ripeness.

---

2 BACON SLICES, HALVED

¼ CUP LOW-FAT BUTTERMILK

1 TABLESPOON FINELY CHOPPED FRESH CHIVES

1 TABLESPOON FINELY CHOPPED FRESH BASIL

2 TABLESPOONS CANOLA MAYONNAISE

2 TEASPOONS CIDER VINEGAR

1 GARLIC CLOVE, MINCED

½ TEASPOON FRESHLY GROUND BLACK PEPPER, DIVIDED

2 EARS SHUCKED CORN

COOKING SPRAY

2 LARGE HEIRLOOM TOMATOES, EACH CUT INTO 4 (½-INCH-THICK) SLICES

2 GLOBE TOMATOES, EACH CUT INTO 4 (½-INCH-THICK) SLICES

⅛ TEASPOON KOSHER SALT

½ RIPE PEELED AVOCADO, THINLY SLICED

4 TEASPOONS EXTRA-VIRGIN OLIVE OIL

Hands-on time: 30 min.
Total time: 30 min.

1. Preheat grill to high heat. Heat a large nonstick skillet over medium heat. Add bacon to pan; cook 8 minutes or until crisp, tossing and turning occasionally to help it curl. Drain bacon on paper towels.

2. Combine buttermilk and next 5 ingredients (through garlic) in a small bowl, stirring with a whisk. Stir in ¼ teaspoon pepper. Set dressing aside.

3. Coat corn with cooking spray. Place corn on grill rack; grill 8 minutes or until well marked, turning occasionally. Remove from grill; cool slightly.

4. Cut corn kernels from cobs.

5. Sprinkle tomato slices evenly with salt.

6. Alternate layers of tomato and avocado on each of 4 plates. Scatter corn evenly onto plates. Drizzle each tomato stack with about 1½ tablespoons dressing and 1 teaspoon oil. Sprinkle remaining ¼ teaspoon black pepper over salads; top each salad with 1 bacon piece. Yield: 4 servings

CALORIES 191; FAT 13g (sat 1.9g, mono 8g, poly 2.2g); PROTEIN 5.1g; CARB 16.1g; FIBER 4.5g; CHOL 5mg; IRON 0.9mg; SODIUM 228mg; CALC 40mg

---

Some of the enzymes that give tomatoes flavor and aroma are destroyed when they drop below 55°F. So avoid refrigerating any variety of tomato.

SUMMER PEACH *and* TOMATO SALAD

A stunning combination of skin-on peaches and heirloom tomatoes of various colors, sizes, and shapes creates a sweet-savory salad that starts off any meal with a bang.

¼ CUP THINLY VERTICALLY SLICED RED ONION

½ POUND RIPE PEACHES, PITTED AND CUT INTO WEDGES

¼ POUND HEIRLOOM TOMATO, CUT INTO THICK WEDGES

¼ POUND HEIRLOOM CHERRY OR PEAR TOMATOES, HALVED

1 TABLESPOON SHERRY VINEGAR

1½ TEASPOONS EXTRA-VIRGIN OLIVE OIL

1 TEASPOON HONEY

⅛ TEASPOON SALT

⅛ TEASPOON FRESHLY GROUND BLACK PEPPER

¼ CUP (1 OUNCE) CRUMBLED FETA CHEESE

2 TABLESPOONS SMALL FRESH BASIL LEAVES OR TORN BASIL

Hands-on time: 19 min.
Total time: 19 min.

1. Combine first 4 ingredients in a large bowl.

2. Combine vinegar, olive oil, honey, salt, and pepper in a small bowl, stirring with a whisk. Drizzle vinegar mixture over peach mixture; toss well to coat. Sprinkle with cheese and basil. Yield: 4 servings (serving size: 1 cup)

CALORIES 75; FAT 3.5g (sat 1.3g, mono 1.6g, poly 0.3g); PROTEIN 2.1g; CARB 9.9g; FIBER 1.7g; CHOL 6mg; IRON 0.4mg; SODIUM 156mg; CALC 47mg

HEIRLOOM TOMATO SALSA

Heirloom tomatoes have a shorter shelf life than regular tomatoes, so buy them within a day or two of when you plan to serve them. This rainbow-hued salsa recipe is a great way to use up ripe heirlooms. Serve as a topping for grilled fish and meats or as a dip for chips.

½ CUP DICED RED ONION

¼ CUP CHOPPED FRESH CILANTRO

2 TABLESPOONS FRESH LIME JUICE

¼ TEASPOON KOSHER SALT

¼ TEASPOON GROUND CUMIN

⅛ TEASPOON GROUND RED PEPPER

1½ POUNDS MIXED HEIRLOOM TOMATOES, SEEDED AND CHOPPED

1 SERRANO CHILE, SEEDED AND MINCED

Hands-on time: 20 min.
Total time: 20 min.

1. Combine all ingredients in a serving bowl; toss gently to mix. Yield: 6 servings (serving size: about ½ cup salsa)

CALORIES 285; FAT 10.2g (sat 1.1g, mono 5.3g, poly 3.2g); PROTEIN 17.9g; CARB 33.4g; FIBER 5g; CHOL 116mg; IRON 3.2mg; SODIUM 466mg; CALC 112mg

HEIRLOOM TOMATOES

Plump, juicy heirloom tomatoes have become much easier to find at farmers' markets and even supermarkets. There are many varieties, shapes, and sizes—from the 2-pound beefsteak to cherry tomatoes as tiny as currants—and colors—red, orange, gold, yellow, purple, even green and nearly white.

BRANDYWINE

This tomato is an excellent multipurpose beefsteak variety. Although it's difficult to verify its exact origin, some experts speculate that it was first cultivated by the Amish more than a century ago. This fruit is grown in yellow-, red-, pink-, and purple-fleshed varieties. With a classic tomato taste, the red Brandywine is full-flavored with a pleasant acidity, a floral aroma similar to roses, and a supple buttery texture.

MORTGAGE LIFTER

This pink-fleshed beefsteak was originally bred by a radiator repairman from West Virginia in the 1930s. Seedlings of the tomato were sold for $1 each, paying off his $6,000 mortgage in six years. This tomato can tip the scale at 2 pounds. It's also known for its mild, sweet flavor.

MR. STRIPEY

A pale yellow tomato with pinkish-orange blush and, occasionally, green stripes, Mr. Stripey is a delicate beefsteak with low acid content that allows its sweetness to shine. The flavor boasts notes of melon, and the firm skin provides a nice contrast to the tender flesh when eaten raw.

PERSIMMON

A prolific rose-orange beefsteak, some say this creamy, meaty, gorgeous tomato was cultivated by Thomas Jefferson. It has a near perfect acid-to-sugar balance.

CHEROKEE PURPLE

As the name implies, this meaty beefsteak variety has a deep purple color that tends toward brown or black. The firm, juicy, sweet-tart flesh, along with its jammy hue, often leads people to find the flavor evocative of a spicy zinfandel wine. Indeed, it has similar vegetal undertones that are balanced with a natural sweetness.

GREEN ZEBRA

At full maturity, this is a yellowish-green tomato with dark green striations. Although it's a beefsteak variety, the fruit is typically smaller than its kin, about the size of a baseball. The flavor is mildly spicy and slightly tart.

OLD IVORY EGG

A mild-flavored yellow plum, this tomato earned its name because it is the size and shape of a chicken's egg. It has a creamy ivory color that turns yellow as it ripens. Enjoy the mild, sweet flavor of this variety either cooked or raw. It's a great garden selection, as it produces fruit up until frost.

SUNGOLD

These little prolific orange cherry tomatoes grow in pretty, long clusters. The flavor is a nice balance of citrusy tartness, with hints of grape, orange, and floral flavors and a pleasant sweetness.

GREEN GRAPE

This delicious little fruit looks like a big Muscat grape. The mild flavor has a nice sweetness balanced by bright acidity, and it's deliciously juicy.

STIR-FRY

Mastering the stir-fry technique is your secret weapon for flavor-packed, healthful meals that are ready in minutes. The key to successful stir-frying is organization, in other words, getting your mise en place together before you begin cooking." Before a drop of oil hits your wok, you want to have all your ingredients cut, measured, and laid out right next to the stove.

Take your organization a step further and combine ingredients where appropriate—if the onions, ginger, and garlic are supposed to be added at the same time, combine them all in a small bowl or ramekin so it's easy to toss them into the pan at once. It's a great excuse to pull out all those cute little bowls you have in the cupboard. As an added bonus, you get to make like your favorite TV chef with all your pre-measured ingredients beautifully laid out. Next on your list: an intern to whisk the empty bowls away and clean them. We wish!

YOU'LL LEARN:

HOW TO MAKE A STIR-FRY • HOW TO CREATE A SAUCE TO FLAVOR YOUR STIR-FRY

MASTER RECIPE:

VEGGIE AND TOFU STIR-FRY

VARIATIONS:

SWEET-SPICY CHICKEN AND VEGETABLE STIR-FRY

ASIAN STIR-FRY QUINOA BOWL

YOUR MISE EN PLACE

PROTEIN
EXTRA-FIRM TOFU, DRAINED

FRESH PRODUCE
LARGE GREEN ONIONS, CUT

GARLIC CLOVES, SLICED

GINGER, CUT

BABY BOK CHOY, QUARTERED LENGTHWISE

CARROTS, PEELED AND CUT

SNOW PEAS, TRIMMED

FLAVOR BOOSTERS/ STAPLES
CANOLA OIL

BLACK PEPPER

CORNSTARCH

SHAOXING (CHINESE RICE WINE)

ORGANIC VEGETABLE BROTH

LOWER-SODIUM SOY SAUCE

HOISIN SAUCE

DARK SESAME OIL

EQUIPMENT NEEDED:

SHARP KNIFE

PAPER TOWELS

LARGE WOK OR HEAVY SKILLET

MEDIUM BOWL

SLOTTED SPOON

SPATULA

SMALL BOWL

WHISK

Veggie and Tofu
STIR-FRY

A handful of common Asian condiments come together to make a sauce that gives this dish a slightly smoky taste that is reminiscent of a good Chinese restaurant stir-fry.

1 (14-OUNCE) PACKAGE WATER-PACKED EXTRA-FIRM TOFU, DRAINED

1 TABLESPOON CANOLA OIL, DIVIDED

¼ TEASPOON BLACK PEPPER

3½ TEASPOONS CORNSTARCH, DIVIDED

3 LARGE GREEN ONIONS, CUT INTO 1-INCH PIECES

3 GARLIC CLOVES, SLICED

1 TABLESPOON JULIENNE-CUT GINGER

4 SMALL BABY BOK CHOY, QUARTERED LENGTHWISE

2 LARGE CARROTS, PEELED AND JULIENNE-CUT

1 CUP SNOW PEAS, TRIMMED

2 TABLESPOONS SHAOXING (CHINESE RICE WINE) OR DRY SHERRY

¼ CUP ORGANIC VEGETABLE BROTH

2 TABLESPOONS LOW-SODIUM SOY SAUCE

1 TABLESPOON HOISIN SAUCE

1 TEASPOON DARK SESAME OIL

Hands-on time: 19 min.
Total time: 49 min.

Don't have a wok? Don't worry; you can make this recipe just as well in a large, heavy skillet.

1. Cut tofu lengthwise into 4 equal pieces; cut each piece crosswise into ½-inch squares. Place tofu on several layers of paper towels; cover with additional paper towels. Let stand 30 minutes, pressing down occasionally.

2. Heat a large wok or large heavy skillet over high heat. Add 1½ teaspoons canola oil to pan; swirl to coat.

3. Combine tofu, pepper, and 2 teaspoons cornstarch in a medium bowl; toss to coat.

4. Add tofu to pan; stir-fry 8 minutes, turning to brown on all sides. Remove tofu from pan with a slotted spoon; place in a medium bowl. Add onions, garlic, and ginger to pan; stir-fry 1 minute. Remove from pan; add to tofu.

5. Add remaining 1½ teaspoons canola oil to pan; swirl to coat. Add bok choy; stir-fry 3 minutes. Add carrots; stir-fry 2 minutes. Add snow peas; stir-fry 1 minute. Add Shaoxing; cook 30 seconds, stirring constantly. Stir in tofu mixture.

6. Combine remaining 1½ teaspoons cornstarch, broth, and remaining ingredients in a small bowl, stirring with a whisk. Add broth mixture to pan; cook until slightly thickened (about 1 minute). Yield: 4 servings (serving size: about 1½ cups)

CALORIES 233; FAT 11.8g (sat 1.8g, mono 3.9g, poly 5.2g); PROTEIN 12.9g; CARB 17.5g; FIBER 3.2g; CHOL 0mg; IRON 3mg; SODIUM 389mg; CALC 227mg

A spicy-sweet sauce made with sambal oelek (chile garlic paste), fish sauce, rice vinegar, and dark sesame oil lends Thai flavors to this stir-fry.

3 TABLESPOONS DARK BROWN SUGAR

1½ TABLESPOONS LOWER-SODIUM SOY SAUCE

1 TABLESPOON FISH SAUCE

1 TABLESPOON RICE VINEGAR

1 TABLESPOON SAMBAL OELEK

1 TEASPOON DARK SESAME OIL

¾ TEASPOON CORNSTARCH

2 TABLESPOONS CANOLA OIL, DIVIDED

1 POUND SKINLESS, BONELESS CHICKEN BREASTS, CUT INTO BITE-SIZED PIECES

8 OUNCES SUGAR SNAP PEAS

1 RED BELL PEPPER, SLICED

½ MEDIUM RED ONION, CUT INTO THIN WEDGES

¼ CUP SLICED GREEN ONIONS

¼ CUP UNSALTED DRY-ROASTED PEANUTS

Hands-on time: 20 min.
Total time: 20 min.

SWEET-SPICY CHICKEN *and* VEGETABLE STIR-FRY

1. Combine first 7 ingredients (through cornstarch), stirring well; set aside.

2. Heat a large wok or large heavy nonstick skillet over high heat. Add 1 tablespoon canola oil to pan; swirl to coat. Add chicken; stir-fry 4 minutes or until browned and done. Remove chicken from wok. Add remaining 1 tablespoon canola oil to wok; swirl to coat. Add sugar snap peas, bell pepper, and red onion; stir-fry 3 minutes or until vegetables are crisp-tender. Stir in brown sugar mixture; cook 1 minute or until thickened. Stir in chicken; toss to coat. Sprinkle with green onions and peanuts. Yield: 4 servings (serving size: 1 cup)

CALORIES 349; FAT 14.2g (sat 1.7g, mono 7.5g, poly 4.3g); PROTEIN 31g; CARB 24.6g; FIBER 3.5g; CHOL 66mg; IRON 2mg; SODIUM 576mg; CALC 69mg

Heat a wok for several minutes until very hot. Use a wok that's cast iron, stainless steel, or rolled carbon steel to stand up to the high temperature.

Add quinoa to fresh veggies and tofu for a healthier dish when you are craving takeout fried rice. Cold quinoa works fine, making this an ideal choice for leftovers.

8 OUNCES EXTRA-FIRM TOFU

2 TABLESPOONS TOASTED SESAME OIL, DIVIDED

1 CUP (1-INCH) SLICES GREEN ONIONS

1 TABLESPOON MINCED FRESH GINGER

5 OUNCES THINLY SLICED SHIITAKE MUSHROOM CAPS

5 GARLIC CLOVES, THINLY SLICED

1 RED BELL PEPPER, THINLY SLICED

3 TABLESPOONS LOWER-SODIUM SOY SAUCE, DIVIDED

2 TABLESPOONS RICE VINEGAR, DIVIDED

¼ TEASPOON KOSHER SALT

2 CUPS COOKED QUINOA

2 CUPS THINLY SLICED NAPA CABBAGE

¼ CUP CHOPPED FRESH CILANTRO

½ TEASPOON SUGAR

Hands-on time: 28 min.
Total time: 28 min.

ASIAN STIR-FRY QUINOA BOWL

1. Arrange tofu on several layers of heavy-duty paper towels. Cover with additional paper towels; let stand 15 minutes. Cut into ½-inch-thick cubes.

2. Heat a large nonstick skillet over medium-high heat. Add 1 tablespoon oil to pan; swirl to coat. Add tofu; sauté 4 minutes or until browned. Place tofu in a bowl. Return pan to medium-high heat. Add remaining 1 tablespoon oil to pan. Add onions and next 4 ingredients (through bell pepper); stir-fry 4 minutes or just until tender. Add 2 tablespoons soy sauce, 1 tablespoon vinegar, and salt; cook 30 seconds. Add mushroom mixture to tofu.

3. Stir in remaining 1 tablespoon soy sauce, remaining 1 tablespoon vinegar, quinoa, cabbage, cilantro, and sugar. Toss well to combine. Yield: 4 (serving size: 1¼ cups)

CALORIES 283; FAT 12.5g (sat 1.7g, mono 3.7g, poly 5.1g); PROTEIN 12g; CARB 32g; FIBER 5g; CHOL 0mg; IRON 3mg; SODIUM 540mg; CALC 99mg

Water is the enemy of crisp, nicely browned food, so remove as much of it as possible from the tofu before cooking. Extra water can also cause violent sputtering of oil in a hot pan.

GRATINS

Nothing quite embodies comfort like a gratin. Bubbling and browned on top as it comes from the oven, there's little question that what lies beneath the crust is going to be tender, creamy, and delicious. Unfortunately, gratins are often synonymous with cringe-inducing amounts of cream and cheese. But they don't have to be. Learn to give gratins a healthy kick by cutting out the unnecessary fat and also layering in veggies that have more to offer than plain white potatoes.

In crafting the perfect gratin, we've cut the fat, upped the nutrition, and given the flavor a boost. We start by swapping out cream for a savory blend of chicken stock and reduced-fat milk. Then we thicken the sauce with a simple roux so you get all the richness of a cream sauce with a fraction of the fat. Including veggies like butternut squash, sweet potatoes, and parsnips adds vitamins A, C, and K, along with fiber.

YOU'LL LEARN:

HOW TO MAKE A GRATIN • HOW TO MAKE DIFFERENT SAUCES

HOW TO GIVE YOUR GRATIN A CRISPY TOP

MASTER RECIPE:

TWO-POTATO GRATIN

VARIATIONS:

TURNIP-PARSNIP GRATIN • SWEET POTATO AND BUTTERNUT GRATIN

YOUR MISE EN PLACE

DAIRY
2% REDUCED-FAT MILK
AGED GRUYÈRE CHEESE, SHREDDED
FRESH PARMESAN CHEESE, GRATED

FRESH PRODUCE
MEDIUM BAKING POTATOES, PEELED AND SLICED
MEDIUM SWEET POTATOES, PEELED AND SLICED
GARLIC CLOVES, CRUSHED
FRESH THYME SPRIGS
FRESH CHIVES, CHOPPED
FRESH THYME, CHOPPED

FLAVOR BOOSTERS/ STAPLES
NO-SALT-ADDED CHICKEN STOCK
CANOLA OIL
ALL-PURPOSE FLOUR
KOSHER SALT
BLACK PEPPER
COOKING SPRAY

EQUIPMENT NEEDED:
VEGETABLE PEELER
SHARP KNIFE
CHEESE GRATER
LARGE STOCKPOT
SLOTTED SPOON
JELLY-ROLL PAN
FINE-MESH SIEVE
MEDIUM BOWL
MEDIUM SAUCEPAN
WHISK
SMALL BOWL
2-QUART CERAMIC DISH

PREHEAT YOUR OVEN TO 350°.

Two-Potato
GRATIN

*Gradually adding the milk to the flour mixture (the roux) will ensure
that your gratin is creamy. Add half the milk and stir until smooth before adding the rest.*

2 MEDIUM BAKING POTATOES, PEELED
    AND CUT INTO ¼-INCH-THICK SLICES
    (ABOUT 3 CUPS)

2 MEDIUM SWEET POTATOES, PEELED
    AND CUT INTO ¼-INCH-THICK SLICES
    (ABOUT 4 CUPS)

2 QUARTS NO-SALT-ADDED CHICKEN STOCK
    (SUCH AS SWANSON)

2 TABLESPOONS CANOLA OIL

3 TABLESPOONS ALL-PURPOSE FLOUR

2 GARLIC CLOVES, CRUSHED

1½ CUPS 2% REDUCED-FAT MILK

2 FRESH THYME SPRIGS

¾ TEASPOON KOSHER SALT, DIVIDED

¼ TEASPOON FRESHLY GROUND BLACK
    PEPPER

3 OUNCES AGED GRUYÈRE CHEESE,
    SHREDDED (ABOUT ¾ CUP)

COOKING SPRAY

2 TABLESPOONS CHOPPED FRESH CHIVES,
    DIVIDED

1½ TEASPOONS CHOPPED FRESH THYME

1 OUNCE FRESH PARMESAN CHEESE,
    GRATED (ABOUT ¼ CUP)

Hands-on time: 30 min.
Total time: 1 hr. 40 min.

1. Preheat oven to 350°. Place potatoes in a large stockpot; cover with stock. Bring mixture to a boil; cook 4 minutes. Remove from heat.

2. Carefully remove potatoes from pot using a slotted spoon, reserving cooking liquid. Arrange potato slices in a single layer on a jelly-roll pan; set aside.

3. Strain cooking liquid through a fine-mesh sieve over a medium bowl; reserve 1 cup cooking liquid. Discard solids and remaining cooking liquid.

4. Heat a medium saucepan over medium heat. Add oil to pan. Sprinkle flour over oil; cook 1 minute, stirring constantly with a whisk. Add garlic; cook 2 minutes, stirring frequently.

5. Combine milk and reserved 1 cup cooking liquid in a small bowl. Gradually pour milk mixture into flour mixture in pan, stirring constantly with a whisk. Add thyme sprigs to pan. Bring mixture to a boil; cook 4 minutes or until slightly thick, stirring frequently. Remove from heat.

6. Strain mixture through a fine-mesh sieve over a bowl, reserving sauce; discard solids. Stir ½ teaspoon salt, pepper, and Gruyère cheese into sauce.

(continued)

7. Spread ½ cup sauce in bottom of a broiler-safe 2-quart ceramic baking dish coated with cooking spray. Arrange a single, flat layer of sweet potato and then baking potato slices over sauce. Over flat layer, alternate baking potato and sweet potato slices, in shingle-like fashion. Sprinkle evenly with remaining ¼ teaspoon salt, 1 tablespoon chives, and chopped thyme; pour remaining sauce over potato mixture. Sprinkle with Parmesan cheese. Bake at 350° for 1 hour or until potatoes are tender when pierced with a knife.

8. Remove gratin from oven. Preheat broiler to high.

9. Place gratin in oven. Broil gratin 3 minutes or until browned. Sprinkle with remaining 1 tablespoon chives. Yield: 8 servings (serving size: about ½ cup)

CALORIES 218; FAT 9g (sat 3.5g, mono 3.8g, poly 1.3g); PROTEIN 9.3g; CARB 25.2g; FIBER 2.7g; CHOL 18mg; IRON 1.2mg; SODIUM 339mg; CALC 228mg

Be gentle when arranging the cooked potatoes in your dish if you want a silky, layered gratin instead of an uninspired dish of broken potatoes.

A mandoline will slice the veggies into uniform thickness. Use a flavorful aged Gruyère cheese or substitute an equally assertive cheese, such as aged cheddar, Gouda, or a pungent soft-ripened cheese like Brie.

3¾ CUPS (⅛-INCH-THICK) SLICES PEELED TURNIP

3¾ CUPS (⅛-INCH-THICK) SLICES PEELED PARSNIP

6 CUPS WATER

COOKING SPRAY

1 CUP WHOLE MILK

⅓ CUP FAT-FREE, LOWER-SODIUM CHICKEN BROTH

2 TABLESPOONS ALL-PURPOSE FLOUR

1 TEASPOON KOSHER SALT

½ TEASPOON FRESHLY GROUND BLACK PEPPER

1 CUP (4 OUNCES) SHREDDED GRUYÈRE CHEESE

2 TABLESPOONS BUTTER

¼ CUP PANKO (JAPANESE BREADCRUMBS)

Hands-on time: 30 min.
Total time: 55 min.

TURNIP-PARSNIP GRATIN

1. Preheat oven to 400°. Combine first 3 ingredients in a large saucepan; bring to a boil. Reduce heat, and simmer 7 minutes or until almost tender. Drain; let stand 5 minutes. Arrange about ½ cup vegetable mixture in each of 8 (5½-inch) round gratin dishes coated with cooking spray.

2. Combine milk, broth, flour, salt, and pepper in a saucepan over medium-high heat; bring to a simmer. Cook 4 minutes, stirring constantly with a whisk until thick. Remove from heat; add cheese, stirring with a whisk until smooth. Spoon about 3 tablespoons sauce over each serving.

3. Melt butter in a medium skillet over medium-high heat. Add panko; toast 2 minutes, stirring constantly. Sprinkle breadcrumb mixture evenly over cheese mixture. Place dishes on a baking sheet. Bake at 400° for 15 minutes or until bubbly and golden brown on top. Let stand 5 minutes before serving. Yield: 8 servings (serving size: 1 gratin)

CALORIES 196; FAT 8.8g (sat 5.1g, mono 2.5g, poly 0.5g); PROTEIN 7.6g; CARB 22.8g; FIBER 5.3g; CHOL 26mg; IRON 0.9mg; SODIUM 424mg; CALC 236mg

SWEET POTATO *and* BUTTERNUT GRATIN

2 TABLESPOONS BUTTER

1 OUNCE PANCETTA, CHOPPED

¼ CUP CHOPPED SHALLOTS

2 GARLIC CLOVES, MINCED

5 TABLESPOONS ALL-PURPOSE FLOUR, DIVIDED

1 TEASPOON CHOPPED FRESH THYME

2 CUPS 2% REDUCED-FAT MILK

¾ CUP (3 OUNCES) GRATED FRESH PARMESAN CHEESE

½ TEASPOON SALT

½ TEASPOON FRESHLY GROUND BLACK PEPPER

⅛ TEASPOON GROUND RED PEPPER

1 POUND BAKING POTATO, PEELED AND CUT INTO ⅛-INCH-THICK SLICES

8 OUNCES SWEET POTATO, PEELED AND CUT INTO ⅛-INCH-THICK SLICES

8 OUNCES BUTTERNUT SQUASH, PEELED AND CUT INTO ⅛-INCH-THICK SLICES

COOKING SPRAY

⅓ CUP (1½ OUNCES) SHREDDED GRUYÈRE CHEESE

Hands-on time: 30 min.
Total time: 1 hr. 10 min.

1. Preheat oven to 375°. Melt butter in a small saucepan over medium-high heat. Add pancetta; cook 1 minute. Add shallots and garlic; cook 2 minutes, stirring constantly. Lightly spoon ¼ cup flour into a dry measuring cup; level with a knife. Add to pan; cook 2 minutes, stirring constantly with a whisk. Stir in thyme. Gradually add milk, stirring constantly with a whisk; cook over medium heat until slightly thick (about 3 minutes), stirring constantly. Stir in Parmesan; cook 3 minutes or until cheese melts. Stir in salt and peppers. Remove from heat.

2. Cook baking potato in boiling water 4 minutes or until almost tender; remove with a slotted spoon. Cook sweet potato in boiling water 4 minutes or until almost tender; remove with a slotted spoon. Cook butternut squash in boiling water 4 minutes or until almost tender; drain. Sprinkle vegetables evenly with remaining 1 tablespoon flour. Arrange potatoes and squash in alternating layers in a broiler-safe 11 x 7–inch baking dish coated with cooking spray; spoon sauce over potato mixture. Top with Gruyère. Bake at 375° for 40 minutes.

3. Remove gratin from oven. Preheat broiler to high. Broil 3 minutes or until golden. Let stand 10 minutes. Yield: 8 servings (serving size: about ½ cup)

CALORIES 220; FAT 8.7g (sat 5.2g, mono 2.2g, poly 0.3g); PROTEIN 9.7g; CARB 26.2g; FIBER 2.6g; CHOL 25mg; IRON 1.3mg; SODIUM 418mg; CALC 259mg

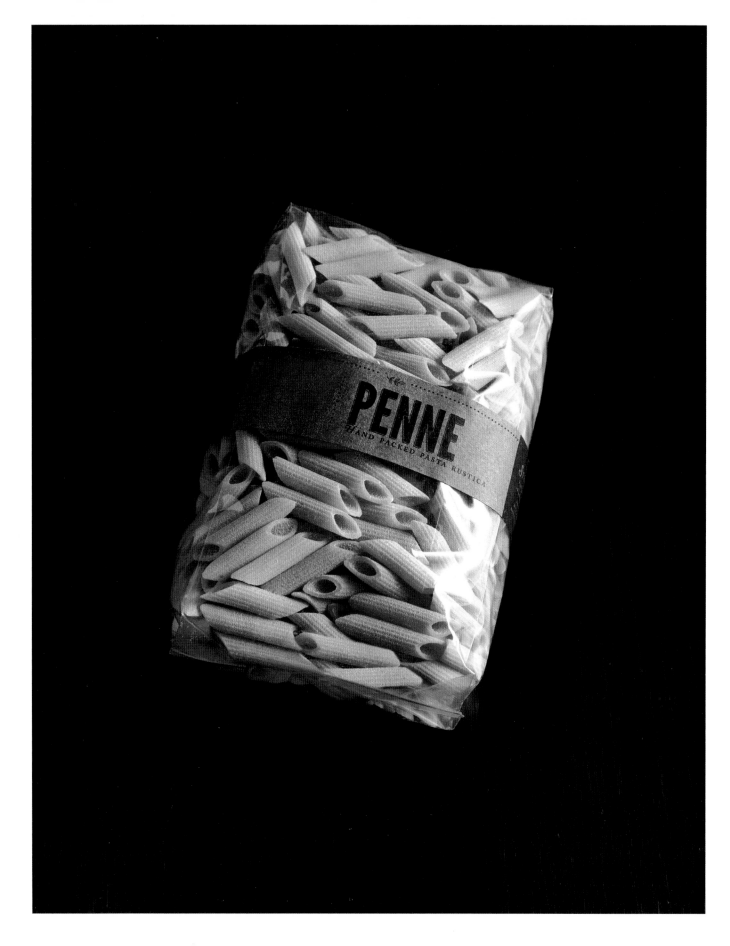

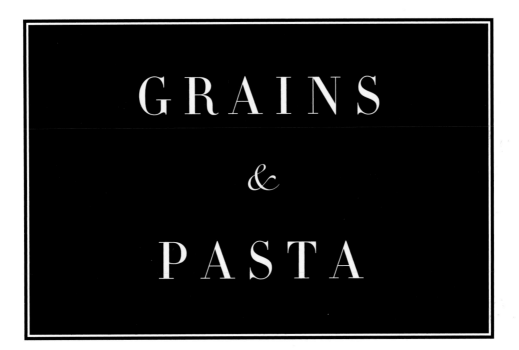

MAC *and* CHEESE

The key to a great "light" mac and cheese is turning the milk into a rich, creamy sauce without any added fat. Well, let's be honest, the real key to these recipes is that they're pasta and lots of cheese. But that part about the milk, it's important too. Whisk together cold milk and flour until it's completely smooth, then bring the mixture to a simmer while constantly stirring. Normally, thickening milk like this would require a roux, which means extra butter, but with careful stirring of the flour and milk, you can eliminate the added fat, and it's all cheesy baked pasta goodness from there on.

To turn this into a one-dish meal-for-the-ages, stir in fresh cooked vegetables like peas or broccoli and cooked lean protein—think grilled chicken or cooked ground turkey. Leftovers? They're just as good cold, with a salad, for lunch the next day. If they last that long.

YOU'LL LEARN:

HOW TO MAKE LOW-FAT WHITE SAUCE • HOW TO TURN WHITE SAUCE INTO A CHEESE SAUCE • TIPS FOR KEEPING MAC AND CHEESE CREAMY

MASTER RECIPE:

CREAMY FOUR-CHEESE MACARONI

VARIATIONS:

CHICKEN-BROCCOLI MAC AND CHEESE WITH BACON

TRUFFLED MAC AND CHEESE

YOUR MISE EN PLACE

DAIRY

LOW-FAT MILK

FONTINA CHEESE, SHREDDED

PARMESAN CHEESE, GRATED

EXTRA-SHARP CHEDDAR CHEESE, SHREDDED

LIGHT PROCESSED CHEESE

FRESH PRODUCE

GARLIC CLOVE, MINCED

FLAVOR BOOSTERS/ STAPLES

ALL-PURPOSE FLOUR

ELBOW MACARONI

SALT

BLACK PEPPER

COOKING SPRAY

CANOLA OIL

MELBA TOASTS, CRUSHED

EQUIPMENT NEEDED:

CHEESE GRATER

LARGE POT

COLANDER

LARGE SAUCEPAN

WHISK

WOODEN SPOON

SMALL BOWL

BAKING DISH

PREHEAT YOUR OVEN TO 375°.

Creamy Four-Cheese
MACARONI

Drain your pasta well, but don't rinse it! Draining keeps moisture to a minimum and allows for a creamier sauce that better coats the pasta. Skipping the rinse leaves a small amount of starch clinging to the noodles and helps marry them to the sauce.

12 OUNCES UNCOOKED ELBOW MACARONI (ABOUT 3 CUPS)

1.5 OUNCES ALL-PURPOSE FLOUR (ABOUT ⅓ CUP)

2⅔ CUPS 1% LOW-FAT MILK

2 OUNCES SHREDDED FONTINA CHEESE (ABOUT ½ CUP)

2 OUNCES GRATED PARMESAN CHEESE (ABOUT ½ CUP)

2 OUNCES SHREDDED EXTRA-SHARP CHEDDAR CHEESE (ABOUT ½ CUP)

3 OUNCES LIGHT PROCESSED CHEESE (SUCH AS LIGHT VELVEETA)

½ TEASPOON SALT

¼ TEASPOON GROUND BLACK PEPPER

COOKING SPRAY

⅓ CUP CRUSHED MELBA TOASTS (ABOUT 12 PIECES)

1 TABLESPOON CANOLA OIL

1 GARLIC CLOVE, MINCED

Hands-on time: 30 min.
Total time: 1 hr.

Why use processed cheese? A small amount is just enough to lend a velvety richness to the sauce without relying on heavy cream.

1. Preheat oven to 375°. Bring 6 quarts water to a boil in a large pot. Add pasta; cook 8 minutes or until al dente; drain.

2. Weigh or lightly spoon flour into dry measuring cup; level with a knife. Place flour in a large saucepan.

3. Gradually add milk, stirring with a whisk until blended. Cook over medium heat until thick (about 8 minutes), stirring constantly with a whisk.

4. Remove from heat; let stand 4 minutes or until sauce cools to 155°. Add cheeses, and stir until the cheeses melt.

5. Stir in cooked macaroni, salt, and black pepper.

6. Spoon mixture into a 2-quart glass or ceramic baking dish coated with cooking spray.

7. Combine crushed toasts, oil, and garlic in small bowl; stir until well blended. Sprinkle over macaroni mixture. Bake at 375° for 30 minutes or until bubbly. Yield: 8 servings (serving size: 1 cup)

CALORIES 347; FAT 11.5 (sat 5.9g, mono 3.4g, poly 1.4g); PROTEIN 17.4g; CARB 43.8g; FIBER 19g; CHOL 29mg; IRON 1.7mg; SODIUM 607mg; CALC 346mg

Cook this one-dish meal on the stovetop and then finish under the broiler. A bit of turmeric enhances the color; it's a slight of hand that makes you perceive the sauce as cheesier than it actually is.

---

6 OUNCES UNCOOKED LARGE OR REGULAR ELBOW MACARONI

3 CUPS PRECHOPPED BROCCOLI FLORETS

3 BACON SLICES, COARSELY CHOPPED

12 OUNCES SKINLESS, BONELESS CHICKEN BREASTS, CUT INTO ½-INCH PIECES

1 TEASPOON KOSHER SALT, DIVIDED

1 TABLESPOON MINCED FRESH GARLIC

⅛ TEASPOON GROUND TURMERIC

1¼ CUPS 1% LOW-FAT MILK

1 CUP UNSALTED CHICKEN STOCK (SUCH AS SWANSON)

¼ CUP PLUS 1 TEASPOON ALL-PURPOSE FLOUR

5 OUNCES SHARP CHEDDAR CHEESE, SHREDDED (ABOUT 1¼ CUPS)

Hands-on time: 25 min.
Total time: 25 min.

CHICKEN-BROCCOLI MAC *and* CHEESE *with* BACON

1. Preheat broiler to high. Cook pasta according to package directions, omitting salt and fat. Add broccoli to pan during last 2 minutes of cooking. Drain.

2. While pasta cooks, place bacon in a large ovenproof skillet over medium-high heat; cook 4 minutes or until browned, stirring occasionally. Remove bacon from pan with a slotted spoon; reserve 1½ teaspoons drippings in pan. Sprinkle chicken with ¼ teaspoon salt. Add chicken to drippings in pan; cook 4 minutes. Sprinkle with garlic; cook 2 minutes, stirring occasionally. Sprinkle with turmeric; cook 30 seconds, stirring frequently.

3. Combine remaining ¾ teaspoon salt, milk, stock, and flour, stirring with a whisk. Add milk mixture to pan; bring to a boil, stirring frequently. Cook 2 minutes or until thickened. Add pasta mixture and 2 ounces cheese; toss to coat. Sprinkle with remaining 3 ounces cheese and bacon. Broil 2 minutes or until cheese melts and just begins to brown. Yield: 6 servings (serving size: about 1 ⅓ cups)

CALORIES 343; FAT 12.2g (sat 6.5g, mono 3.7g, poly 0.9g); PROTEIN 26g; CARB 31g; FIBER 2g; CHOL 64mg; IRON 2mg; SODIUM 647mg; CALC 265mg

TRUFFLED MAC *and* CHEESE

Steeping the milk with onion and bay leaf imparts a subtle background flavor to the cheese sauce that complements the intense earthy flavor of truffle oil. (Measure truffle oil carefully; a little bit goes a long way!)

2¼ CUPS 1% LOW-FAT MILK, DIVIDED

2 CUPS SLICED ONION (ABOUT 1 MEDIUM)

1 BAY LEAF

12 OUNCES UNCOOKED ELBOW MACARONI (ABOUT 3 CUPS)

2 TABLESPOONS ALL-PURPOSE FLOUR

¾ TEASPOON KOSHER SALT

¾ CUP (3 OUNCES) SHREDDED FONTINA CHEESE

½ CUP (2 OUNCES) SHREDDED COMTÉ OR GRUYÈRE CHEESE

1½ TEASPOONS WHITE TRUFFLE OIL

2 OUNCES FRENCH BREAD BAGUETTE, TORN

2 TABLESPOONS GRATED FRESH PARMESAN CHEESE

2 GARLIC CLOVES, CRUSHED

1 TABLESPOON OLIVE OIL

Hands-on time: 36 min.
Total time: 44 min.

1. Heat 1¾ cups milk, onion, and bay leaf in a large saucepan to 180° or until tiny bubbles form around edges (do not boil). Cover and remove from heat; let stand 15 minutes.

2. Bring 6 quarts water to a boil in a large pot. Add pasta; cook 8 minutes or until al dente; drain.

3. Strain milk mixture through a colander over a bowl; discard solids. Return milk to saucepan over medium heat. Combine remaining ½ cup milk and flour in a small bowl, stirring with a whisk until well blended. Gradually stir flour mixture and salt into warm milk, stirring constantly with a whisk. Bring mixture to a boil, stirring frequently; cook 1 minute, stirring constantly. Remove from heat; let stand 6 minutes or until mixture cools to 155°. Gradually add fontina and Comté cheeses, stirring until cheeses melt. Stir in pasta and truffle oil. Spoon mixture into a 2-quart broiler-safe glass or ceramic baking dish.

4. Preheat broiler. Place bread, Parmesan cheese, and garlic in a food processor; process until coarse crumbs form. Drizzle with olive oil; pulse until fine crumbs form. Sprinkle breadcrumb mixture over pasta. Place dish on middle rack in oven; broil 2 minutes or until golden brown. Yield: 6 servings (serving size: about 1 cup)

CALORIES 418; FAT 13.2g (sat 6.1g, mono 5.2g, poly 1.1g); PROTEIN 18.9g; CARB 55.2g; FIBER 2.1g; CHOL 33mg; IRON 2.4mg; SODIUM 528mg; CALC 325mg

STUFFED & BAKED PASTAS

Curious cook: Get ready to meet crème fraîche. It's destined to be your new this-sauce-is-so-creamy-and-delicious secret weapon. Never tried crème fraîche? Think of it as sour cream's sophisticated cousin. It's naturally soured so it's richer and creamier (and has a bit more fat) than sour cream. But that richness keeps it from separating and becoming watery when cooked, making it the perfect addition (in small amounts) to baked pastas.

Now that you've got your creamy pasta sauce down, let's talk about a nutrient-packed, one-dish meal that is completely irresistible. With kale (antioxidants; fiber; vitamins K, A, and C) and butternut squash (beta-carotene, potassium, vitamin B_6), you'd be hard pressed to find a way to pack more goodness into one simple meal. Roasting vegetables, like the butternut squash, separately before incorporating them into a baked dish is a great way to concentrate their flavor and cut down cooking time. Did we mention the bacon and cheese? Perfection reached.

YOU'LL LEARN:

HOW TO MAKE A SAVORY PASTA SAUCE • HOW LONG TO COOK PASTA THAT WILL ALSO BE BAKED • HOW TO TELL WHEN A CASSEROLE IS "DONE"

MASTER RECIPE:

BACON AND BUTTERNUT PASTA

VARIATIONS:

SHRIMP STUFFED SHELLS • MUSHROOM LASAGNA

YOUR MISE EN PLACE

PROTEIN
BACON SLICES

DAIRY
CRÈME FRAÎCHE
GRUYÈRE CHEESE, SHREDDED

FRESH PRODUCE
BUTTERNUT SQUASH, CUBED
KALE, CHOPPED
ONION, VERTICALLY SLICED
GARLIC CLOVES, MINCED

FLAVOR BOOSTERS/STAPLES
OLIVE OIL
COOKING SPRAY
ZITI
SALT
FAT-FREE, LOWER-SODIUM CHICKEN BROTH
ALL-PURPOSE FLOUR
CRUSHED RED PEPPER

EQUIPMENT NEEDED:
SHARP KNIFE
CHEESE GRATER
LARGE BOWL
BAKING SHEET
LARGE POT
NONSTICK SKILLET
SMALL SAUCEPAN
SMALL BOWL
WHISK
BAKING DISH

PREHEAT YOUR OVEN TO 400°.

Bacon and Butternut
PASTA

Pasta should be slightly undercooked when it goes into a baked casserole. The sauce helps to finish cooking the baked pasta, so it needs enough liquid—like broth, tomato sauce, or flour-thickened milk—for the noodles to absorb as they bake.

---

5 CUPS (½-INCH) CUBED PEELED BUTTERNUT SQUASH

1 TABLESPOON OLIVE OIL

COOKING SPRAY

12 OUNCES UNCOOKED ZITI (SHORT TUBE-SHAPED PASTA), CAMPANILE, OR OTHER SHORT PASTA

4 CUPS CHOPPED KALE

2 BACON SLICES

2 CUPS VERTICALLY SLICED ONION

1 TEASPOON SALT, DIVIDED

5 GARLIC CLOVES, MINCED

2 CUPS FAT-FREE, LOWER-SODIUM CHICKEN BROTH, DIVIDED

2 TABLESPOONS ALL-PURPOSE FLOUR

½ TEASPOON CRUSHED RED PEPPER

1 CUP CRÈME FRAÎCHE

⅓ CUP (ABOUT 1½ OUNCES) SHREDDED GRUYÈRE CHEESE

Hands-on time: 38 min.
Total time: 1 hr. 15 min.

To prevent mushy noodles, boil pasta until it's almost al dente so it will be soft and perfect after baking.

1. Preheat oven to 400°. Combine squash and oil in a large bowl; toss well. Arrange squash mixture in a single layer on a baking sheet coated with cooking spray. Bake at 400° for 30 minutes or until squash is tender.

2. Bring 6 quarts water to a boil in a large pot. Add pasta; cook 7 minutes or until almost al dente. Add kale to pan during last 2 minutes of cooking. Drain pasta mixture.

3. Cook bacon in a large nonstick skillet over medium heat until crisp. Remove bacon from pan; crumble.

4. Add onion to drippings in pan; cook 6 minutes, stirring occasionally. Add ½ teaspoon salt and garlic; cook 1 minute, stirring occasionally.

5. Bring 1¾ cups broth to a boil in a small saucepan. Combine remaining ¼ cup broth and flour in a small bowl, stirring with a whisk. To broth in pan, add flour mixture, remaining ½ teaspoon salt, and pepper. Cook 2 minutes or until slightly thickened. Remove from heat; stir in crème fraîche.

6. Combine squash, pasta mixture, bacon, onion mixture, and sauce in a large bowl; toss gently.

7. Place pasta mixture in a 13 x 9–inch glass or ceramic baking dish coated with cooking spray; sprinkle evenly with cheese. Bake at 400° for 25 minutes or until bubbly and slightly browned. Yield: 8 servings (serving size: about 1½ cups)

CALORIES 388; FAT 15.4g (sat 8.3g, mono 2.2g, poly 0.7g); PROTEIN 12.1g; CARB 51.4g; FIBER 4.8g; CHOL 36mg; IRON 2.9mg; SODIUM 475mg; CALC 166mg

Shrimp goes into these pasta shells raw to prevent it from overcooking while the pasta bakes. Potato starch is used because it tolerates higher baking temperatures than cornstarch.

---

20 UNCOOKED JUMBO PASTA SHELLS (ABOUT 8 OUNCES)

1½ TABLESPOONS OLIVE OIL

½ CUP CHOPPED SHALLOTS

2 TABLESPOONS MINCED GARLIC (ABOUT 6 CLOVES)

½ CUP (4 OUNCES) ⅓-LESS-FAT CREAM CHEESE

¼ CUP 2% REDUCED-FAT MILK

¼ TEASPOON GROUND RED PEPPER

⅓ CUP CHOPPED FRESH BASIL

1 POUND MEDIUM SHRIMP, PEELED, DEVEINED, AND COARSELY CHOPPED

1 TABLESPOON POTATO STARCH

COOKING SPRAY

3 CUPS LOWER-SODIUM MARINARA SAUCE, DIVIDED

⅓ CUP (1½ OUNCES) GRATED FRESH PARMESAN CHEESE

Hands-on time: 22 min.
Total time: 1hr. 10 min.

SHRIMP STUFFED SHELLS

1. Preheat oven to 400°. Bring 6 quarts water to a boil in a large pot. Add pasta; cook 7 minutes or until almost al dente. Drain well.

2. Heat a medium skillet over medium heat. Add oil to pan; swirl to coat. Add shallots; cook 4 minutes, stirring occasionally. Add garlic; cook 1 minute, stirring constantly. Add cream cheese, milk, and pepper; cook until cheese melts, stirring until smooth. Remove from heat. Stir in basil. Place shrimp in a bowl. Sprinkle with potato starch; toss well to coat. Add cream cheese mixture to shrimp; toss well.

3. Divide shrimp mixture evenly and stuff into pasta shells. Coat a 13 x 9–inch glass or ceramic baking dish with cooking spray; spread 1 cup marinara over bottom of dish. Arrange shells in prepared dish; top with remaining 2 cups marinara. Sprinkle shells evenly with Parmesan cheese. Bake at 400° for 30 minutes or until shrimp is done. Yield: 5 servings (serving size: 4 stuffed shells)

CALORIES 496; FAT 16g (sat 6.2g, mono 5.3g, poly 1.4g); PROTEIN 31.1g; CARB 85.6g; FIBER 1.6g; CHOL 163mg; IRON 4.1mg; SODIUM 575mg; CALC 208mg

1 CUP BOILING WATER

1 OUNCE DRIED PORCINI MUSHROOMS

1 TABLESPOON BUTTER

2 TABLESPOONS OLIVE OIL, DIVIDED

1¼ CUPS CHOPPED SHALLOTS (ABOUT 4)

1 (8-OUNCE) PACKAGE PRESLICED
CREMINI MUSHROOMS

1 (4-OUNCE) PACKAGE PRESLICED EXOTIC
MUSHROOM BLEND

1 TEASPOON SALT, DIVIDED

½ TEASPOON FRESHLY GROUND BLACK
PEPPER, DIVIDED

1½ TABLESPOONS CHOPPED FRESH THYME

6 GARLIC CLOVES, MINCED AND DIVIDED

½ CUP WHITE WINE

⅓ CUP (3 OUNCES) ⅓-LESS-FAT CREAM
CHEESE

2 TABLESPOONS CHOPPED FRESH CHIVES,
DIVIDED

3 CUPS 2% REDUCED-FAT MILK, DIVIDED

1.1 OUNCES ALL-PURPOSE FLOUR (ABOUT
¼ CUP)

COOKING SPRAY

9 NO-BOIL LASAGNA NOODLES

½ CUP (2 OUNCES) GRATED PARMIGIANO-
REGGIANO CHEESE

Hands-on time: 40 min.
Total time: 1 hr. 25 min.

MUSHROOM LASAGNA

1. Preheat oven to 350°. Combine 1 cup boiling water and porcini. Cover and let stand 30 minutes; strain through a cheesecloth-lined sieve over a bowl, reserving liquid and mushrooms.

2. Melt butter in a large skillet over medium-high heat. Add 1 tablespoon oil to pan; swirl to coat. Add shallots to pan; sauté 3 minutes. Add cremini mushrooms and mushroom blend, ½ teaspoon salt, and ¼ teaspoon pepper; sauté 6 minutes or until mushrooms are browned. Add thyme and half the garlic; sauté 1 minute. Stir in wine; bring to a boil. Cook 1 minute or until liquid almost evaporates, scraping pan to loosen browned bits. Remove from heat; stir in cream cheese and 1 tablespoon chives. Add reserved porcini mushrooms.

3. Heat a saucepan over medium-high heat. Add remaining 1 tablespoon oil to pan; swirl to coat. Add remaining garlic; sauté 30 seconds. Add the reserved porcini liquid, 2¾ cups milk, remaining ½ teaspoon salt, and remaining ¼ teaspoon pepper; bring to a boil. Combine remaining ¼ cup milk and flour in a small bowl; stir with a whisk. Add flour mixture to milk mixture, and simmer 2 minutes or until slightly thick, stirring constantly with a whisk.

4. Spoon ½ cup milk sauce into an 11 x 7–inch glass or ceramic baking dish coated with cooking spray, and top with 3 noodles. Spread half of mushroom mixture over noodles. Repeat layers once, then top with 3 noodles and end with remaining sauce. Sprinkle cheese over top. Bake at 350° for 45 minutes or until golden. Top with remaining 1 tablespoon chopped chives. Yield: 6 servings

CALORIES 396; FAT 15.4g (sat 7.1g, mono 5.5g, poly 0.8g); PROTEIN 17.1g;
CARB 43.5g; FIBER 3.2g; CHOL 33mg; IRON 3.1mg; SODIUM 668mg;
CALC 288mg

HOMEMADE PASTA

If the idea of making fresh pasta dough intimidates you, quit making excuses. Imagine a mound of flour on a countertop, fresh eggs carefully added, and the whole mixture gently coaxed into soft, silky sheets of pasta. Then imagine taking a shortcut, utilizing a mess-free option for pasta-making enjoyment. Carefully measure the ingredients, add them all to a food processor, and run the machine in three- to four-second bursts until a ball forms, then knead until just smooth. It may sound like an all-day venture, but this way of making fresh pasta is shockingly simple and addictively fun.

It's really no more difficult than measuring flour and letting the machine do the work of mixing it with a few eggs.

It's a job that can get a touch messy—with sticky hands from kneading and flour-covered countertops—but the end result makes it all worthwhile. Did you just read that and think only of how long it will take you to scrub your counter clean? We get it, and we've got the answer for you. You can tape a piece of parchment paper to the countertop and knead on the paper if you'd like. Like we said, no excuses: Make your own noodles or ravioli tonight!

YOU'LL LEARN:

HOW TO MAKE FRESH PASTA DOUGH • HOW TO ROLL DOUGH WITH A PASTA MACHINE • HOW TO CUT PASTA BY HAND

MASTER RECIPE:

FRESH PASTA DOUGH

VARIATIONS:

RAVIOLI WITH HERBED RICOTTA FILLING

WHOLE WHEAT TAGLIOLINI WITH FRESH CHERRY TOMATO SAUCE

YOUR MISE EN PLACE

PROTEIN
LARGE EGGS

FLAVOR BOOSTERS/ STAPLES
SOFT WHEAT FLOUR

SEA SALT

EQUIPMENT NEEDED:
FOOD PROCESSOR

PLASTIC WRAP

PASTA MACHINE

Fresh
PASTA DOUGH

Hand-cranked Italian pasta machines are easy to use and yield pasta with smooth exterior surfaces. But you can also use a rolling pin and make the noodle sheets by hand. Use noodle sheets to make ravioli or cut it into thin strips of spaghetti or other shapes.

5.6 OUNCES SOFT WHEAT FLOUR (ABOUT 1¼ CUPS)

⅛ TEASPOON FINE SEA SALT

2 LARGE EGGS

Hands-on time: 28 min.
Total time: 48 min.

The Italians use a finely ground soft wheat flour (called 00) for pasta dough and pizza because it results in a silkier texture. But all-purpose flour works fine.

1. Weigh or lightly spoon flour into dry measuring cups; level with a knife. Combine flour, salt, and eggs in a food processor; pulse 10 times or until mixture is crumbly (dough will not form a ball).

2. Turn dough out onto a lightly floured surface; knead until smooth and elastic (about 4 minutes).

3. Shape dough into a disk; wrap with plastic wrap. Let dough stand at room temperature for 20 minutes.

4. Unwrap dough. Divide dough into 8 equal portions.

5. Working with 1 portion (keep remaining dough covered to prevent drying), pass dough through pasta rollers of a pasta machine on the widest setting.

6. Fold dough in half crosswise; fold in half again.

7. Pass dough through rollers again. Move width gauge to next setting; pass pasta through rollers. Continue moving width gauge to narrower settings, passing dough through rollers once at each setting to form a 15 x 3–inch pasta strip. Lay strip flat on a lightly floured surface; cover.

8. Repeat procedure with remaining dough portions to make 8 pasta strips. Yield: 4 servings (serving size: 2 ounces uncooked pasta)

CALORIES 178; FAT 2.9g (sat 0.8g, mono 1g, poly 0.3g); PROTEIN 6.9g; CARB 30.2g; FIBER 0.2g; CHOL 106mg; IRON 0.9mg; SODIUM 107mg; CALC 21mg

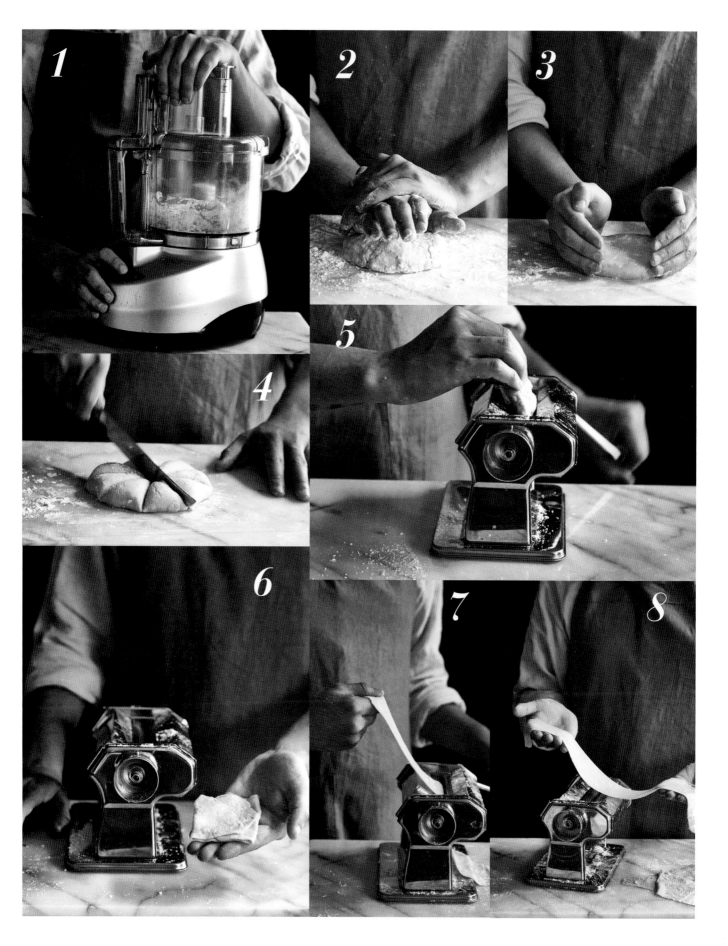

You can shape and fill ravioli and freeze it for up to a month.

RAVIOLI:

¾ CUP (6 OUNCES) PART-SKIM RICOTTA CHEESE

¼ CUP (1 OUNCE) GRATED FRESH PARMESAN CHEESE

2 TABLESPOONS FINELY CHOPPED FRESH BASIL

½ TEASPOON GRATED LEMON RIND

¼ TEASPOON FRESHLY GROUND BLACK PEPPER

1 LARGE EGG

FRESH PASTA DOUGH (PAGE 254)

6 QUARTS WATER

2 TABLESPOONS FINE SEA SALT

SAUCE:

2 TABLESPOONS EXTRA-VIRGIN OLIVE OIL

2 GARLIC CLOVES, MINCED

¼ CUP CHOPPED FRESH BASIL

1 OUNCE SHAVED FRESH PARMESAN CHEESE

Hands-on time: 1 hr.
Total time: 1 hr. 30 min.

RAVIOLI *with* HERBED RICOTTA FILLING

1. To prepare ravioli, place ricotta in a cheesecloth-lined colander; drain 30 minutes. Combine ricotta, ¼ cup Parmesan, and next 4 ingredients (through egg), stirring until well combined.

2. Place 1 (15 x 3–inch) sheet Fresh Pasta Dough on a lightly floured surface. Spoon 1½ teaspoons filling in the center of sheet 1½ inches from one end. Spoon 4 more portions of 1½ teaspoons filling at 3-inch intervals along the length of sheet. Moisten edges and in between each filling portion with water; place 1 (15 x 3–inch) pasta sheet on top, pressing to seal. Cut pasta sheet crosswise into 5 (3 x 3–inch) ravioli, trimming edges with a sharp knife. Place ravioli on a lightly floured baking sheet (cover with a damp towel to prevent drying). Repeat procedure with remaining pasta sheets and filling to form 20 ravioli.

3. Bring 6 quarts water and salt to a boil in an 8-quart pot. Add half of ravioli to pot; cook 1½ minutes, until no longer translucent. Remove ravioli from water with slotted spoon. Repeat procedure with remaining ravioli.

4. To prepare sauce, heat oil in a large skillet over low heat. Add garlic to pan; cook 6 minutes or until garlic is tender. Remove from heat. Place 5 ravioli in each of 4 bowls; drizzle each serving with 1½ teaspoons garlic oil. Top each serving with 1 tablespoon chopped basil and one-fourth of the shaved Parmesan. Serve immediately. Yield: 4 servings

CALORIES 375; FAT 18.4g (sat 6.7g, mono 8g, poly 1.5g); PROTEIN 19.8g; CARB 34.1g; FIBER 4.1g; CHOL 169.1mg; IRON 1.4mg; SODIUM 734.7mg; CALC 283.9mg

WHOLE WHEAT TAGLIOLINI
with FRESH CHERRY TOMATO SAUCE

The nutty, slightly sweet flavor of whole-wheat flour is a tasty addition to a basic pasta recipe. It also boosts the protein and fiber content of your noodles.

PASTA:

4.5 OUNCES ALL-PURPOSE FLOUR (ABOUT 1 CUP)

4.75 OUNCES WHOLE-WHEAT FLOUR (ABOUT 1 CUP)

1 TABLESPOON PLUS ¼ TEASPOON SALT, DIVIDED

5 TABLESPOONS WATER

2 TABLESPOONS EXTRA-VIRGIN OLIVE OIL

2 LARGE EGGS

6 QUARTS WATER

SAUCE:

2 TABLESPOONS OLIVE OIL

2 GARLIC CLOVES, MINCED

5 CUPS QUARTERED CHERRY TOMATOES

½ CUP THINLY SLICED FRESH BASIL

3 TABLESPOONS DRAINED CAPERS

1 TEASPOON GRATED LEMON RIND

¼ TEASPOON CRUSHED RED PEPPER

Hands-on time: 55 min.
Total time: 1 hr. 15 min.

1. Combine flours and ¼ teaspoon salt in a food processor; process 30 seconds. Combine 5 tablespoons water, olive oil, and eggs in a bowl, stir well. With processor running, pour water mixture through the food chute, processing just until dough forms a ball. Turn dough out onto a lightly floured surface; knead 5 or 6 times. Shape into a disk. Dust lightly with flour; wrap in plastic wrap. Let stand 30 minutes.

2. Divide dough into 3 equal portions. Working with 1 portion at a time (cover remaining dough to prevent drying), press dough into a flat rectangle. Roll dough into a 14–inch square, dusting with flour if necessary. Lay dough sheet flat; fold ends so they meet in the middle. Fold the sheet in half like closing a book. Fold in half again to form 8 layers. With a sharp knife, cut the pasta crosswise into ¼-inch-wide noodles. Separate noodles, and dust with flour. Place noodles on a jelly-roll pan dusted with flour. Repeat procedure with remaining dough portions.

3. Bring 6 quarts water and remaining 1 tablespoon salt to a boil in a large Dutch oven. Place noodles in a sieve; shake off excess flour. Add to pan. Cook 1½ minutes or until done; drain.

4. To prepare sauce, heat 2 tablespoons oil in a large non-stick skillet over medium-low heat. Add garlic to pan; cook 3 minutes, stirring frequently (do not brown). Remove from heat. Stir in tomatoes and remaining ingredients. Toss with noodles. Yield: 4 servings (serving size: 1¼ cups).

CALORIES 408; FAT 17.1g (sat 2.8g, mono 11.2g, poly 2.6g); PROTEIN 12.7g; CARB 53.5g; FIBER 7.3g; CHOL 93mg; IRON 4mg; SODIUM 565mg; CALC 58mg

QUINOA

What makes a "superfood" like quinoa so super? Is it because it's incredibly simple, almost foolproof, to prepare? Is it because it's gluten-free? Or is it quinoa's versatility that makes it stand out above the grain crowd? In these recipes, quinoa plays the starring role in a refreshing veggie-packed salad, lends its superior nutrition to a stuffing for baked tomatoes, and adds pop to a vegetarian chili. No matter how you choose to use quinoa, there is a lot to love—it is quick-cooking, packed with flavor, and loaded with good nutrition and texture.

For you history buffs, quinoa has been growing in the high elevations of the Andes mountains for nearly 3,000 years. Its dietary value was quickly realized by the Incan people, who made the crop a part of sacred ceremonies. Quinoa is the only plant-based source of all nine essential amino acids, making it a key component of vegetarian diets. High in fiber, quinoa also has lots of magnesium, iron, and vitamin B_6. It doesn't matter which of these super reasons you choose for getting this superfood into your diet. You can't go wrong with these recipes!

YOU'LL LEARN:

HOW (AND WHY) TO RINSE QUINOA • HOW TO COOK QUINOA

HOW TO DETERMINE WHEN QUINOA IS "DONE"

MASTER RECIPE:

RED QUINOA SALAD

VARIATIONS:

BAKED TOMATOES WITH QUINOA, CORN, AND GREEN CHILES

QUINOA AND ROASTED PEPPER CHILI

YOUR MISE EN PLACE

DAIRY
FETA CHEESE, CRUMBLED

FRESH PRODUCE
SHALLOT, MINCED
TOMATOES, DICED AND SEEDED
CUCUMBER, DICED AND SEEDED
FRESH MINT, CHOPPED
FRESH OREGANO, CHOPPED
LEMON, CUT IN WEDGES

FLAVOR BOOSTERS/ STAPLES
RED QUINOA
OLIVE OIL
RED WINE VINEGAR
KOSHER SALT
BLACK PEPPER
CANNED CHICKPEAS, RINSED AND DRAINED

EQUIPMENT NEEDED:
SHARP KNIFE
FINE MESH SIEVE/STRAINER
LARGE BOWL
SAUCEPAN
SMALL BOWL
WHISK
SALAD TOSSERS

RED QUINOA SALAD

Rinsing quinoa before cooking it helps remove a bitter-tasting sap that's released during the harvesting process. Some supermarket quinoa is pre-rinsed, but it never hurts to give it another washing.

1 CUP UNCOOKED RED QUINOA

2 CUPS WATER

⅓ CUP OLIVE OIL

2 TABLESPOONS RED WINE VINEGAR

1½ TEASPOONS FINELY MINCED SHALLOT

¼ TEASPOON KOSHER SALT

¼ TEASPOON FRESHLY GROUND BLACK PEPPER

2 CUPS (½-INCH) DICED SEEDED TOMATO

½ CUP (½-INCH) DICED SEEDED CUCUMBER

3 TABLESPOONS CHOPPED FRESH MINT

1 TABLESPOON CHOPPED FRESH OREGANO

1 (15-OUNCE) CAN CHICKPEAS (GARBANZO BEANS), RINSED AND DRAINED

2 OUNCES CRUMBLED FETA CHEESE (ABOUT ½ CUP)

4 LEMON WEDGES

Hands-on time: 20 min.
Total time: 1 hr. 20 min.

When is quinoa fully cooked? When the grains pop open to reveal the kernel's germ, a little white tail that looks like an apostrophe.

1. Place quinoa in a fine sieve, and place sieve in a large bowl. Cover quinoa with water. Using your hands, rub the grains together for 30 seconds; rinse and drain. Repeat the procedure twice. Drain well.

2. Combine quinoa and 2 cups water in a 1½-quart saucepan; bring to a boil. Reduce heat, cover, and simmer for 15 minutes or until water is absorbed. Drain and place in a large bowl. Let cool 1 hour.

3. While quinoa cools, combine oil and next 4 ingredients (through pepper) in a small bowl, stirring with a whisk. Let dressing stand 20 minutes.

4. Add dressing, tomato, and next 4 ingredients (through chickpeas) to quinoa; toss well. Add cheese, and toss gently. Serve with lemon wedges. Yield: 4 servings (serving size: about 1¾ cups salad and 1 lemon wedge)

CALORIES 460; FAT 24.7g (sat 5g, mono 14.7g, poly 3.8g); PROTEIN 12.5g; CARB 48.4g; FIBER 7.4g; CHOL 13mg; IRON 3.5mg; SODIUM 499mg; CALC 133mg

Unlike pasta, quinoa retains its firm texture during baking, making it a perfect whole-grain stuffing for all kinds of vegetables—think tomatoes, as well as bell peppers, eggplant, and zucchini.

2 POBLANO CHILES

2 CUPS FRESH CORN KERNELS (ABOUT 4 EARS)

1 CUP CHOPPED ONION

1 TABLESPOON CHOPPED FRESH OREGANO

1 TABLESPOON OLIVE OIL

1 TABLESPOON FRESH LIME JUICE

1 TEASPOON SALT, DIVIDED

¾ TEASPOON GROUND CUMIN

¼ TEASPOON FRESHLY GROUND BLACK PEPPER

6 LARGE RIPE TOMATOES (ABOUT 4 POUNDS)

1 CUP UNCOOKED QUINOA

¼ CUP WATER

4 OUNCES COLBY-JACK CHEESE, SHREDDED (ABOUT 1 CUP)

Hands-on time: 55 min.
Total time: 1hr. 20 min.

BAKED TOMATOES
with QUINOA, CORN, *and* GREEN CHILES

1. Preheat broiler to high. Cut the chiles in half lengthwise; discard seeds and membranes. Place chile halves, skin side up, on a foil-lined baking sheet; flatten with hand. Broil 8 minutes or until blackened. Place in paper bag; close tightly. Let stand 10 minutes. Peel chiles. Coarsely chop chiles; place in a bowl. Add corn and onion to pan; broil 10 minutes, stirring twice. Add corn mixture to chopped chiles; stir in oregano, oil, lime juice, ¼ teaspoon salt, cumin, and black pepper.

2. Cut tops off tomatoes; set aside. Carefully scoop out tomato pulp, leaving shells intact. Strain pulp through a sieve over a bowl, pressing with the back of a spoon to extract liquid. Reserve 1¼ cups liquid, and discard remaining liquid. Sprinkle tomatoes with ½ teaspoon salt. Invert tomatoes on a wire rack; let stand 30 minutes. Dry insides of tomatoes with a paper towel.

3. Place quinoa in a fine sieve, and place sieve in a large bowl. Cover quinoa with water. Rub the grains together for 30 seconds; rinse and drain. Repeat procedure twice. Drain well. Combine reserved tomato liquid, quinoa, ¼ cup water, and remaining ¼ teaspoon salt in a medium saucepan; bring to a boil. Cover, reduce heat, and simmer for 15 minutes or until liquid is absorbed. Remove from heat; fluff with a fork. Add quinoa mixture to corn mixture; toss well.

4. Preheat oven to 350°. Spoon about ¾ cup corn mixture into each tomato. Divide cheese evenly among tomatoes. Place tomatoes and tops, if desired, on a jelly-roll pan.

5. Bake at 350° for 15 minutes. Remove from oven. Preheat broiler. Broil the tomatoes 1½ minutes or until cheese melts. Place tomato tops on tomatoes, if desired. Yield: 6 servings (serving size: 1 stuffed tomato)

CALORIES 320; FAT 11.2g (sat 4.1g, mono 2.4g, poly 2g); PROTEIN 13.4g; CARB 46.3g; FIBER 8.8g; CHOL 17mg; IRON 3.2mg; SODIUM 550mg; CALC 195mg

QUINOA *and* ROASTED PEPPER CHILI

Make sure to keep quinoa cooking at a simmer, as boiling too rapidly will cause the grain to expand quickly and burst, losing its distinctive texture.

2 RED BELL PEPPERS

2 POBLANO CHILES

4 TEASPOONS OLIVE OIL

3 CUPS CHOPPED ZUCCHINI

1½ CUPS CHOPPED ONION

4 GARLIC CLOVES, MINCED

1 TABLESPOON CHILI POWDER

1 TEASPOON GROUND CUMIN

½ TEASPOON SPANISH SMOKED PAPRIKA

½ CUP WATER

⅓ CUP UNCOOKED QUINOA, RINSED

¼ TEASPOON KOSHER SALT

1 (14.5-OUNCE) CAN FIRE-ROASTED DICED TOMATOES WITH CHIPOTLES, UNDRAINED

1 (15-OUNCE) CAN NO-SALT-ADDED PINTO BEANS, RINSED AND DRAINED

1 CUP LOW-SODIUM VEGETABLE JUICE

Hands-on time: 25 min.
Total time: 45 min.

1. Preheat broiler. Cut bell peppers and chiles in half lengthwise; discard seeds and membranes. Place halves, skin sides up, on a foil-lined baking sheet, and flatten with hand.

2. Broil 10 minutes or until blackened. Place in a paper bag; fold to close tightly. Let stand 10 minutes. Peel and coarsely chop.

3. Heat a large Dutch oven over medium-high heat. Add oil to pan; swirl to coat. Add zucchini, onion, and garlic; sauté 4 minutes. Stir in chili powder, cumin, and paprika; sauté for 30 seconds. Add roasted peppers and chiles, ½ cup water, and remaining ingredients; bring to a boil. Reduce heat to medium-low; cover and simmer for 20 minutes or until quinoa is tender. Yield: 4 servings (serving size: 1½ cups)

CALORIES 258; FAT 6.3g (sat 0.9g, mono 3.6g, poly 1.2g); PROTEIN 9.7g; CARB 42.1g; FIBER 9.8g; CHOL 0.0mg; IRON 3.7mg; SODIUM 430mg; CALC 108mg

BREADS

MUFFINS

Making a great muffin is a lot like the first few years working in a professional kitchen—you're going to take some lumps. Whether it's that tray of bread that toasted just a little too long, or knocking that perfectly finished sauce over at just the wrong time, there are bound to be a few bumps (or lumps!) on the road to muffin greatness. You can accept and learn from them or toss in your side towel and walk off discouraged. If you want to bake muffins that are tender and perfectly moist, learn to take your lumps.

Things to remember: Don't be tempted to stir and stir until the batter is perfectly smooth; you'll end up with muffins that are tough, almost bread-like. It's a gently stirred batter that yields the perfect muffin. And be sure not to overfill your muffin cups—they should be filled between two-thirds and three-fourths full for perfectly peaked muffins rather than ones that spill over their tops. (A great batter means nothing if half of it winds up on the floor of your oven!)

YOU'LL LEARN:

HOW TO MIX A MUFFIN BATTER • HOW TO ACHIEVE UNIFORM TEXTURE (INSTEAD OF TUNNELS)

MASTER RECIPE:

PARMESAN CORN MUFFINS

VARIATIONS:

TUSCAN LEMON MUFFINS • CHERRY–WHEAT GERM MUFFINS

YOUR MISE EN PLACE

WET
BUTTERMILK
OLIVE OIL
LARGE EGG, LIGHTLY BEATEN
COOKING SPRAY

DRY
ALL-PURPOSE FLOUR
YELLOW CORNMEAL
SUGAR
SALT
GROUND RED PEPPER

LEAVENING AGENTS
BAKING POWDER
BAKING SODA

MIX-INS
PARMIGIANO-REGGIANO CHEESE,
    GRATED
FRESH CHIVES, FINELY CHOPPED

EQUIPMENT NEEDED:
SHARP KNIFE
CHEESE GRATER
SMALL BOWL
LARGE BOWL
WHISK
WOODEN SPOON
12-CUP MUFFIN TIN
WOODEN PICK
WIRE COOLING RACK

PREHEAT YOUR OVEN TO 400°.

Parmesan
CORN MUFFINS

The key to a nice even crumb—and no tunnels or air pockets—is all in the mixing. For the best results, stir "wet" and "dry" ingredients together gently, and quit before you think you're finished.

1¼ CUPS FAT-FREE BUTTERMILK

¼ CUP OLIVE OIL

1 LARGE EGG, LIGHTLY BEATEN

4.5 OUNCES ALL-PURPOSE FLOUR (ABOUT 1 CUP)

¾ CUP YELLOW CORNMEAL

1 TABLESPOON SUGAR

2 TEASPOONS BAKING POWDER

¼ TEASPOON BAKING SODA

¼ TEASPOON SALT

⅛ TEASPOON GROUND RED PEPPER

3 OUNCES GRATED FRESH PARMIGIANO-REGGIANO CHEESE (ABOUT ¾ CUP), DIVIDED

3 TABLESPOONS FINELY CHOPPED FRESH CHIVES, DIVIDED

COOKING SPRAY

Hands-on time: 15 min.
Total time: 28 min.

Resist using your handheld or stand-up mixer for muffin batter. It is best stirred by hand.

1. Preheat oven to 400°. Combine the first 3 ingredients in a small bowl.

2. Weigh or lightly spoon flour into dry measuring cups; level with a knife. Combine flour and next 6 ingredients (through pepper) in a large bowl, stirring well with a whisk.

3. Make a well in center of flour mixture. Add buttermilk mixture; stir just until moist. Stir in 2 ounces cheese (about ½ cup) and 2 tablespoons chives.

4. Spoon batter into 12 muffin cups coated with cooking spray.

5. Sprinkle muffins evenly with remaining 1 ounce cheese and remaining 1 tablespoon chives. Bake at 400° for 13 minutes or until a wooden pick inserted in center comes out with moist crumbs clinging. Remove muffins from tin; cool on a wire rack. Yield: 12 servings (serving size: 1 muffin)

CALORIES 164; FAT 7.1g (sat 1.8g, mono 3.5g, poly 0.7g); PROTEIN 6.3g; CARB 18.5g; FIBER 0.7g; CHOL 20mg; IRON 1mg; SODIUM 300mg; CALC 177mg

TUSCAN LEMON MUFFINS

Using ricotta cheese ensures a light and fluffy texture as well as a moist and delicious muffin that's almost sweet enough to satisfy a craving for cake.

7.9 OUNCES ALL-PURPOSE FLOUR (ABOUT 1¾ CUPS)

¾ CUP GRANULATED SUGAR

2½ TEASPOONS BAKING POWDER

¼ TEASPOON SALT

¾ CUP PART-SKIM RICOTTA CHEESE

½ CUP WATER

¼ CUP OLIVE OIL

1 TABLESPOON GRATED LEMON RIND

2 TABLESPOONS FRESH LEMON JUICE

1 LARGE EGG, LIGHTLY BEATEN

COOKING SPRAY

2 TABLESPOONS TURBINADO SUGAR

Hands-on time: 13 min.
Total time: 34 min.

1. Preheat oven to 375°. Weigh or lightly spoon flour into dry measuring cups; level with a knife. Combine flour and next 3 ingredients (through salt) in a large bowl; make a well in center. Combine ricotta and next 5 ingredients (through egg) in a small bowl. Add ricotta mixture to flour mixture, stirring just until moist.

2. Place 12 muffin-cup liners in muffin cups and coat liners with cooking spray. Divide batter among muffin cups. Sprinkle turbinado sugar over batter. Bake at 375° for 16 minutes or until a wooden pick inserted in center comes out clean. Cool 5 minutes in pan on a wire rack. Yield: 12 servings (serving size: 1 muffin)

CALORIES 186; FAT 6.2 (sat 1.5g, mono 3.4g, poly 0.6g); PROTEIN 4g; CARB 29.5g; FIBER 0.6g; CHOL 21mg; IRON 1mg; SODIUM 160mg; CALC 81mg

Wheat germ boosts fiber while dried cherries add a hit of sweet-tart flavor. Substitute other dried fruit for the cherries, but keep amounts the same.

6.75 OUNCES ALL-PURPOSE FLOUR (ABOUT 1½ CUPS)

¾ CUP DRIED CHERRIES, COARSELY CHOPPED

½ CUP TOASTED WHEAT GERM

½ CUP PACKED DARK BROWN SUGAR

1 TEASPOON BAKING POWDER

1 TEASPOON BAKING SODA

½ TEASPOON SALT

¼ TEASPOON GROUND ALLSPICE

1 CUP LOW-FAT BUTTERMILK

¼ CUP CANOLA OIL

1 LARGE EGG, LIGHTLY BEATEN

COOKING SPRAY

Hands-on time: 12 min.
Total time: 32 min.

CHERRY–WHEAT GERM MUFFINS

1. Preheat oven to 400°. Weigh or lightly spoon flour into dry measuring cups; level with a knife. Combine flour and next 7 ingredients (through allspice) in a large bowl, stirring with a whisk. Make a well in center of mixture. Combine buttermilk, oil, and egg in a bowl, stirring well with a whisk. Add buttermilk mixture to flour mixture, stirring just until moist.

2. Place 12 muffin-cup liners in muffin cups, and coat liners with cooking spray. Divide batter evenly among prepared muffin cups. Bake at 400° for 15 minutes or until a wooden pick inserted in center comes out clean. Cool 5 minutes in pan on a wire rack. Yield: 12 servings (serving size: 1 muffin)

CALORIES 202; FAT 5.9 (sat 0.7g, mono 3.3g, poly 1.8g); PROTEIN 4.5g; CARB 32.4g; FIBER 2.2g; CHOL 16mg; IRON 1.5mg; SODIUM 268mg; CALC 68mg

---

If you can't find buttermilk at your grocery store, stir together 1 cup milk with 1 tablespoon lemon juice or white vinegar. Let the mixture stand 5 minutes, then add to your recipe.

How to Become a
GREAT BAKER

Baking demands precision. If a cake recipe calls for the cook to fold in flour in six batches, a shortcut of four will compromise the crumb. Even one tablespoon too much flour can change the texture of a reduced-fat cake. Here are some fundamentals to keep in mind.

1. WEIGH AND MEASURE. Learn the difference between weight and volume. Flour needs to be weighed. If you don't have a kitchen scale, buy one. Weight is the only accurate way to measure flour. Depending on how tightly flour is packed into a measuring cup, you can end up with double the amount intended. That's why we give flour measurements in ounces first. (In a pinch, you can use measuring cups. To improve accuracy, stir flour gently with a large spoon before measuring, then level with a knife or small metal spatula.)

Water, oil, milk, and other wet ingredients should be poured into a clear measuring cup on a level counter, then checked at eye level, not from above.

2. FOLLOW THE RECIPE. You've heard that baking is as much science as art, so to prevent disastrous results, read through the recipe from start to finish. If you want to experiment (and we do it all the time), regard it as an experiment, and expect a few failures along the way.

3. USE THE PROPER PAN. Your recipe calls for two 9-inch round cake pans, but you only have 8-inch pans. What to do? Go get two 9-inch pans. Pan size is specified in recipes because a cake or quick bread increases in volume 50 to 100 percent during baking; if your loaf pan or cake pan is too small, the batter could overflow. Color is important, too; glass or dark nonstick pans usually require a 25-degree reduction in baking temperature versus silver-colored aluminum pans.

4. CHECK YOUR OVEN. Oven temperatures need to be spot on. To prevent an under- or over-done baked good, get an oven thermometer—it's the best way to be sure your oven is calibrated correctly. In addition, check your oven for hot spots. Use the bread test: Place bread slices on the middle rack and bake at 350° for a few minutes. Check if any get singed, if so, you've found the oven's hot spot. Try to avoid these areas or rotate pans accordingly.

Bake muffins, cakes, and quick breads in the middle (too close to the top or bottom can cause overbrowning). Gently close the oven door—a slam can release air bubbles trapped in the batter.

5. PREHEAT THE OVEN. An oven that hasn't been preheated may not drastically affect a casserole, but it will have an effect on your baking. Baked goods need that initial blast of heat to activate the leavening. Although it's tempting, don't put your pan in before the oven is properly preheated. If it isn't at the correct temperature, your recipe will take longer to bake and you run the risk of having a dry texture and low volume.

6. CHECK FOR DONENESS. Each recipe provides a suggested baking time, and some include a doneness test. We recommend that you check for doneness a few minutes earlier than the recipe states to allow for variations in your oven or other factors. For muffins, quick breads, and some cakes, insert a wooden pick; it should come out clean. For other recipes, it is a visual cue like a certain degree of browning. Completely baked bread will have a beautiful golden-brown color and sound hollow when tapped on the bottom.

BANANA BREAD

Should we consider calling this banana cake? The word bread feels like a bit of a misnomer when you think about it. We're talking about dense, moist, soul-warming goodness with just the right touch of sweetness. It doesn't feel like bread. Whatever you call it, there is a lot to love here. With all those bananas providing texture and moisture, there is very little need for added fat in the recipe. The recipe is stunningly simple to make and packed with good-for-you things like flaxseed and yogurt.

It's the perfect thing to enjoy with your morning coffee, but you'll probably find yourself snacking on it around lunchtime or maybe even consider toasting it to top with a scoop of Salted Caramel Ice Cream (page 344) after dinner. When you find something you love this much, why not share it? It's a great gift for housewarming, new baby, get-well-soon, or thinking-of-you. There's no wrong time to bake a loaf of this delicious bread for someone.

YOU'LL LEARN:

HOW TO MIX A QUICK BREAD BATTER • HOW TO TEST FOR DONENESS

HOW TO COOL A QUICK BREAD

MASTER RECIPE:

BASIC BANANA BREAD

VARIATIONS:

BANANAS FOSTER BREAD • PEANUT BUTTER-BANANA BREAD

YOUR MISE EN PLACE

WET
MASHED RIPE BANANA
PLAIN FAT-FREE YOGURT
BUTTER, MELTED
LARGE EGGS
COOKING SPRAY
1% LOW-FAT MILK

DRY
GRANULATED SUGAR
BROWN SUGAR
ALL-PURPOSE FLOUR
GROUND FLAXSEED
SALT
GROUND CINNAMON
GROUND ALLSPICE
POWDERED SUGAR

LEAVENING AGENTS
BAKING SODA

EQUIPMENT NEEDED:
LARGE BOWL
ELECTRIC MIXER
SMALL BOWL
LOAF PAN
SPATULA
WOODEN PICK
WIRE COOLING RACK
SPOON

PREHEAT YOUR OVEN TO 350°.

Basic

BANANA BREAD

Rich in heart-healthy fats, flaxseed adds moistness and a nutty flavor to this bread.
Look for whole ground flaxseed (sometimes labeled flaxseed meal) in the baking aisle.

1½ CUPS MASHED RIPE BANANA

⅓ CUP PLAIN FAT-FREE YOGURT

5 TABLESPOONS BUTTER, MELTED

2 LARGE EGGS

½ CUP GRANULATED SUGAR

½ CUP PACKED BROWN SUGAR

6.75 OUNCES ALL-PURPOSE FLOUR
(ABOUT 1½ CUPS)

¼ CUP GROUND FLAXSEED

¾ TEASPOON BAKING SODA

½ TEASPOON SALT

½ TEASPOON GROUND CINNAMON

⅛ TEASPOON GROUND ALLSPICE

COOKING SPRAY

⅓ CUP POWDERED SUGAR

1½ TEASPOONS 1% LOW-FAT MILK

Hands-on time: 15 min.
Total time: 1 hr. 20 min.

Don't be tempted to puree your bananas perfectly smooth. A slightly chunky mash will yield the best texture in your bread.

1. Preheat oven to 350°. Combine first 4 ingredients in a large bowl; beat with an electric mixer at medium speed. Add granulated and brown sugars; beat until combined.

2. Weigh or lightly spoon flour into dry measuring cups; level with a knife. Combine flour and next 5 ingredients (through ground allspice) in a small bowl. Add flour mixture to banana mixture; beat just until blended.

3. Pour batter into a 9 x 5–inch loaf pan coated with cooking spray. Bake at 350° for 55 minutes or until a wooden pick inserted in center comes out clean. Remove from oven; cool 10 minutes in pan on a wire rack.

4. Remove bread from pan; cool completely.

5. Combine powdered sugar and milk in a small bowl, stirring until smooth; drizzle over bread. Yield: 16 servings (serving size: 1 slice)

CALORIES 167; FAT 5.1 (sat 2.5g, mono 1.3g, poly 0.9g); PROTEIN 2.9g; CARB 28.3g; FIBER 1.5g; CHOL 32mg; IRON 1mg; SODIUM 173mg; CALC 24mg

BANANAS FOSTER BREAD

This adult interpretation switches all the sugar to brown sugar and cooks the mashed bananas with cognac or dark rum. If you don't like a boozy-flavored glaze, substitute apple cider for the alcohol.

1½ CUPS MASHED RIPE BANANA

1 CUP PACKED BROWN SUGAR, DIVIDED

6 TABLESPOONS BUTTER, MELTED AND DIVIDED

¼ CUP COGNAC OR DARK RUM, DIVIDED

⅓ CUP PLAIN FAT-FREE YOGURT

2 LARGE EGGS

6.75 OUNCES ALL-PURPOSE FLOUR (ABOUT 1½ CUPS)

¼ CUP GROUND FLAXSEED

¾ TEASPOON BAKING SODA

½ TEASPOON SALT

½ TEASPOON GROUND CINNAMON

⅛ TEASPOON GROUND ALLSPICE

COOKING SPRAY

⅓ CUP POWDERED SUGAR

Hands-on time: 18 min.
Total time: 1 hr. 28 min.

1. Preheat oven to 350°. Combine banana, ½ cup brown sugar, 5 tablespoons butter, and 3 tablespoons cognac in a nonstick skillet. Cook over medium heat until mixture begins to bubble. Remove from heat; cool. Place banana mixture in a large bowl. Add yogurt, remaining ½ cup brown sugar, and eggs. Beat with a mixer at medium speed.

2. Weigh or lightly spoon flour into dry measuring cups; level with a knife. Combine flour and next 5 ingredients (through allspice) in a small bowl. Add flour mixture to banana mixture; beat just until blended. Pour batter into a 9 x 5–inch loaf pan coated with cooking spray. Bake at 350° for 1 hour or until a wooden pick inserted in center comes out clean. Remove from oven; cool 10 minutes in pan on a wire rack. Remove bread from pan; place on wire rack.

3. Combine remaining 1 tablespoon melted butter, remaining 1 tablespoon cognac, and powdered sugar in a small bowl; stir until well blended. Drizzle over the warm bread. Yield: 16 servings (serving size: 1 slice)

CALORIES 194; FAT 5.8 (sat 3g, mono 1.5g, poly 0.9g); PROTEIN 2.9g; CARB 31.1g; FIBER 1.5g; CHOL 34mg; IRON 1.1mg; SODIUM 181mg; CALC 32mg

---

Even the best banana bread will turn out dry if overbaked. It will continue cooking after it is removed from the oven, so if your bread is close to being ready, go ahead and let it rest.

PEANUT BUTTER– BANANA BREAD

Peanut butter is whipped into the basic banana bread recipe along with roasted peanuts to add a nutty flavor.

1½ CUPS MASHED RIPE BANANA

⅓ CUP PLAIN FAT-FREE YOGURT

⅓ CUP PLUS 1 TABLESPOON CREAMY PEANUT BUTTER, DIVIDED

3 TABLESPOONS BUTTER, MELTED

2 LARGE EGGS

½ CUP GRANULATED SUGAR

½ CUP PACKED BROWN SUGAR

6.75 OUNCES ALL-PURPOSE FLOUR (ABOUT 1½ CUPS)

¼ CUP GROUND FLAXSEED

¾ TEASPOON BAKING SODA

½ TEASPOON SALT

½ TEASPOON GROUND CINNAMON

⅛ TEASPOON GROUND ALLSPICE

2 TABLESPOONS CHOPPED DRY-ROASTED PEANUTS

COOKING SPRAY

⅓ CUP POWDERED SUGAR

1 TABLESPOON 1% LOW-FAT MILK

Hands-on time: 20 min.
Total time: 1 hr. 35 min.

1. Preheat oven to 350°. Combine banana, yogurt, ⅓ cup peanut butter, butter, and eggs in a large bowl; beat with a mixer at medium speed. Add granulated and brown sugars; beat until blended.

2. Weigh or lightly spoon flour into dry measuring cups; level with a knife. Combine flour and next 5 ingredients (through allspice) in a small bowl. Add flour mixture to banana mixture; beat just until blended. Stir in nuts. Pour batter into a 9 x 5–inch loaf pan coated with cooking spray. Bake at 350° for 1 hour and 5 minutes or until a wooden pick inserted in center comes out clean. Remove from oven; cool 10 minutes in pan on a wire rack. Remove bread from pan; cool.

3. Combine powdered sugar, milk, and remaining 1 tablespoon peanut butter in a small bowl, stirring with a whisk. Drizzle glaze over bread. Yield: 16 servings (serving size: 1 slice)

CALORIES 198; FAT 7.4 (sat 2.3g, mono 2.7g, poly 1.8g); PROTEIN 4.7g; CARB 29.7g; FIBER 1.9g; CHOL 28mg; IRON 1.1mg; SODIUM 200mg; CALC 27mg

It is important that your bread cools completely to room temperature before adding the glaze. The sugar mixture will roll right off a warm cake.

BUTTERMILK BISCUITS

When you're looking to kick up the excitement level around your brunch table, a platter of tender, flaky biscuits should cement your legacy as breakfast royalty. I challenge you to just say "buttermilk biscuits" without smiling. It can't be done. Warm from the oven, they're the ultimate crowd pleaser, and if you run across someone who doesn't get excited about homemade biscuits, you probably don't want to be friends with them anyway.

Making the perfect biscuit is all about learning to handle the dough properly. Don't mix or knead too much. You want your dough to be moist lumps of flour and butter that just barely hold together. When you pat the dough into shape, use your rolling pin sparingly. Your restraint will be rewarded with the most tender and flaky biscuits you've ever tasted. Once you've perfected your biscuit technique, don't let them be pigeon-holed to the hours before noon. Mini biscuits with thin slices of ham deserve a place in the Hors d'Oeuvre Hall of Fame. Or omit the salt and drizzle baked biscuits with honey, then fill with fresh fruit and lightly whipped cream or yogurt. No matter how you eat them, you win.

YOU'LL LEARN:

HOW TO CUT BUTTER INTO FLOUR • HOW TO PRODUCE FLAKY, TENDER BISCUITS

MASTER RECIPE:

FLAKY BUTTERMILK BISCUITS

VARIATIONS:

PARMESAN PEPPER BISCUITS • SPICED PUMPKIN BISCUITS

YOUR MISE EN PLACE

WET
CHILLED BUTTER, CUT
BUTTERMILK
HONEY

DRY
ALL-PURPOSE FLOUR
SALT

LEAVENING AGENTS
BAKING POWDER

EQUIPMENT NEEDED:
LARGE BOWL
PASTRY BLENDER (OR 2 KNIVES)
SMALL BOWL
WHISK
ROLLING PIN
BISCUIT CUTTER
BAKING SHEET
PARCHMENT PAPER
WIRE COOLING RACKS

PREHEAT YOUR OVEN TO 400°.

Flaky Buttermilk
BISCUITS

To maximize the number of biscuits you get from the recipe, gather the dough scraps after cutting, gently pat or reroll to a ¾-inch thickness, and cut out additional biscuits.

9 OUNCES ALL-PURPOSE FLOUR (ABOUT 2 CUPS)

2½ TEASPOONS BAKING POWDER

½ TEASPOON SALT

5 TABLESPOONS CHILLED BUTTER, CUT INTO SMALL PIECES

¾ CUP FAT-FREE BUTTERMILK

3 TABLESPOONS HONEY

Hands-on time: 12 min.
Total time: 30 min.

These biscuits are low in fat, but you'd never suspect it. Buttermilk is the secret; it keeps low-fat baked goods moist and tender.

1. Preheat oven to 400°. Weigh or lightly spoon flour into dry measuring cups; level with a knife. Combine flour, baking powder, and salt in a large bowl; cut in butter with a pastry blender or 2 knives until mixture resembles coarse meal. Chill 10 minutes.

2. Combine buttermilk and honey in a small bowl, stirring with a whisk until well blended. Add buttermilk mixture to flour mixture; stir just until moist.

3. Turn dough out onto a lightly floured surface; knead lightly 4 times.

4. Roll dough into a (½-inch-thick) 9 x 5–inch rectangle; dust top of dough with flour.

5. Fold dough crosswise into thirds (as if folding a piece of paper to fit into an envelope). Re-roll dough into a (½-inch-thick) 9 x 5–inch rectangle; dust top of dough with flour.

6. Fold dough crosswise into thirds; gently roll or pat to a ¾-inch thickness.

7. Cut dough with a 1¾-inch biscuit cutter to form 14 dough rounds (rerolling if necessary). Place dough rounds, 1 inch apart, on a baking sheet lined with parchment paper. Bake at 400° for 12 minutes or until golden.

8. Remove from pan; cool 2 minutes on wire racks. Serve warm. Yield: 14 servings (serving size: 1 biscuit)

CALORIES 122; FAT 4.3g (sat 2.6g, mono 1.1g, poly 0.2g); PROTEIN 2.3g; CARB 18.9g; FIBER 0.9g; CHOL 11mg; IRON 1.1mg; SODIUM 192mg; CALC 59mg

The sharp, nutty flavor of Parmesan and the spicy bite of black pepper make these biscuits a standout pairing for roasted meats or the perfect vehicle for a breakfast sandwich.

9 OUNCES ALL-PURPOSE FLOUR
(ABOUT 2 CUPS)

2½ TEASPOONS BAKING POWDER

1 TEASPOON FRESHLY GROUND
BLACK PEPPER

½ TEASPOON SALT

¼ CUP CHILLED BUTTER, CUT INTO
SMALL PIECES

¾ CUP FAT-FREE BUTTERMILK

3 TABLESPOONS HONEY

½ CUP (2 OUNCES) GRATED FRESH
PARMESAN CHEESE

Hands-on time: 26 min.
Total time: 40 min.

PARMESAN PEPPER BISCUITS

1. Preheat oven to 400°. Weigh or lightly spoon flour into dry measuring cups; level with a knife. Combine flour, baking powder, pepper, and salt in a large bowl; cut in butter with a pastry blender or 2 knives until mixture resembles coarse meal. Chill 10 minutes.

2. Combine buttermilk and honey in a small bowl, stirring with a whisk until well blended; add cheese. Add buttermilk mixture to flour mixture; stir just until moist.

3. Turn dough out onto a lightly floured surface; knead lightly 4 times. Roll dough into a (½-inch-thick) 9 x 5–inch rectangle; dust top of dough with flour. Fold dough crosswise into thirds (as if folding a piece of paper to fit into an envelope). Re-roll dough into a (½-inch-thick) 9 x 5–inch rectangle; dust top of dough with flour. Fold dough crosswise into thirds; gently roll or pat to a ¾-inch thickness. Cut dough with a 1¾-inch biscuit cutter to form 14 dough rounds.

4. Place dough rounds, 1 inch apart, on a baking sheet lined with parchment paper. Bake at 400° for 13 minutes or until golden. Remove from pan; cool 2 minutes on wire racks. Serve warm. Yield: 14 servings (serving size: 1 biscuit)

CALORIES 131; FAT 4.7 (sat 2.9g, mono 0.9g, poly 0.2g); PROTEIN 4.2g; CARB 18.5g; FIBER 0.5g; CHOL 13mg; IRON 0.9mg; SODIUM 239mg; CALC 98mg

SPICED PUMPKIN BISCUITS

You'll find many different methods for rolling biscuit dough, but the folding technique used in these recipes helps create the most irresistible, flaky layers.

---

9 OUNCES ALL-PURPOSE FLOUR
   (ABOUT 2 CUPS)

2½ TEASPOONS BAKING POWDER

1¼ TEASPOONS PUMPKIN PIE SPICE

½ TEASPOON SALT

5 TABLESPOONS CHILLED BUTTER,
   CUT INTO SMALL PIECES

⅓ CUP FAT-FREE BUTTERMILK

3 TABLESPOONS HONEY

¾ CUP CANNED PUMPKIN

Hands-on time: 26 min.
Total time: 40 min.

1. Preheat oven to 400°. Weigh or lightly spoon flour into dry measuring cups; level with a knife. Combine flour, baking powder, pumpkin pie spice, and salt in a large bowl; cut in butter with a pastry blender or 2 knives until mixture resembles coarse meal. Chill 10 minutes.

2. Combine buttermilk and honey in a small bowl, stirring with a whisk until well blended; add canned pumpkin. Add buttermilk mixture to flour mixture; stir just until moist.

3. Turn dough out onto a lightly floured surface; knead lightly 4 times. Roll dough into a (½-inch-thick) 9 x 5–inch rectangle; dust top of dough with flour. Fold dough crosswise into thirds (as if folding a piece of paper to fit into an envelope). Re-roll dough into a (½-inch-thick) 9 x 5–inch rectangle; dust top of dough with flour. Fold dough crosswise into thirds; gently roll or pat to a ¾-inch thickness. Cut dough with a 1¾-inch biscuit cutter to form 14 dough rounds.

4. Place dough rounds, 1 inch apart, on a baking sheet lined with parchment paper. Bake at 400° for 14 minutes or until golden. Remove from pan; cool 2 minutes on wire racks. Serve warm. Yield: 14 servings (serving size: 1 biscuit)

CALORIES 122; FAT 4.3 (sat 2.6g, mono 1.1g, poly 0.2g); PROTEIN 2.3g;
CARB 18.9g; FIBER 0.9g; CHOL 11mg; IRON 1.1mg; SODIUM 192mg;
CALC 59mg

DINNER ROLLS

You know the feeling. You walk into your local bakery or pastry shop and see the gorgeous display of simple, handmade breads and baked goods. It's a "wow" moment. Then you daydream for a minute about making them yourself. How a basket of perfectly formed rolls sitting in the center of your dinner table would knock the socks off your family and friends. But you snap yourself out of it. Nah, you think, I could never make those myself. Yes, you can. It's time to get your hands—and countertops—dirty (well, covered in flour at least).

Working with yeast dough can be one of the most satisfying journeys in the kitchen. The alchemy of transforming flour and water into perfectly light, buttery rolls or chewy, pillow-soft breadsticks goes beyond cooking. It's art. And as with any worthwhile endeavor, mastery comes with practice. It's about touch and smell, the way the dough feels as you gently coax it into the proper form, and the scent that fills your kitchen as the bread rises and bakes to the moment of golden perfection. With our step-by-step guidance, your first batch will be great; your second will be even better. Forget your doubts—dive in and enjoy.

YOU'LL LEARN:

HOW TO MAKE A YEAST DOUGH • HOW TO SET UP DOUGH TO RISE
HOW TO FASHION DOUGH INTO VARIOUS SHAPES

MASTER RECIPE:

DINNER ROLLS

VARIATIONS:

ORANGE-BUTTERMILK DINNER ROLLS
TWISTED FENNEL AND COARSE SALT BREADSTICKS

YOUR MISE EN PLACE

WET
EGG, LIGHTLY BEATEN

COOKING SPRAY

MELTED BUTTER

EVAPORATED FAT-FREE MILK,
WARMED

DRY
SUGAR

ALL-PURPOSE FLOUR

SALT

CORNMEAL

LEAVENING AGENTS
DRY YEAST

TOPPING
POPPY SEEDS (OPTIONAL)

EQUIPMENT NEEDED:
LARGE BOWL

WOODEN SPOON

KITCHEN TOWEL

2 BAKING SHEETS

PASTRY BRUSH

PLASTIC WRAP

PASTRY CUTTER

WIRE COOLING RACKS

DINNER ROLLS

Extra rolls can be shaped, then frozen for up to eight weeks. Pull as many as you need out of the freezer, without thawing, and follow instructions for the second rise (Step 12), adding another 90 to 120 minutes for rising.

2 TEASPOONS SUGAR

1 PACKAGE DRY YEAST (ABOUT 2¼ TEASPOONS)

1 (12-OUNCE) CAN EVAPORATED FAT-FREE MILK, WARMED (100° TO 110°)

18 OUNCES ALL-PURPOSE FLOUR (ABOUT 4 CUPS), DIVIDED

1 LARGE EGG, LIGHTLY BEATEN

1 TEASPOON SALT

COOKING SPRAY

1 TEASPOON CORNMEAL

2 TABLESPOONS BUTTER, MELTED AND COOLED

POPPY SEEDS (OPTIONAL)

Hands-on time: 25 min.
Total Time: 2 hr. 10 min.

Worried about getting the milk temperature just right? Your finger makes a great thermometer—if you can't put your finger in, it's too hot. If it feels cool, it's too cold.

1. Dissolve sugar and yeast in warm milk in a large bowl; let stand 5 minutes.

2. Weigh or lightly spoon flour into dry measuring cups; level with a knife. Stir 13.5 ounces flour and egg into the milk mixture, stirring until smooth. Cover flour mixture; let stand 15 minutes.

3. Uncover and add 3.38 ounces flour and salt; stir until a soft dough forms.

4. Turn the dough out onto a floured surface. Knead until smooth and elastic (about 8 minutes); add enough of the remaining flour, 1 tablespoon at a time, to prevent the dough from sticking to hands (dough will feel tacky).

5. Place the dough in a large bowl coated with cooking spray, turning to coat top. Cover with a kitchen towel and let rise in a warm place (85°), free from drafts, for 40 minutes or until doubled in size. (Press two fingers into the dough. If an indentation remains, the dough has risen enough.)

6. Punch dough down; cover and let rest for 5 minutes.

7. Divide dough into 16 equal portions.

8. Working with 1 portion at a time (cover remaining dough to prevent drying), shape each portion into desired form: basic round ball, knot, snail, or twist.

(continued)

9. For knot: Shape each portion into an 8-inch rope *(a)*. Tie each rope into a single knot; tuck top end of rope under bottom edge of roll *(b)*.

10. For snail: Shape each portion into a 20-inch rope. Working on a flat surface, coil each rope around itself in a spiral; pinch tail of coil to seal.

11. For twist: Shape each portion into an 18-inch rope. Fold each rope in half so that both ends meet. Hold ends of rope in one hand and folded end in the other hand; gently twist.

12. Place shaped dough portions on each of 2 baking sheets lightly sprinkled with ½ teaspoon cornmeal. Lightly coat shaped dough portions with cooking spray; cover with plastic wrap. Let rise in a warm place (85°), free from drafts, for 20 minutes or until doubled in size.

13. Preheat oven to 400°. Gently brush dough portions with butter; sprinkle with poppy seeds, if desired.

14. Place 1 baking sheet on bottom oven rack and 1 baking sheet on middle oven rack. Bake at 400° for 10 minutes; rotate baking sheets. Bake an additional 10 minutes or until lightly browned on top and hollow-sounding when tapped on bottom. Place on wire racks. Serve warm, or cool completely on wire racks. Yield: 16 servings (serving size: 1 roll)

CALORIES 151; FAT 2.1g (sat 1.1g, mono 0.5g, poly 0.2g); PROTEIN 5.4g; CARB 27g; FIBER 0.9g; CHOL 18mg; IRON 1.7mg; SODIUM 187mg; CALC 69mg

Not fond of orange? Try substituting dried rosemary, or lemon rind with dried dill. Keep experimenting and create your own signature rolls.

1¼ CUPS WARM BUTTERMILK (100° TO 110°)

2 TABLESPOONS SUGAR

1 TABLESPOON HONEY

1 PACKAGE DRY YEAST (ABOUT 2¼ TEASPOONS)

3 TABLESPOONS BUTTER, MELTED AND DIVIDED

4 TEASPOONS GRATED ORANGE RIND

1 TEASPOON KOSHER SALT

14 OUNCES ALL-PURPOSE FLOUR (ABOUT 3 CUPS)

COOKING SPRAY

Hands-on time: 20 min.
Total time: 2 hr. 20 min.

VARIATION

ORANGE-BUTTERMILK DINNER ROLLS

---

1. Combine first 3 ingredients in bowl of an electric mixer. Sprinkle yeast over mixture; let stand 5 minutes or until bubbly. Stir in 2 tablespoons butter, rind, and salt. Weigh or lightly spoon flour into dry measuring cups; level with a knife. Add flour to yeast mixture; mix on low speed with a dough hook until a soft, elastic dough forms (about 5 minutes). Dough will be sticky. Place dough in a large bowl coated with cooking spray, turning to coat top. Cover with a kitchen towel and let rise in a warm place (85°) for 1 hour or until doubled in size.

2. Punch dough down; turn out onto a lightly floured surface. Cut dough into 13 equal pieces. Working with 1 piece at a time, roll dough into a ball by cupping your hand and pushing against dough and surface while rolling. Arrange dough balls 2 inches apart on a baking sheet coated with cooking spray. Brush lightly with remaining 1 tablespoon butter. Cover; let rise 1 hour or until doubled in size.

3. Preheat oven to 375°. Bake at 375° for 20 minutes or until rolls are golden. Remove rolls from pan; cool slightly on a wire rack. Yield: 13 servings (serving size: 1 roll)

CALORIES 163; FAT 3.7g (sat 2.2g, mono 0.7g, poly 0.2g); PROTEIN 4.2g; CARB 28.1g; FIBER 1g; CHOL 10mg; IRON 1.5mg; SODIUM 192mg; CALC 7mg

TWISTED FENNEL *and* COARSE SALT BREADSTICKS

Substitute poppy or sesame seeds for the fennel seeds or sprinkle on a combination of all three.

---

1 TABLESPOON SUGAR

1 PACKAGE DRY YEAST (ABOUT 2¼ TEASPOONS)

1 CUP PLUS 2 TABLESPOONS WARM FAT-FREE MILK (100° TO 110°)

3 TABLESPOONS EXTRA-VIRGIN OLIVE OIL

12.3 OUNCES ALL-PURPOSE FLOUR (ABOUT 2¾ CUPS), DIVIDED

½ CUP YELLOW CORNMEAL

¾ TEASPOON SALT

COOKING SPRAY

1 TABLESPOON WATER

1 EGG WHITE, LIGHTLY BEATEN

1 TABLESPOON FENNEL SEEDS

1½ TEASPOONS KOSHER SALT

Hands-on time: 27 min.
Total time: 1 hr. 17 min.

Kneading dough by hand lets you feel when it becomes smooth and elastic, a sign of proper gluten development.

1. Dissolve sugar and yeast in warm milk in a bowl; let stand 5 minutes. Stir in olive oil. Lightly spoon flour into dry measuring cups; level with a knife. Combine 2½ cups flour, cornmeal, and salt in a large bowl. Add yeast mixture; stir until a soft dough forms. Turn dough out onto a lightly floured surface. Knead until smooth and elastic (about 10 minutes); add enough of remaining flour, 1 tablespoon at a time, to prevent dough from sticking to hands (the dough will feel sticky). Place dough in a large bowl coated with cooking spray, turning to coat top. Cover with a kitchen towel and let rise in a warm place (85°), free from drafts, 1 hour or until doubled in size. (Gently press two fingers into dough. If indentation remains, dough has risen enough.)

2. Punch dough down; turn out onto a lightly floured surface. Divide dough into 24 equal portions. Working with 1 portion at a time (cover remaining portions), shape each into a 9-inch rope. Twist 2 ropes together; pinch ends to seal. Repeat with remaining dough. Place on 2 baking sheets lined with parchment paper. Cover dough, and let rise 30 minutes or until doubled in size.

3. Preheat oven to 425°. Combine 1 tablespoon water and egg white in a small bowl. Combine fennel seeds and kosher salt in another bowl. Brush breadsticks with egg white mixture, and sprinkle evenly with fennel seed mixture. Bake at 425° for 15 minutes or until puffed and lightly golden. Cool on a wire rack before serving. Yield: 12 servings (serving size: 1 breadstick)

CALORIES 164; FAT 4g (sat 0.6g, mono 2.8g, poly 0.5g); PROTEIN 4.6g; CARB 27g; FIBER 1.5g; CHOL 0mg; IRON 1.7mg; SODIUM 399mg; CALC 58mg

DESSERTS

BROWNIES

Get ready. You are about to vault to superhero status. Legends will be told of your baking greatness as friends gather around the dessert buffet. Your invitations to potlucks and bake sales will go through the roof. That's because we are going to show you how to master the gooey, chocolate-studded, outrageously delicious world of light brownies.

Brownies are the ideal place to begin testing your hand at light baking. If you're already well versed in home-crafted goodies, you'll barely notice the healthful tweaks—a little less fat, a little fewer nuts, fat-free milk. If you're a brownie-baking novice, we'll have you looking like a pro in no time. Brownies call for the most basic of mixing methods: Simply combine all of the dry ingredients in one bowl and the wet in another. Add all of the wet ingredients to the dry, and stir until just combined. Get the whole mix into the oven, then just sit back and wait to be showered with praise and thanks.

YOU'LL LEARN:

**HOW TO MIX A BROWNIE BATTER • HOW TO MAKE BLONDIES
HOW TO CHECK FOR DONENESS**

MASTER RECIPE:

CLASSIC FUDGE-WALNUT BROWNIES

VARIATIONS:

SALTED CARAMEL BROWNIES • PEANUT-BUTTER-CUP BLONDIES

YOUR MISE EN PLACE

WET
FAT-FREE MILK
BUTTER, MELTED
VANILLA EXTRACT
EGGS, LIGHTLY BEATEN
COOKING SPRAY

DRY
ALL-PURPOSE FLOUR
GRANULATED SUGAR
UNSWEETENED COCOA
BROWN SUGAR
BAKING POWDER
SALT

MIX-INS
CHOCOLATE CHUNKS
CHOPPED WALNUTS

EQUIPMENT NEEDED:
LARGE BOWL
WHISK
MICROWAVE-SAFE BOWL
LARGE SPOON
RUBBER SPATULA
SQUARE BAKING PAN
WOODEN PICK
WIRE COOLING RACK

PREHEAT YOUR OVEN TO 350°.

Classic Fudge-Walnut
BROWNIES

Bake brownies just until set and remove them from the oven before they can dry out.
The best test of doneness is to insert a wooden pick into the center of the pan.
When moist crumbs cling to the pick when you pull it out, the brownies are perfectly baked.

3.38 OUNCES ALL-PURPOSE FLOUR
   (ABOUT ¾ CUP)

1 CUP GRANULATED SUGAR

¾ CUP UNSWEETENED COCOA

½ CUP PACKED BROWN SUGAR

½ TEASPOON BAKING POWDER

¼ TEASPOON SALT

1 CUP BITTERSWEET CHOCOLATE
   CHUNKS, DIVIDED

⅓ CUP FAT-FREE MILK

6 TABLESPOONS BUTTER, MELTED

1 TEASPOON VANILLA EXTRACT

2 LARGE EGGS, LIGHTLY BEATEN

½ CUP CHOPPED WALNUTS, DIVIDED

COOKING SPRAY

Hands-on time: 15 min.
Total time: 45 min.

Until you know how long brownies take in your oven, begin checking the brownies for doneness 2 to 3 minutes before the recommended time in the recipe.

1. Preheat oven to 350°. Weigh or lightly spoon flour into dry measuring cups; level with a knife. Combine flour and next 5 ingredients (through salt) in a large bowl, stirring well with a whisk.

2. Combine ½ cup chocolate chunks and milk in a microwave-safe bowl; microwave at HIGH 1 minute or until melted, stirring after 30 seconds.

3. Stir butter, vanilla, and eggs into milk mixture. Add milk mixture, remaining ½ cup chocolate, and ¼ cup nuts to flour mixture; stir to combine.

4. Scrape the batter into a 9-inch square metal baking pan coated with cooking spray; sprinkle with remaining ¼ cup nuts.

5. Bake at 350° for 22 minutes or until a wooden pick inserted in center comes out with moist crumbs clinging. Cool in pan on a wire rack. Cut into 20 pieces. Yield: 20 servings (serving size: 1 brownie)

CALORIES 186; FAT 9.1g (sat 4.2g, mono 2.2g, poly 1.7g); PROTEIN 2.8g; CARB 25.4g; FIBER 1.4g; CHOL 30mg; IRON 0.9mg; SODIUM 74mg; CALC 23mg

The brownies need to be completely cool before spreading on the thin caramel glaze.

BROWNIES:

3.38 OUNCES ALL-PURPOSE FLOUR (ABOUT ¾ CUP)

1 CUP GRANULATED SUGAR

¾ CUP UNSWEETENED COCOA

½ CUP PACKED BROWN SUGAR

½ TEASPOON BAKING POWDER

6 TABLESPOONS BUTTER, MELTED

2 LARGE EGGS, LIGHTLY BEATEN

1 TEASPOON VANILLA EXTRACT

COOKING SPRAY

TOPPINGS:

¼ CUP BUTTER

¼ CUP PACKED BROWN SUGAR

3½ TABLESPOONS EVAPORATED FAT-FREE MILK, DIVIDED

¼ TEASPOON VANILLA EXTRACT

½ CUP POWDERED SUGAR

1 OUNCE BITTERSWEET CHOCOLATE, COARSELY CHOPPED

⅛ TEASPOON COARSE SEA SALT

Hands-on time: 30 min.
Total time: 1 hr. 30 min.

SALTED CARAMEL BROWNIES

1. Preheat oven to 350°. To prepare brownies, weigh or lightly spoon flour into dry measuring cups; level with a knife. Combine flour and next 4 ingredients (through baking powder) in a large bowl, stirring well with a whisk.

2. Combine 6 tablespoons melted butter, eggs, and 1 teaspoon vanilla in a small bowl. Add butter mixture to flour mixture; stir to combine. Scrape batter into a 9-inch square metal baking pan lightly coated with cooking spray. Bake at 350° for 19 minutes or until a wooden pick inserted in center comes out with moist crumbs clinging. Cool in pan on a wire rack.

3. To prepare toppings, melt ¼ cup butter in a saucepan over medium heat. Add ¼ cup brown sugar and 1½ tablespoons milk; cook 2 minutes. Remove from heat. Add ¼ teaspoon vanilla and powdered sugar; stir with a whisk until smooth. Spread mixture evenly over cooled brownies. Let stand 20 minutes or until set.

4. Combine remaining 2 tablespoons milk and chocolate in a microwave-safe bowl; microwave at HIGH for 45 seconds or until melted, stirring after 20 seconds. Stir just until smooth; drizzle over caramel. Sprinkle with sea salt; let stand until set. Cut into 20 pieces. Yield: 20 servings (serving size: 1 brownie)

CALORIES 180; FAT 7.2g (sat 4.1g, mono 1.7g, poly 0.3g); PROTEIN 2.1g; CARB 27.8g; FIBER 0.8g; CHOL 37mg; IRON 0.9mg; SODIUM 76mg; CALC 26mg

PEANUT-BUTTER-CUP BLONDIES

Be careful not to overmix; a slightly lumpy batter is much better than one that has been mixed too much. Overworked batter turns out dry, tough blondies.

5.6 OUNCES ALL-PURPOSE FLOUR (ABOUT 1¼ CUPS)

1 CUP GRANULATED SUGAR

½ TEASPOON BAKING POWDER

¼ TEASPOON SALT

⅓ CUP CREAMY PEANUT BUTTER

¼ CUP BUTTER, MELTED AND COOLED SLIGHTLY

2 TABLESPOONS 2% REDUCED-FAT MILK

1 TEASPOON VANILLA EXTRACT

2 LARGE EGGS, LIGHTLY BEATEN

¼ CUP SEMISWEET CHOCOLATE CHIPS

COOKING SPRAY

4 (0.75-OUNCE) PEANUT BUTTER CUPS, COARSELY CHOPPED

Hands-on time: 20 min.
Total time: 2 hr.

1. Preheat oven to 350°. Weigh or lightly spoon flour into dry measuring cups; level with a knife. Combine flour and next 3 ingredients (through salt) in a large bowl, stirring well with a whisk.

2. Combine peanut butter and next 4 ingredients (through eggs) in a medium bowl, stirring well. Add peanut butter mixture to flour mixture; stir until combined. Stir in chocolate chips.

3. Scrape the batter into a 9-inch square metal baking pan lightly coated with cooking spray, and arrange the peanut butter cups over batter. Bake at 350° for 19 minutes or until a wooden pick inserted in center comes out with moist crumbs clinging. Cool in pan on a wire rack. Cut into 20 pieces. Yield: 20 servings (serving size: 1 brownie)

CALORIES 153; FAT 7g (sat 2.9g, mono 2g, poly 0.8g); PROTEIN 3.2g; CARB 20.8g; FIBER 0.7g; CHOL 28mg; IRON 0.7mg; SODIUM 98mg; CALC 17mg

CLASSIC PIES

Nothing says old-school comfort like a handmade pie. Tender flaky crust, luscious filling, crisp or creamy topping, it's the sweet stuff that after-dinner dreams are made of. And crafting a beautiful pie is way easier than you think. The crust takes a little effort. (But if you're not ready to tackle making your own crust, feel free to buy a premade one for your first few forays into pie making.) Fillings can be as simple as chopping up fresh fruit and tossing it in a bowl with a few other ingredients, or stirring together pecans, bourbon, and eggs. In the only-slightly-more-challenging category, you can whisk up a silky chiffon filling.

Whether you're a novice or you truly know your way around a rolling pin, there's some deep-dish wisdom to be gained from our test kitchen pros. You'll learn the finer points of constructing the perfect crust. We'll show you some sneaky tricks for rolling dough out flawlessly. It involves plastic wrap, which helps with the rolling process for a thinner, lower-fat crust like this one. And you'll get the essential technique behind a light-as-air filling. When the dusting flour settles, you'll be pulling better-than-you-ever-imagined pies out of your oven.

YOU'LL LEARN:

HOW TO MAKE A LIGHTER PIECRUST • HOW TO SHAPE AND ROLL PIECRUST
HOW TO MAKE SEVERAL PIE FILLINGS AND TOPPINGS

MASTER RECIPE:

CRANBERRY-APPLE PIE

VARIATIONS:

SPICED PUMPKIN CHIFFON PIE • MAPLE-BOURBON PECAN PIE

YOUR MISE EN PLACE

DAIRY
BUTTER, CHILLED AND CUT

PRODUCE
FRESH CRANBERRIES
GALA APPLES, PEELED AND CUT

FLAVOR BOOSTERS/ STAPLES
ALL-PURPOSE FLOUR
GRANULATED SUGAR
SALT
VEGETABLE SHORTENING, CHILLED AND CUT
DARK BROWN SUGAR
GROUND CINNAMON
GRADE B MAPLE SYRUP
COOKING SPRAY
ICE WATER

EQUIPMENT NEEDED:
SHARP KNIFE
LARGE BOWL
WHISK
PASTRY BLENDER (OR 2 KNIVES)
FORK
HEAVY-DUTY PLASTIC WRAP
ROLLING PIN
PIE PLATE
LARGE SPOON
ALUMINUM FOIL
BAKING SHEET
WIRE COOLING RACK

CRANBERRY-APPLE PIE

Be ready for the aromas of fall to fill your kitchen as this beautiful pie bakes.
We call for grade B maple syrup because it's less refined and so has a stronger,
more "maple-y" flavor. If you use milder grade A syrup, stir in a single scrape
of fresh nutmeg to boost the maple flavor.

ALL-PURPOSE LIGHT PIECRUST DOUGH:

9 OUNCES ALL-PURPOSE FLOUR (ABOUT 2 CUPS)

2 TEASPOONS GRANULATED SUGAR

1¼ TEASPOONS SALT, DIVIDED

6 TABLESPOONS CHILLED BUTTER, CUT INTO SMALL PIECES

6 TABLESPOONS CHILLED VEGETABLE SHORTENING, CUT INTO SMALL PIECES

6 TABLESPOONS ICE WATER

FILLING:

1½ CUPS FRESH CRANBERRIES

⅓ CUP PACKED DARK BROWN SUGAR

5 TABLESPOONS ALL-PURPOSE FLOUR

¼ TEASPOON SALT

¼ TEASPOON GROUND CINNAMON

2½ POUNDS GALA APPLES (ABOUT 6), PEELED AND CUT INTO ½-INCH PIECES

⅔ CUP GRADE B MAPLE SYRUP

COOKING SPRAY

Hands-on time: 50 min.
Total time: 3 hr.

1. To prepare dough, weigh or lightly spoon 9 ounces flour into dry measuring cups; level with a knife. Combine flour, 2 teaspoons sugar, and 1 teaspoon salt in a large bowl, stirring well with a whisk; cut in butter and shortening with a pastry blender or 2 knives until mixture resembles coarse meal.

2. Gradually add ice water; toss with a fork until flour mixture is moist.

3. Divide the dough into 2 equal portions. Gently press each portion into a 5-inch circle on heavy-duty plastic wrap; cover and chill 1 hour.

4. To prepare filling, combine cranberries and next 5 ingredients (through apples) in a large bowl, tossing gently to coat. Add syrup, tossing to coat.

5. Slightly overlap 2 sheets of plastic wrap on a damp surface. Unwrap and place 1 portion of chilled dough on plastic wrap. Cover dough with 2 additional sheets of overlapping plastic wrap. Roll dough, still covered, into a 12-inch circle. Chill dough in freezer 5 minutes or until plastic wrap can be easily removed.

(continued)

Chilling the dough after it's shaped in the pan will help ensure your crust doesn't leak during baking and results in perfectly crafted edges.

6. Remove top sheets of plastic wrap; fit dough, plastic wrap side up, into a 9-inch pie plate coated with cooking spray. Remove remaining plastic wrap.

7. Spoon apple mixture into prepared crust.

8. Slightly overlap 2 sheets of plastic wrap on a slightly damp surface. Unwrap and place remaining portion of chilled dough on plastic wrap. Cover dough with 2 additional sheets of overlapping plastic wrap. Roll dough, still covered, into an 11-inch circle. Chill dough in freezer 5 minutes or until plastic wrap can be easily removed. Remove top sheets of plastic wrap; fit dough, plastic wrap side up, over apple mixture. Remove remaining plastic wrap.

9. Press edges of dough together. Fold edges under, and flute. Cut several slits in top of dough to allow steam to escape. Chill pie in refrigerator for 10 minutes.

10. Preheat oven to 425°. Place pie plate on a foil-lined baking sheet. Place baking sheet on bottom oven rack; bake at 425° for 25 minutes. Reduce oven temperature to 375° (do not remove pie from oven); bake an additional 45 minutes or until browned. Cool on a wire rack. Yield: 12 servings (serving size: 1 wedge)

CALORIES 312; FAT 12.2g (sat 5.2g, mono 3.5g, poly 1.9g); PROTEIN 2.9g; CARB 49.2g; FIBER 2.3g; CHOL 15mg; IRON1.5mg; SODIUM 291mg; CALC 28mg

Cut the recipe for All-Purpose Light Piecrust in half to make a single crust for this pie.

½ RECIPE ALL-PURPOSE LIGHT PIECRUST DOUGH (PAGE 318), PREPARED THROUGH STEP 5

COOKING SPRAY

1¼ CUPS CANNED PUMPKIN

½ CUP PACKED BROWN SUGAR

¾ TEASPOON GROUND CINNAMON

½ TEASPOON GRATED LEMON RIND

¼ TEASPOON SALT

⅛ TEASPOON GROUND NUTMEG

2 LARGE EGG YOLKS

⅔ CUP EVAPORATED LOW-FAT MILK

1 ENVELOPE UNFLAVORED GELATIN

¼ CUP FRESH ORANGE JUICE

2 LARGE EGG WHITES

⅛ TEASPOON CREAM OF TARTAR

5 TABLESPOONS GRANULATED SUGAR, DIVIDED

3 TABLESPOONS WATER

½ CUP HEAVY WHIPPING CREAM

½ OUNCE SHAVED BITTERSWEET CHOCOLATE

Hands-on time: 40 min.
Total time: 5 hr. 25 min.

SPICED PUMPKIN CHIFFON PIE

1. Preheat oven to 400°. Remove 2 sheets of plastic from All-Purpose Light Piecrust Dough. Fit dough, plastic wrap side up, into a 9-inch pie plate coated with cooking spray. Remove top sheet of plastic wrap. Fold edges under; flute. Pierce bottom and sides of dough with a fork; freeze 10 minutes. Line bottom of dough with a piece of foil; arrange pie weights or dried beans on foil. Bake at 400° for 25 minutes or until browned. Remove weights and foil. Cool completely on a wire rack.

2. Combine pumpkin and next 6 ingredients (through egg yolks) in a medium saucepan, stirring with a whisk. Stir in milk; bring to a boil. Reduce heat, and simmer 4 minutes or until slightly thick, stirring frequently. Remove from heat. Sprinkle gelatin over orange juice in a small microwave-safe bowl; let stand 1 minute. Microwave at HIGH 15 seconds, stirring until gelatin dissolves. Stir gelatin mixture into pumpkin mixture. Cool.

3. Place 2 egg whites and cream of tartar in a bowl; beat with a mixer at high speed until frothy. Gradually add 1 tablespoon granulated sugar, beating until soft peaks form. Combine remaining ¼ cup granulated sugar and 3 tablespoons water in a saucepan; bring to a boil. Cook, without stirring, until candy thermometer registers 250°. Pour hot sugar syrup in a thin stream over egg whites, beating at high speed until stiff peaks form. Gently stir one-fourth of egg white mixture into pumpkin mixture; gently fold in remaining egg white mixture. Pour into cooled crust. Refrigerate 4 hours or until set.

4. Place cream in a medium bowl; beat with a mixer at high speed until soft peaks form. Spread evenly over pie; top with chocolate. Yield: 10 servings (serving size: 1 wedge)

CALORIES 274; FAT 13.2g (sat 5.8g, mono 3.8g, poly 1.6g); PROTEIN 5.3g; CARB 34.5g; FIBER 1.4g; CHOL 63mg; IRON 1.5mg; SODIUM 173mg; CALC 82mg

*Using refrigerated piecrust adds
a little more fat to the bottom
line, but we tweak the remaining ingredients so that a slice
delivers less than half the fat and
calories of traditional pecan pie.*

½ (14.1-OUNCE) PACKAGE REFRIGERATED
    PIE DOUGH

COOKING SPRAY

¾ CUP PECAN HALVES

¼ CUP FINELY CHOPPED PECANS

½ CUP MAPLE SYRUP

½ CUP DARK CORN SYRUP

3 TABLESPOONS BROWN SUGAR

2 TABLESPOONS BUTTER, MELTED

2 TABLESPOONS BOURBON

1 TEASPOON VANILLA EXTRACT

¼ TEASPOON KOSHER SALT

2 LARGE EGGS, LIGHTLY BEATEN

2 LARGE EGG WHITES, LIGHTLY BEATEN

Hands-on time: 12 min.
Total time: 1 hr. 23 min.

MAPLE-BOURBON
PECAN PIE

1. Preheat oven to 350°. Roll dough into a 12-inch
circle. Fit dough into a 9-inch pie plate coated with
cooking spray, draping excess dough over edges. Fold
edges under, and flute. Chill in freezer 15 minutes.

2. Combine pecans and remaining ingredients in a
bowl, stirring well to combine. Pour filling into prepared
crust.

3. Bake at 350° for 38 minutes or until center of pie is
almost set (shield edges of piecrust with foil if crust gets
too brown). Cool on wire rack. Yield: 10 servings (serving size: 1 wedge)

CALORIES 308; FAT 16.2g (sat 4.4g, mono 7g, poly 3.8g); PROTEIN 3.3g;
CARB 37.6g; FIBER 1g; CHOL 51mg; IRON 0.7mg; SODIUM 203mg; CALC 29mg

LAYER CAKES

L ayer cake is the answer. No matter what the question or occasion may be, layer cake is inevitably the welcome dessert solution. Whether you are celebrating one of life's special events or simply commemorating the fact that everyone is together for a meal, a rich-tasting, tender, moist cake layered with fluffy, creamy icing is a dramatic and memorable way to conclude. But questions remain, such as: Really? Me? In my kitchen? Make it myself? Again, the answer is yes, layer cake. We're here to show you how.

We'll not only take you through the steps to turn out a professional-looking cake, but we'll shave off extra fat and calories along the way. So you just ran out of excuses. You'll start baking the cake layers, using brilliant techniques and ingredients to get perfect flavor and texture without loads of butter. Then, finish it all off with the perfect icing: fluffy meringue, bittersweet chocolate glaze, or deeply flavored maple—it's up to you.

YOU'LL LEARN:

HOW TO MIX A CAKE BATTER • HOW TO BAKE A CAKE

HOW TO MAKE SEVERAL KINDS OF FROSTING

MASTER RECIPE:

VANILLA CAKE WITH ITALIAN MERINGUE FROSTING

VARIATIONS:

CHOCOLATE-ORANGE LAYER CAKE • PECAN SPICE CAKE WITH MAPLE FROSTING

YOUR MISE EN PLACE

WET
COOKING SPRAY
BUTTERMILK
1% REDUCED-FAT MILK
BUTTER, SOFTENED
CANOLA OIL
EGG YOLKS
VANILLA EXTRACT
LARGE EGG WHITES
WATER
LEMON CURD

DRY
CAKE FLOUR
SALT
SUGAR
CREAM OF TARTAR

LEAVENING AGENTS
BAKING POWDER
BAKING SODA

EQUIPMENT NEEDED:
ROUND CAKE PANS
WAX PAPER
MIXING BOWLS
WHISK
ELECTRIC MIXER (HANDHELD OR STAND)
WOODEN PICK
WIRE COOLING RACKS
SMALL SAUCEPAN
WOODEN SPOON
CANDY THERMOMETER
SPATULA

VANILLA CAKE

with Italian Meringue Frosting

Precision is important when baking, especially light baking where there's less margin for error. For absolute accuracy, get in the habit of weighing the flour (for tips, see page 276).

CAKE:

COOKING SPRAY

2 TEASPOONS CAKE FLOUR

11 OUNCES CAKE FLOUR (ABOUT 2¾ CUPS)

½ TEASPOON BAKING POWDER

½ TEASPOON BAKING SODA

½ TEASPOON SALT

1 CUP NONFAT BUTTERMILK

¼ CUP 1% REDUCED-FAT MILK

1 CUP PLUS 2 TABLESPOONS SUGAR, DIVIDED

5 TABLESPOONS BUTTER, SOFTENED

2 TABLESPOONS CANOLA OIL

3 LARGE EGG YOLKS

1 TEASPOON VANILLA EXTRACT

3 LARGE EGG WHITES

FROSTING:

⅔ CUP PLUS 2 TABLESPOONS SUGAR, DIVIDED

¼ CUP WATER

DASH OF SALT

¼ TEASPOON CREAM OF TARTAR

3 LARGE EGG WHITES

½ TEASPOON VANILLA EXTRACT

FILLING:

½ CUP BOTTLED LEMON CURD

Hands-on time: 45 min.
Total time: 1 hr. 25 min.

1. Preheat oven to 350°. To prepare cake, lightly coat 2 (8-inch) round metal cake pans with cooking spray; line bottoms of pans with wax paper. Coat wax paper with cooking spray; dust each pan with 1 teaspoon flour.

2. Weigh or lightly spoon 11 ounces flour into dry measuring cups; level with a knife. Combine flour, baking powder, baking soda, and ½ teaspoon salt in a medium bowl, stirring well with a whisk. Combine buttermilk and reduced-fat milk in a small bowl.

3. Combine 1 cup sugar and butter in a large bowl; beat with mixer at medium speed until well blended. Add canola oil and egg yolks, 1 at a time, beating well after each addition. Beat in 1 teaspoon vanilla extract.

4. Add flour mixture and milk mixture alternately to butter mixture, beginning and ending with flour mixture and beating just until combined.

5. Place 3 egg whites in a medium bowl; beat with a mixer at high speed until foamy, using clean, dry beaters. Gradually add remaining 2 tablespoons sugar, beating until stiff peaks form.

(continued)

Cream of tartar is your insurance policy when whipping egg whites for a fluffy frosting. It helps stabilize the whites while adding volume.

Prevent the layers from sticking to the pan and crumbling by spraying with cooking spray, lining with paper, spraying again, and dusting with flour.

6. Gently fold egg white mixture into batter.

7. Divide batter evenly between prepared pans. Bake at 350° for 28 minutes or until a wooden pick inserted into center comes out clean.

8. Cool in pans 10 minutes on wire racks. Loosen edges with a knife, and invert cakes onto racks. Cool completely; discard wax paper.

9. To prepare frosting, combine ⅔ cup sugar, ¼ cup water, and dash of salt in a small saucepan over medium-high heat; bring to a boil, stirring just until sugar dissolves. Cook, without stirring, until a thermometer registers 240°, about 4 minutes.

10. Combine cream of tartar and 3 egg whites in a clean large bowl; beat with a mixer with clean, dry beaters at high speed until foamy. Gradually add the remaining 2 tablespoons sugar, beating at high speed until medium peaks form. Gradually pour the hot sugar syrup into the egg white mixture, beating first at medium speed and then at high speed until stiff peaks form. Beat in ½ teaspoon vanilla extract into the meringue frosting.

11. To prepare filling, place lemon curd in a medium bowl. Gently fold ⅓ cup meringue into the curd. Fold an additional ⅔ cup meringue into curd mixture.

12. Place 1 cake layer on a plate; spread filling over top of cake, leaving a ¼-inch border. Top with remaining cake layer. Spread the remaining frosting over sides and top of cake. Yield: 16 servings (serving size: 1 wedge)

CALORIES 274; FAT 7.5g (sat 3.3g, mono 2.4g, poly 0.8g); PROTEIN 4.2g; CARB 48.4g; FIBER 1.3g; CHOL 59mg; IRON 1.7mg; SODIUM 214mg; CALC 23mg

If need be, you can pop well-wrapped baked cake layers (minus frosting) in the fridge for up to a week, or in the freezer for up to three months. Best of all, baking the cake in advance will actually make it easier to assemble and no one (we promise) will be able to taste the difference.

CAKE:

1 CUP BOILING WATER

⅔ CUP UNSWEETENED COCOA

2 OUNCES BITTERSWEET CHOCOLATE, FINELY CHOPPED

COOKING SPRAY

2 TEASPOONS ALL-PURPOSE FLOUR

1¾ CUPS SUGAR

6 TABLESPOONS BUTTER, SOFTENED

1 TEASPOON VANILLA EXTRACT

3 LARGE EGG WHITES

½ CUP FAT-FREE SOUR CREAM

7.4 OUNCES CAKE FLOUR (ABOUT 1⅔ CUPS)

1 TEASPOON BAKING POWDER

¾ TEASPOON BAKING SODA

½ TEASPOON SALT

CHOCOLATE-ORANGE LAYER CAKE

1. Preheat oven to 350°. To prepare cake, combine 1 cup boiling water and ⅔ cup cocoa in a bowl, stirring until smooth. Add 2 ounces bittersweet chocolate; stir until smooth. Cool to room temperature.

2. Coat 2 (8-inch) round metal cake pans with cooking spray; line bottoms of pans with wax paper. Coat wax paper with cooking spray; dust each pan with 1 teaspoon flour.

3. Place 1¾ cups sugar, 6 tablespoons butter, and 1 teaspoon vanilla in a large bowl; beat with a mixer at medium speed 1 minute. Add egg whites, 1 at a time, beating well after each addition. Add sour cream; beat at medium speed 2 minutes. Weigh or lightly spoon 7.4 ounces cake flour into dry measuring cups; level with a knife. Combine flour, baking powder, baking soda, and ½ teaspoon salt in a bowl, stirring well. Add flour mixture and cocoa mixture alternately to sugar mixture, beginning and ending with flour mixture and beating just until combined.

4. Divide batter evenly between prepared pans. Bake at 350° for 30 minutes or until a wooden pick inserted into center comes out clean. Cool in pans 10 minutes on wire racks. Invert cake layers onto racks; cool completely. Discard wax paper.

FILLING:

⅓ CUP ORANGE JUICE

3 TABLESPOONS SUGAR

1½ TEASPOONS CORNSTARCH

2½ TEASPOONS UNSWEETENED COCOA

¾ TEASPOON ALL-PURPOSE FLOUR

DASH OF SALT

¼ OUNCE BITTERSWEET CHOCOLATE,
   FINELY CHOPPED

¾ CUP FROZEN FAT-FREE WHIPPED
   TOPPING, THAWED

GLAZE:

2 TABLESPOONS EVAPORATED
   LOW-FAT MILK

1 TABLESPOON BUTTER

4 OUNCES BITTERSWEET CHOCOLATE,
   FINELY CHOPPED

Hands-on time: 45 min.
Total time: 2 hr. 15 min.

5. To prepare filling, combine juice and next 6 ingredients (through ¼ ounce bittersweet chocolate) in a small saucepan over low heat; bring mixture to a boil, stirring frequently. Cook 1 minute, stirring constantly. Pour into a bowl. Cover and chill. Uncover; fold in whipped topping.

6. To prepare glaze, combine milk, 1 tablespoon butter, and 4 ounces bittersweet chocolate in a medium microwave-safe bowl; microwave at HIGH for 1 minute, stirring every 15 seconds until smooth.

7. Place 1 cake layer on a plate. Spread filling over top, leaving a ¼-inch border. Top with remaining cake layer. Spoon warm glaze over top of cake, allowing it to drip over the edges of cake. Yield: 16 servings (serving size: 1 wedge)

CALORIES 280; FAT 10.4g (sat 5.7g, mono 1.3g, poly 0.3g); PROTEIN 4.2g; CARB 46g; FIBER 1.9g; CHOL 14mg; IRON 1.5mg; SODIUM 229mg; CALC 38mg

PECAN SPICE CAKE *with* MAPLE FROSTING

Work quickly to spread the warm frosting over the first layer, stack the second on top, and then spread the remaining frosting over the top and sides before it sets.

CAKE:

COOKING SPRAY

2 TEASPOONS ALL-PURPOSE FLOUR

9 OUNCES ALL-PURPOSE FLOUR (ABOUT 2 CUPS)

½ TEASPOON BAKING SODA

½ TEASPOON SALT

½ TEASPOON GROUND CINNAMON

¼ TEASPOON GROUND NUTMEG

DASH OF GROUND CLOVES

1 CUP PACKED BROWN SUGAR

½ CUP BUTTER, SOFTENED

3 LARGE EGGS

1 TEASPOON VANILLA EXTRACT

1 CUP BUTTERMILK

⅓ CUP CHOPPED PECANS, TOASTED

1. Preheat oven to 350°. To prepare cake, coat 2 (8-inch) round metal cake pans with cooking spray. Line bottoms of pans with wax paper; coat with cooking spray. Dust each pan with 1 teaspoon flour.

2. Weigh or lightly spoon 9 ounces flour into dry measuring cups; level with a knife. Combine flour, baking soda, and next 4 ingredients (through cloves) in a medium bowl, stirring well with a whisk.

3. Place 1 cup brown sugar and ½ cup butter in a large mixing bowl; beat with a mixer at medium-high speed until light and fluffy, about 3 minutes. Add eggs, 1 at a time, beating well after each addition. Beat in 1 teaspoon vanilla. Add flour mixture and buttermilk alternately to butter mixture, beginning and ending with flour mixture and beating just until combined. Fold in ⅓ cup pecans. Divide batter evenly between prepared pans.

4. Bake at 350° for 24 minutes or until a wooden pick inserted in center comes out clean. Cool in pans 5 minutes on wire racks. Invert cake layers onto racks; cool completely. Discard wax paper.

5. To prepare frosting, place ½ cup brown sugar, heavy whipping cream, maple syrup, 1 tablespoon butter, and dash of salt in a heavy saucepan over medium-high heat; bring to a boil, stirring just until sugar dissolves. Cook 3 minutes, without stirring. Scrape brown sugar mixture

FROSTING:

½ CUP PACKED BROWN SUGAR

¼ CUP HEAVY WHIPPING CREAM

¼ CUP MAPLE SYRUP

1 TABLESPOON BUTTER

DASH OF SALT

2 CUPS POWDERED SUGAR

½ TEASPOON VANILLA EXTRACT

2 TABLESPOONS CHOPPED PECANS,
   TOASTED

Hands-on time: 40 min.
Total time: 1 hr. 15 min.

into a bowl. Add powdered sugar; beat with a mixer at high speed 2 minutes or until slightly cooled and thick. Beat in ½ teaspoon vanilla.

6. Place 1 cake layer on a plate. Spread about ¾ cup frosting evenly over layer; top with second layer. Spread remaining frosting over sides and top of cake; sprinkle with 2 tablespoons pecans. Let cake stand until frosting sets. Yield: 16 servings (serving size: 1 wedge)

CALORIES 325; FAT 11.8g (sat 5.7g, mono 3.8g, poly 1.2g); PROTEIN 3.8g; CARB 52.1g; FIBER 0.8g; CHOL 64mg; IRON 1.5mg; SODIUM 209mg; CALC 36mg

How to Bake a
BETTER CAKE

A cake is essentially a chemistry experiment—a series of ingredients mixed in a specific order to cause reactions that produce specific effects. Most layer cakes get their soft, fine texture, and moistness—called a crumb—by first creaming together fat and sugar, adding eggs, and slowly incorporating dry ingredients into the mixture while alternating with a liquid, such as milk or buttermilk. Angel food, sponge, and chiffon cakes get their signature airy, foamlike textures when whole eggs or egg whites (depending on the cake) are whipped until voluminous, then folded into the batter. The air incorporated by whipping the eggs gives these cakes volume, making them springy and elastic.

1. USE THE RIGHT FLOUR FOR THE RECIPE.
Different flours contain varying percentages of protein—the more protein, the more gluten. Cake flour has the least protein and yields extra-light baked goods, like angel food cake. Bread flour has the most and is used for denser items; all-purpose is in the middle and produces tender cakes.

2. ALTERNATE WET AND DRY INGREDIENTS WHEN MIXING CAKE BATTER.
It's all about batter bubbles. When you beat sugar and softened butter or eggs into a frothy foam, this adds air to the batter. Bubbles give cakes a tender, open crumb. Gradually adding the dry ingredients keeps those bubbles from popping. For a fluffy cake, you have to alternate, carefully and patiently, to keep the bubbles at their best.

3. GIVE YOUR CAKE A COOLDOWN.
Cool cakes in the pan on a wire rack for 20 minutes, then remove from pan. Once cooled, place a plate on top, invert the pan, and gently tap or shake it to release the cake. For example, angel food cakes are usually baked in tube pans, then inverted either on feet attached to the pan or over a bottle to cool upside down while still in the pan—gravity helps the cake keep its volume. When it has cooled, run a narrow spatula around the edges, and release onto a plate.

4. FROST LIKE A PROFESSIONAL.
Put a small dollop of frosting in the center of the cake plate, and place the first cake layer on top. This will keep the cake from moving as you work. Use an offset spatula to frost the top, add the next layer, then coat the whole cake with a thin layer of frosting. (This "crumb coat" holds loose crumbs in place.) Place the cake in the freezer for 15 minutes, then remove and finish frosting, starting with the top, then the sides.

CAKE CHEMISTRY

Successful cake baking begins in the mixing bowl with the chemistry among key ingredients striking a balance between form and structure.

FLOUR thickens the batter and provides gluten, a protein that gives the cake structure. It forms when flour is combined with a liquid and agitated. Don't overmix, which can cause your cake to turn tough.

LEAVENERS, like baking soda or powder, produce carbon dioxide bubbles, which are trapped by the starch in the batter and expand during baking, causing the cake to rise.

FATS, like butter, shortening, or oil, help retard gluten formation while providing moisture for the cake. This ensures a tender texture. Some fats can be used to add flavors of their own, as in olive oil cake.

SUGAR has three functions: It breaks up gluten, keeping the texture tender; it absorbs liquid, keeping the cake moist; and it caramelizes in baking, enriching the flavors and helping the cake brown.

EGGS firm up when cooked due to the protein they contain, helping cake batters set in the oven. Egg yolks contain fat, as well as lecithin, an emulsifier that allows fats and water to mix smoothly and ensures even texture.

ICE CREAM

Ice cream is one of the simplest, most delicious things you're probably not making at home. Too intimidated to give it a try? Don't be; making ice cream requires no specialized skills in the kitchen besides the ability to turn on the stove and stir a few ingredients in a pot. Still not convinced? Flip through this lesson, and imagine yourself scooping out a frosty bowl of strawberry-rhubarb, salted caramel, or chocolate ice cream at the end of a hot day.

Now that you are imagining luscious homemade ice cream, it's time to get churning. Ice cream can be made in several ways. There's the old-fashioned method that requires ice and rock salt and churns (either powered by hand or electricity) to make large quantities, up to 4 quarts. Or there are the smaller 1- or 2-quart tabletop makers that skip the ice and rock salt in favor of special bowls that you place in your freezer for 24 hours; they "churn" your ice cream base with a plastic mixing paddle powered by electricity.

No matter what type of ice cream maker you use, a few tricks will ensure a smooth, rich-tasting batch every time: Chill your base thoroughly before spinning in an ice cream maker. Ideally, make the base and chill overnight in the refrigerator. Follow the proportions in the recipes and don't overfill your maker. It may look a little empty, but that space is needed for proper aeration; an overfilled ice cream maker will make dense, icy ice cream.

YOU'LL LEARN:

HOW TO MAKE A CUSTARD ICE CREAM BASE • HOW TO MAKE ICE CREAM IN AN OLD-FASHIONED CHURN • HOW TO MAKE ICE CREAM IN A TABLETOP MAKER

MASTER RECIPE:

STRAWBERRY-RHUBARB ICE CREAM

VARIATIONS:

SALTED CARAMEL ICE CREAM • DOUBLE CHOCOLATE ICE CREAM

YOUR MISE EN PLACE

PROTEIN
LARGE EGG YOLKS

DAIRY
WHOLE MILK

HALF-AND-HALF

PRODUCE
FRESH RHUBARB, CHOPPED

FRESH STRAWBERRIES, CHOPPED

FLAVOR BOOSTERS/ STAPLES
SUGAR

FRUITY RED WINE

EQUIPMENT NEEDED:
SHARP KNIFE

HEAVY SAUCEPAN

CANDY THERMOMETER

LARGE BOWL

WHISK

LARGE, ICE-FILLED BOWL

MEDIUM SAUCEPAN

BLENDER

FINE-MESH SIEVE

WOODEN SPOON

KITCHEN TOWELS

OLD-FASHIONED ICE CREAM MAKER

ROCK SALT

Strawberry-Rhubarb
ICE CREAM

*This recipe uses an old-fashioned churn; we like these ice cream makers
because they typically whip more air into the custard base, yielding light and fluffy results.*

2½ CUPS WHOLE MILK

¾ CUP HALF-AND-HALF

1 CUP SUGAR, DIVIDED

3 LARGE EGG YOLKS

2 CUPS CHOPPED FRESH RHUBARB

⅓ CUP FRUITY RED WINE (SUCH AS
    MERLOT) OR CRANBERRY JUICE
    COCKTAIL

3 CUPS CHOPPED FRESH STRAWBERRIES
    (ABOUT 1 POUND)

Hands-on time: 15 min.
Total time: 1 hr. 5 min.

*Steal a tip from the pros
by blitzing the chilled base
mixture in a blender for 15
to 30 seconds before adding
to an ice cream maker. Your
reward: extra lift.*

1. Combine milk and half-and-half in a heavy saucepan over
medium-high heat. Heat milk mixture to 180° or until tiny
bubbles form around edge (do not boil).

2. Combine ½ cup sugar and egg yolks in a large bowl, whisk-
ing until pale yellow. Gradually add half of hot milk mixture
to egg yolk mixture, stirring constantly with a whisk.

3. Pour the egg yolk mixture into pan with remaining milk
mixture; cook over medium-low heat until a thermometer
registers 160° (about 2 minutes), stirring constantly.

4. Place pan in a large, ice-filled bowl for 20 minutes or until
custard cools completely, stirring occasionally.

5. Combine remaining ½ cup sugar, rhubarb, and wine in
a saucepan over medium-high heat; bring to a boil. Reduce
heat, and simmer 8 minutes or until rhubarb is tender and
liquid is syrupy. Remove from heat; let stand 10 minutes.

6. Combine rhubarb mixture and strawberries in a blender;
process until smooth. Strain mixture through a sieve over
a bowl, pressing with a wooden spoon; discard solids. Stir
rhubarb mixture into custard mixture.

7. Pour custard into the freezer can of an old-fashioned ice
cream maker; churn according to manufacturer's instructions.

8. Drain ice water from freezer bucket; repack with salt and
ice. Cover with kitchen towels, and let stand 1 hour or until
firm. Yield: 10 servings (serving size: about ¾ cup)

CALORIES 173; FAT 5.6 g (sat 2.9g, mono 1.7g, poly 0.5g); PROTEIN 3.8g;
CARB 28.2g; FIBER 1.3g; CHOL 74mg; IRON 0.4mg; SODIUM 36mg; CALC 123mg

SALTED CARAMEL ICE CREAM

This ice cream is made in an old-fashioned churn ice cream maker. You'll make a quick caramel on the stovetop to stir into a traditional custard-style ice cream. A sprinkle of flake salt added just before serving delivers that sweet-salty hit of ice cream nirvana.

3½ CUPS 2% REDUCED-FAT MILK

3 LARGE EGG YOLKS

1¼ CUPS PACKED BROWN SUGAR

¼ CUP HEAVY CREAM

1 TABLESPOON BUTTER

½ TEASPOON SEA SALT

½ TEASPOON FLAKE SALT

Hands-on time: 35 min.
Total time: 2 hr. 5 min.

1. Place milk in a medium saucepan over medium-high heat. Heat to 180° or until tiny bubbles form around edge of pan (do not boil). Place egg yolks in a large bowl; stir with a whisk. Gradually add half of hot milk to yolks, stirring constantly. Return yolk mixture to pan. Remove from heat.

2. Combine sugar, cream, and butter in a large saucepan over medium heat; bring to a boil, stirring until sugar melts. Cook 3 minutes without stirring. Remove from heat; stir in sea salt. Gradually add caramel mixture to milk mixture in the pan, stirring constantly. Return pan to low heat; cook until a thermometer registers 160°. Place pan in a large, ice-filled bowl until completely cooled, stirring occasionally.

3. Pour mixture into the freezer can of an old-fashioned ice cream freezer; churn according to manufacturer's instructions. Drain ice water from freezer bucket; repack with salt and ice. Cover with kitchen towels, and let stand 1 hour or until firm. Scoop about ½ cup ice cream into each of 10 dishes; sprinkle evenly with flake salt. Yield: 10 servings

CALORIES 241; FAT 7.9g (sat 4.5g, mono 2.5g, poly 0.5g); PROTEIN 4.7g; CARB 39g; FIBER 0g; CHOL 99mg; IRON 0.9mg; SODIUM 370mg; CALC 173mg

VARIATION

DOUBLE CHOCOLATE ICE CREAM

This recipe uses a tabletop ice cream maker, the kind with a bowl that needs to be stashed in the freezer for at least 24 hours. After churning, you'll need to transfer the softer finished product to a container and freeze until firm. The combo of low-fat milk and a small amount of heavy cream lends richness without an overload of fat.

1⅓ CUPS SUGAR

⅓ CUP UNSWEETENED COCOA

2½ CUPS 2% REDUCED-FAT MILK, DIVIDED

3 LARGE EGG YOLKS

⅓ CUP HEAVY WHIPPING CREAM

2.5 OUNCES BITTERSWEET CHOCOLATE, CHOPPED

Hands-on time: 35 min.
Total time: 2 hr. 5 min.

1. Combine sugar and cocoa in a medium, heavy saucepan over medium-low heat. Add ½ cup milk and egg yolks, stirring well. Stir in remaining 2 cups milk. Cook 12 minutes or until a thermometer registers 160°, stirring constantly. Remove from heat.

2. Place cream in a medium microwave-safe bowl; microwave at HIGH 1½ minutes or until cream boils. Add chocolate to cream; stir until smooth. Add cream mixture to pan; stir until smooth. Place pan in a large, ice-filled bowl. Cool completely, stirring occasionally.

3. Pour mixture into the prepared freezer can of a tabletop ice cream maker; mix according to manufacturer's instructions. Spoon ice cream into a freezer-safe container; cover and freeze 1 hour or until firm. Yield: 10 servings (serving size: about ½ cup)

CALORIES 226; FAT 8.9g (sat 4.6g, mono 1.5g, poly 0.3g); PROTEIN 4g; CARB 35.6g; FIBER 1g; CHOL 79mg; IRON 0.7mg; SODIUM 37mg; CALC 75mg

SOUFFLÉS

Mastering the soufflé ranks as a major culinary achievement, but for all the mystique and lore, they are really quite simple. A soufflé is made up of two parts: a base, the thick mixture that gives the dish its flavor; and an aerator which gives its light texture, here the billowy froth of egg whites. Sounds easy enough, right? Well, pulling off the perfect soufflé is all about timing.

In most restaurants the soufflé base is made to order because it needs to be at the right temperature for mixing. If the base is too cold, it won't mix smoothly with the egg whites. If the base is too hot, the whipped whites will begin to soften and lose air, which results in a soufflé that is unlikely to rise. The whites also need to be used within five minutes of whipping or they will begin to lose stability. While these two steps can be temperamental, with a little practice, you'll get it in no time. The last crucial step in the soufflé is to serve immediately. Remember your gorgeous, delicate creation is leavened only by steam; once that steam dissipates, the soufflé will begin to sink. Now, get ready to whip up soaring soufflés to impress the pants off your dinner guests.

YOU'LL LEARN:

HOW TO MAKE A SOUFFLÉ • HOW TO PERFECTLY FOLD IN EGG WHITES
HOW MAKE CRÈME ANGLAISE

MASTER RECIPE:

BROWN SUGAR SOUFFLÉS WITH CRÈME ANGLAISE

VARIATIONS:

BITTERSWEET CHOCOLATE SOUFFLÉS • LEMON-ALMOND SOUFFLÉS

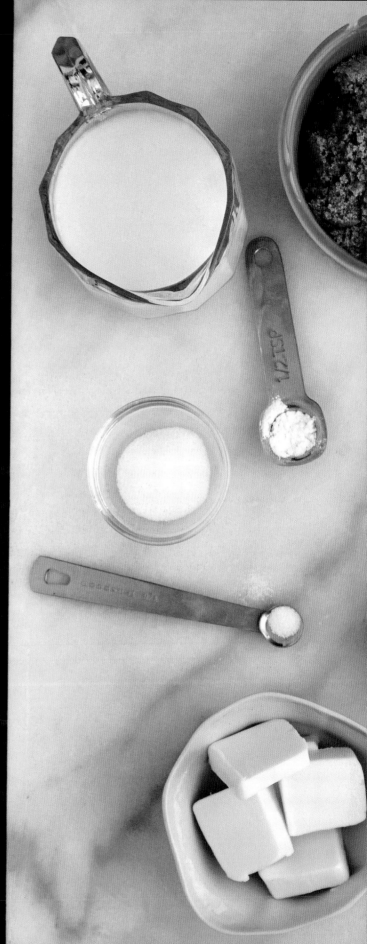

YOUR MISE EN PLACE

PROTEIN
LARGE EGG, LIGHTLY BEATEN
LARGE EGGS, SEPARATED

DAIRY
FAT-FREE MILK
BUTTER

PRODUCE
VANILLA BEAN, SPLIT LENGTHWISE

FLAVOR BOOSTERS/ STAPLES
GRANULATED SUGAR
COOKING SPRAY
BROWN SUGAR
ALL-PURPOSE FLOUR
SALT
VANILLA EXTRACT
CREAM OF TARTAR

EQUIPMENT NEEDED:
MEDIUM HEAVY SAUCEPAN
WHISK
MEDIUM AND LARGE BOWLS
BAKING SHEET
RAMEKINS
MIXER
SPATULA

PREHEAT YOUR OVEN TO 425°.

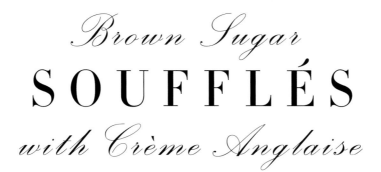

Brown Sugar
SOUFFLÉS
with Crème Anglaise

*The butter develops a deep nutty taste when cooked until the solids fall
to the bottom of the pan and become toasted. The combination of brown sugar
and browned butter gives this rich dessert an intense caramel flavor.*

1¾ CUPS FAT-FREE MILK, DIVIDED

1 (2-INCH) PIECE VANILLA BEAN,
   SPLIT LENGTHWISE

4½ TABLESPOONS GRANULATED SUGAR,
   DIVIDED

1 LARGE EGG, LIGHTLY BEATEN

COOKING SPRAY

½ CUP PACKED BROWN SUGAR

3 TABLESPOONS ALL-PURPOSE FLOUR

⅛ TEASPOON SALT

4½ TABLESPOONS BUTTER

1 TEASPOON VANILLA EXTRACT

1 LARGE EGG YOLK

6 LARGE EGG WHITES

½ TEASPOON CREAM OF TARTAR

Hands-on time: 48 min.
Total time: 1 hr. 18 min.

1. Pour ½ cup milk into a medium saucepan over medium heat. Scrape seeds from vanilla bean; add seeds and bean to milk. Cook 6 minutes (do not boil); discard bean.

2. Combine 2 tablespoons granulated sugar and egg in a bowl. Gradually add hot milk mixture to bowl, stirring constantly with a whisk. Return the mixture to pan. Cook over medium heat for 4 minutes or until mixture coats the back of a spoon, stirring constantly. Immediately pour into a bowl. Cover the crème Anglaise and chill.

3. Place a baking sheet in oven. Preheat oven to 425°. Lightly coat 6 (8-ounce) ramekins with cooking spray. Sprinkle evenly with 2½ tablespoons granulated sugar, tilting and turning dishes to coat sides.

(continued)

Soufflés are leavened only by egg whites; separate the eggs carefully and allow the whites to come to room temperature so they whip nicely.

Wiping clean the rim of the soufflé dish may seem trivial, but it is essential if you want your soufflé to rise tall and straight. Small bits of batter on the rim of the dish will brown quickly and act like an anchor, holding down a side or potentially the entire soufflé.

4. Combine brown sugar, flour, and salt. Place butter in a medium heavy saucepan over medium heat; cook for 3 minutes or until butter browns slightly. Stir in brown sugar mixture and remaining 1¼ cups milk; bring to a boil. Cook for 2 minutes or until slightly thick, stirring constantly; remove from heat. Let stand 5 minutes. Stir in vanilla extract and egg yolk.

5. Combine egg whites and cream of tartar in a large bowl; let stand at room temperature 15 minutes. Beat with a mixer at high speed until medium peaks form. (Test to see if they stand at a 45° angle to be sure.)

6. Gently stir one-fourth of egg whites into milk mixture, pulling the heavier custard mixture up and over the whites, using a sweeping S motion as you work. Gently fold in remaining egg whites. Gently spoon mixture into prepared ramekins. Sharply tap dishes 2 or 3 times on counter.

7. Place dishes on preheated baking sheet and return baking sheet to 425° oven. Immediately reduce oven temperature to 350°; bake soufflés at 350° for 30 minutes or until puffy and golden. Serve immediately with crème Anglaise. Yield: 6 servings (serving size: 1 soufflé and 2 tablespoons crème)

CALORIES 274; FAT 11.1g (sat 6.2g, mono 3.2g, poly 0.7g); PROTEIN 9.1g; CARB 34.9g; FIBER 0.1g; CHOL 125mg; IRON 0.8mg; SODIUM 225mg; CALC 123mg

These chocolaty soufflés, which are airy and elegant, garnered our test kitchens' highest rating.

COOKING SPRAY

2 TABLESPOONS PLUS ¾ CUP GRANULATED SUGAR, DIVIDED

½ CUP DUTCH PROCESS COCOA

2 TABLESPOONS ALL-PURPOSE FLOUR

⅛ TEASPOON SALT

½ CUP 1% LOW-FAT MILK

1 TEASPOON VANILLA EXTRACT

2 LARGE EGG YOLKS

4 LARGE EGG WHITES

⅛ TEASPOON CREAM OF TARTAR

3 OUNCES BITTERSWEET CHOCOLATE, FINELY CHOPPED

1 TABLESPOON POWDERED SUGAR

Hands-on time: 15 min.
Total time: 30 min.

BITTERSWEET CHOCOLATE SOUFFLÉS

1. Preheat oven to 350°. Coat 8 (4-ounce) ramekins with cooking spray, and sprinkle with the 2 tablespoons granulated sugar.

2. Combine ½ cup granulated sugar, cocoa, flour, and salt in a small saucepan. Gradually add milk, stirring with a whisk until blended. Bring to a boil over medium heat; cook until thick (about 3 minutes), stirring constantly. Remove from heat; let stand 3 minutes. Gradually stir in vanilla and egg yolks. Spoon cocoa mixture into a large bowl; cool.

3. Place egg whites in a large bowl; beat with a mixer at high speed until foamy. Gradually add remaining ¼ cup granulated sugar and cream of tartar, beating mixture until stiff peaks form. Gently stir one-fourth of egg white mixture into cocoa mixture; gently fold in remaining egg white mixture and the chopped chocolate. Spoon into prepared ramekins.

4. Bake at 350° for 15 minutes or until puffy and set. Sprinkle with powdered sugar. Yield: 8 servings (serving size: 1 soufflé)

CALORIES 206; FAT 5.5g (sat 3g, mono 1g, poly 0.3g); PROTEIN 5.2g; CARB 34.1g; FIBER 2.3g; CHOL 55mg; IRON 1mg; SODIUM 75mg; CALC 33mg

VARIATION

LEMON-ALMOND SOUFFLÉS

COOKING SPRAY

½ CUP PLUS 2 TABLESPOONS GRANULATED SUGAR, DIVIDED

2 LARGE EGG YOLKS

¾ CUP LOW-FAT BUTTERMILK

1 TABLESPOON GRATED LEMON RIND

⅓ CUP FRESH LEMON JUICE

2 TABLESPOONS BUTTER, MELTED

1.13 OUNCES ALL-PURPOSE FLOUR (ABOUT ¼ CUP)

6 LARGE EGG WHITES

½ TEASPOON CREAM OF TARTAR

¼ CUP SLICED ALMONDS, LIGHTLY TOASTED

Hands-on time: 16 min.
Total time: 36 min.

Beating the egg whites just to medium peaks allows them room to expand as the soufflé cooks, rising to dramatic heights.

1. Place a baking sheet in oven. Preheat oven to 425°. Lightly coat 6 (8-ounce) ramekins with cooking spray; sprinkle evenly with 2 tablespoons sugar, tilting dishes to coat sides completely.

2. Combine ¼ cup sugar and egg yolks in a large bowl; beat with a mixer at high speed until thick and pale (about 2 minutes). Add buttermilk and next 4 ingredients (through flour); beat at medium speed just until blended.

3. Combine egg whites and cream of tartar in a large bowl; let stand at room temperature 15 minutes. Using clean dry beaters, beat with a mixer at high speed until soft peaks form. Gradually add remaining ¼ cup sugar, 1 tablespoon at a time, beating until medium peaks form.

4. Gently stir one-fourth of egg whites into lemon mixture; gently fold in remaining egg whites. Gently spoon mixture into prepared ramekins. Sharply tap dishes 2 or 3 times on counter to level. Sprinkle evenly with almonds.

5. Place dishes on preheated baking sheet; return baking sheet to 425° oven. Immediately reduce oven temperature to 350°; bake soufflés at 350° for 20 minutes or until puffy and lightly browned. Serve immediately. Yield: 6 servings (serving size: 1 soufflé)

CALORIES 207; FAT 7.6g (sat 3.3g, mono 2.9g, poly 0.9g); PROTEIN 7g; CARB 29.2g; FIBER 0.8g; CHOL 81mg; IRON 0.6mg; SODIUM 117mg; CALC 60mg

NUTRITIONAL ANALYSIS

HOW TO USE IT AND WHY: Glance at the end of any *Cooking Light* recipe, and you'll see how committed we are to helping you make the best of today's light cooking. With chefs, registered dietitians, home economists, and a computer system that analyzes every ingredient we use, *Cooking Light* gives you authoritative dietary detail like no other magazine. We go to such lengths so you can see how our recipes fit into your healthful eating plan. If you're trying to lose weight, the calorie and fat figures will probably help most. But if you're keeping a close eye on the sodium, cholesterol, and saturated fat in your diet, we provide those numbers, too. And because many women don't get enough iron or calcium, we can help there, as well. Finally, there's a fiber analysis for those of us who don't get enough roughage. Here's a helpful guide to put our nutritional analysis numbers into perspective. Remember, one size doesn't fit all, so take your lifestyle, age, and circumstances into consideration when determining your nutrition needs. For example, pregnant or breast-feeding women need more protein, calories, and calcium. And women older than 50 need 1,200mg of calcium daily, 200mg more than the amount recommended for younger women.

IN OUR NUTRITIONAL ANALYSIS, WE USE THESE ABBREVIATIONS

sat	saturated fat	CHOL	cholesterol
mono	monounsaturated fat	CALC	calcium
poly	polyunsaturated fat	g	gram
CARB	carbohydrates	mg	milligram

DAILY NUTRITION GUIDE

	Women ages 25 to 50	Women over 50	Men ages 24 to 50	Men over 50
Calories	2,000	2,000 or less	2,700	2,500
Protein	50g	50g or less	63g	60g
Fat	65g or less	65g or less	88g or less	83g or less
Saturated Fat	20g or less	20g or less	27g or less	25g or less
Carbohydrates	304g	304g	410g	375g
Fiber	25g to 35g	25g to 35g	25g to 35g	25g to 35g
Cholesterol	300mg or less	300mg or less	300mg or less	300mg or less
Iron	18mg	8mg	8mg	8mg
Sodium	2,300mg or less	1,500mg or less	2,300mg or less	1,500mg or less
Calcium	1,000mg	1,200mg	1,000mg	1,000mg

The nutritional values used in our calculations either come from The Food Processor, Version 10.4 (ESHA Research), or are provided by food manufacturers.

METRIC EQUIVALENTS

The information in the following charts is provided to help cooks outside the United States successfully use the recipes in this book. All equivalents are approximate.

COOKING/OVEN TEMPERATURES

	Fahrenheit	Celsius	Gas Mark
Freeze Water	32° F	0° C	
Room Temp.	68° F	20° C	
Boil Water	212° F	100° C	
Bake	325° F	160° C	3
	350° F	180° C	4
	375° F	190° C	5
	400° F	200° C	6
	425° F	220° C	7
	450° F	230° C	8
Broil			Grill

LIQUID INGREDIENTS BY VOLUME

¼ tsp	=						1 ml		
½ tsp	=						2 ml		
1 tsp	=						5 ml		
3 tsp	=	1 Tbsp	=	½ fl oz	=		15 ml		
2 Tbsp	=	⅛ cup	=	1 fl oz	=		30 ml		
4 Tbsp	=	¼ cup	=	2 fl oz	=		60 ml		
5⅓ Tbsp	=	⅓ cup	=	3 fl oz	=		80 ml		
8 Tbsp	=	½ cup	=	4 fl oz	=		120 ml		
10⅔ Tbsp	=	⅔ cup	=	5 fl oz	=		160 ml		
12 Tbsp	=	¾ cup	=	6 fl oz	=		180 ml		
16 Tbsp	=	1 cup	=	8 fl oz	=		240 ml		
1 pt	=	2 cups	=	16 fl oz	=		480 ml		
1 qt	=	4 cups	=	32 fl oz	=		960 ml		
				33 fl oz	=		1000 ml	=	1 l

DRY INGREDIENTS BY WEIGHT

(To convert ounces to grams, multiply the number of ounces by 30.)

1 oz	=	¹⁄₁₆ lb	=	30 g
4 oz	=	¼ lb	=	120 g
8 oz	=	½ lb	=	240 g
12 oz	=	¾ lb	=	360 g
16 oz	=	1 lb	=	480 g

LENGTH

(To convert inches to centimeters, multiply the number of inches by 2.5.)

1 in	=				2.5 cm		
6 in	=	½ ft		=	15 cm		
12 in	=	1 ft		=	30 cm		
36 in	=	3 ft	=	1 yd	=	90 cm	
40 in	=				100 cm	=	1 m

EQUIVALENTS FOR DIFFERENT TYPES OF INGREDIENTS

Standard Cup	Fine Powder (ex. flour)	Grain (ex. rice)	Granular (ex. sugar)	Liquid Solids (ex. butter)	Liquid (ex. milk)
1	140 g	150 g	190 g	200 g	240 ml
¾	105 g	113 g	143 g	150 g	180 ml
⅔	93 g	100 g	125 g	133 g	160 ml
½	70 g	75 g	95 g	100 g	120 ml
⅓	47 g	50 g	63 g	67 g	80 ml
¼	35 g	38 g	48 g	50 g	60 ml
⅛	18 g	19 g	24 g	25 g	30 ml

ACKNOWLEDGMENTS

Thanks to Shaun Chavis for asking me to be a part of this amazing project, and to Betty Wong who brought everything you see on these pages to life. To the entire *Cooking Light* team, thank you for the incredible work on this book with your thoughtful, delicious recipes and gorgeous, vibrant photos. Finally, to my wife Brooke and daughter Parker, thank you for always being there to make me smile and share a plate of something yummy!

–James Briscione

ABOUT THE AUTHOR

James Briscione is a chef, author, and culinary instructor. He is Food Network's first *Chopped* champion and the co-author of *Just Married & Cooking*. James is the Director of Culinary Development at the Institute of Culinary Education and lives in New York with his wife and daughter. Visit him at www.thecoupleskitchen.com.

INDEX

©2015 by Time Home Entertainment Inc.

1271 Avenue of the Americas, New York, NY 10020
Cooking Light is a registered trademark of Time Inc. Lifestyle Group.

All rights reserved. No part of this book may be reproduced in any form or by any means without the prior written permission of the publisher, excepting brief quotations in connection with reviews written specifically for inclusion in magazines or newspapers, or limited excerpts strictly for personal use.

ISBN-13: 978-0-8487-3991-1
ISBN-10: 0-8487-3991-4
Library of Congress Control Number: 2015930569
Printed in the United States of America
First Printing 2015

OXMOOR HOUSE

Creative Director: Felicity Keane
Art Director: Christopher Rhoads
Executive Photography Director: Iain Bagwell
Executive Food Director: Grace Parisi
Senior Editor: Betty Wong
Managing Editor: Elizabeth Tyler Austin
Assistant Managing Editor: Jeanne de Lathouder

THE GREAT COOK

Editorial Assistant: April Smitherman
Assistant Test Kitchen Manager:
    Alyson Moreland Haynes
Food Stylists: Nathan Carrabba,
    Victoria E. Cox, Margaret Monroe Dickey,
    Catherine Crowell Steele
Photo Editor: Kellie Lindsey
Senior Photographer: Hélène Dujardin

Senior Photo Stylists: Kay E. Clarke,
    Mindi Shapiro Levine
Senior Production Manager: Greg A. Amason
Associate Production Manager: Kimberly Marshall

CONTRIBUTORS

Author: James Briscione
Editor: Maureen Callahan
Assistant Project Editor: Melissa Brown
Compositors: AnnaMaria Jacob, Anna Ramia
Copy Editors: Julie Bosche, Deri Reed
Proofreader: Jacqueline Giovanelli
Indexer: Mary Ann Laurens
Fellows: Laura Arnold, Kylie Dazzo, Nicole Fisher,
    Loren Lorenzo, Caroline Smith, Amanda Widis
Food Stylists: Tami Hardeman, Katelyn Hardwick,
    Erica Hopper, Ana Price Kelly, Julia Rutland
Photographers: Jim Bathie, Brian Woodcock
Photo Stylist: Mary Clayton Carl

COOKING LIGHT

Editor: Hunter Lewis
Executive Editor, Food: Ann Taylor Pittman

TIME HOME ENTERTAINMENT INC.

Publisher: Margot Schupf
Vice President, Finance: Vandana Patel
Executive Director, Marketing Services: Carol Pittard
Publishing Director: Megan Pearlman
Assistant General Counsel: Simone Procas